# Bananas and Business

# Bananas and Business

*The United Fruit Company in Colombia, 1899–2000*

Marcelo Bucheli

NEW YORK UNIVERSITY PRESS
*New York and London*

NEW YORK UNIVERSITY PRESS
New York and London
www.nyupress.org

Library of Congress Cataloging-in-Publication Data
Bucheli, Marcelo.
Bananas and business : the United Fruit Company
in Colombia, 1899-2000 / Marcelo Bucheli.
p. cm.
Includes bibliographical references and index.
ISBN 0–8147–9934–5 (cloth : alk. paper)
1. United Fruit Company—History.  2. Banana trade—Colombia—
Magdalena (Dept.)—History—20th century.  3. Banana trade—
Colombia—Urabá, Gulf of, Region—History—20th century.
I. Title.
HD9259.B3C7228     2004
338.7'634772'098610904—dc22          2004017316
New York University Press books are printed on acid-free paper,
and their binding materials are chosen for strength and durability.

Manufactured in the United States of America

10 9 8 7 6 5 4 3 2 1

Colombia in the twentieth century. (Map by Daniel Cardoso)

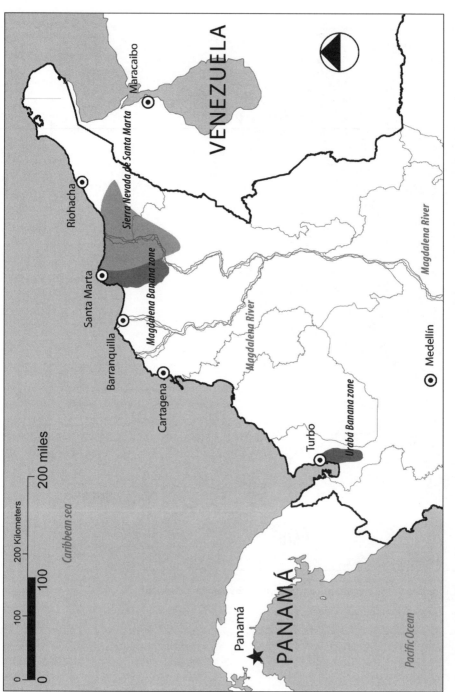

Colombia, Llanura del Caribe. The Magdalena Banana Zone was created in the late-nineteenth century and the Uraba Banana Zone was created in the early 1960s. (Map by Daniel Cardoso)

# Contents

# Acknowledgments

This book is the outcome of a research project that began almost ten years ago. Since I started this project I have enjoyed the generous help, advice, assistance, and support of many people and institutions in Colombia and the United States. My list of acknowledgments includes a wide number of people ranging from academics to businessmen, political activists to government officials, and plantation field workers to former members of the Colombian guerrillas. I certainly can not complain of a lack of attention from these people. I am unable to mention the names of many of those who kindly and enthusiastically helped me during my field research in several Colombian towns. The country's current international reputation as one of the most dangerous places in the world strongly contrasted with the warmth and friendliness I found across the country as I conducted my research.

This book would not have been possible without the guidance of Stephen Haber, my doctoral advisor at Stanford University. He patiently and meticulously read drafts of this book over several years and gave me valuable advice on how to conduct my research and show my results. I appreciate the time, energy, and enthusiasm he invested in this project.

I received crucial feedback from other scholars on early versions of the arguments made in this book. I am particularly grateful to William Childs, Zephyr Frank, Avner Greif, James Robinson, Steve Striffler, Luis Fernando Medina, Mark Moberg, John Wirth, and Gavin Wright. I also thank my two anonymous readers for their comments on the last drafts of this manuscript.

My research process benefited from enriching discussions I had with Norma Alvarez, Claudia Linares, Moramay López, Noël Maurer, Adolfo Meisel, Francisco Monaldi, Aldo Mussachio, Eduardo Posada-Carbó, Ian Read, Michael Tomz, and Martín Valadez.

In the early stages of my research, I received valuable organizational and editing suggestions from Petra Hammerl and Megan McCarthy. I am particularly indebted to Patty Fong for her careful editing. I thank Juan Carlos Echeverry and Fabio Sánchez from the Universidad de los Andes in Bogotá for providing me with the time and resources to finish this book. I also thank the people who believed in this project in its early stages, particularly Carlos Dávila, Alberto Flórez, Catherine LeGrand, Gerard Martin, and Adolfo Meisel.

It would have been impossible for me to obtain the material used in this book had it not been for the generosity of many people. I express my gratitude to former United Fruit officials William Mason and Thomas McCann. In Bogotá, I thank Irving Bernal, Aurelio Correa, Luis Mauricio Cuervo, and Andrés and Eliseo Restrepo. In Medellín, José Fernando Acevedo, Sabina Alvarez, Gabriel Jaime Arango, Fernando Botero, Reynaldo Escobar, and Martha Valencia. In Urabá, Mario Agudelo, Oswaldo Cuadrado, Gabriel Jaime Elejalde, Samuel Fernández, Santiago Gómez, José María Otálora, and Guillermo Rivera. In Santa Marta, Arturo Bermúdez, Adriana Corso, José Rafael Dávila, Edgar Rey, Luis Riascos, and Eduardo Solano. In Ciénaga, María Teresa de Caneva, and Guillermo and Ismael Correa. In Aracataca, Aramis Bermúdez. My field research was pleasant thanks to the hospitality and generosity of Reynaldo, Bertha, and Javier Posada in Medellín, and Lucy Peñaranda in Santa Marta.

I could not have finished a project of this many years without personal support. Several people made the years I spent writing this book more pleasant and less stressful than they could have been. Luis Fernando Medina, Claudia Linares, and their daughter, Alejandra, were a constant source of emotional and material support. In addition to his academic feedback, Zephyr Frank also gave me his kind and strong support. I was also fortunate to have the long-distance, but constant, presence of old friends Andrés Páez and Corey Tyrrell. Friends in San Francisco made the years living in that city some of the most enjoyable of my life. For this, I thank Jorge and Pedro Bachman, Javier Cardoso, Silvia Cristancho, Hernán Galperín, Federico Gutiérrez-Schott, Miguel Hadelich, Juan Maya, Tatiana Melguizo, Paula Razquin, and Amelia Sosa. I am also grateful to my family, Raúl, Guillermina, Marietta, Adriana, and Andrea Bucheli for their constant support and faith in this project. Last, I want to thank Ericka Beckman for sharing the stress and joys of the last months spent revising the book, which made all the difference.

This book would not exist without the enthusiasm and professionalism of Alison Waldenberg and Deborah Gershenowitz, my editors at New York University Press. I also thank Jennifer Yoon of NYU Press for her patience in the last stages of this project.

The research for this book was financed by the generosity of the Stanford Center for Latin American Studies, the Social Science History Institute at Stanford, the Mellon Summer Research Grant, and the Stanford History Department.

# 1

# Introduction

In 1967, Colombian novelist Gabriel García Márquez published *One Hundred Years of Solitude*, a work for which he was awarded the Nobel Prize. *One Hundred Years of Solitude* soon became obligatory reading for anyone interested in Latin America.[1]

The novel tells of the inhabitants of an imaginary Colombian-Caribbean town, Macondo—a quiet village inhabited by people from different parts of Colombia who settled there after the country's nineteenth-century civil wars. The town's calm is disturbed by the sudden arrival of what García Márquez calls the "leaf storm." The "leaf storm" represents the arrival of an American banana company that changes Macondo forever—the foreigners build nice towns with white houses surrounded by high fences, build a railroad, and open banana plantations. Thousands of workers pour into the region looking for jobs with the foreign fruit company. Macondo is never the same again.

García Márquez has said the main inspiration for his writings were the stories he heard as a child from his grandmother when growing up in the banana town of Aracataca (in the Magdalena region of Colombia). He took the name "Macondo" from a banana farm located close to Aracataca that was owned by the American multinational corporation, the United Fruit Company. In his novel, García Márquez re-creates one of the most infamous events in Colombian history: the massacre of the United Fruit banana workers demonstrating in the city of Ciénaga by the Colombian army in 1928. In fact, when telling the story of the workers demonstrating in Macondo's main plaza, García Márquez mentions the name General Cortés Vargas. Cortés Vargas was the military commander who led the army's encounter with the strikers, opening fire and killing thousands of demonstrators. This is the only historically accurate name used in the novel; the actual mission to pacify the

Magdalena region in 1928 was commanded by General Carlos Cortés Vargas.[2]

The banana region of Magdalena (where García Márquez grew up) still resembles the time when United Fruit operated there. The towns in the region are still accessible by the railway built by United Fruit in the early twentieth century, and the fenced-in white houses built for the company's managers are still used by some of the locals. On the streets of Ciénaga, the center of the banana region, one still can see the decaying French-style mansions that were the residences of the local planter families. They are now used as cheap restaurants and dance clubs with big, fluorescent, soft drink billboards covering the old, well-crafted façades. Some of the older upper-class residents who remain in the city, their fading European diplomas still hang proudly in living rooms in which the imported furniture has not been replaced in decades, remember with nostalgia the times of the "banana boom" in which they could travel to Paris easily.

When García Márquez was asked why he wrote about the events that took place in Magdalena in the late 1920s, he replied, "I wanted to write about it before the historians come."[3] García Márquez was successful; before 1967, no serious historical studies had been written about the 1928 strike or about the social dynamics surrounding the banana industry in Colombia. However, the spectacular success of *One Hundred Years of Solitude* inspired several scholars to study the magical region they learned of from García Márquez. Just two years after the novel was published, British researcher Judith White wrote the first historical study of the social conflicts leading to the 1928 strike and to the subsequent massacre. White closes her study with a passage taken from *One Hundred Years of Solitude*. In the passage, two of the characters remember the thousands of deaths from the massacre but fall into a mindset of denial by trying to forget it ever happened.

The influence that García Márquez's work has had on scholars interested in the history of United Fruit is enormous. It can not be denied that if García Márquez had not written his work, the history of United Fruit in Colombia would have interested few scholars. No book or article of United Fruit in Magdalena fails to mention García Márquez; all of them take his version of the 1928 massacre seriously. The acceptance of the novel's image of these events as reality has gone far beyond what García Márquez ever imagined. Even now, the portrayal of the thousands of casualties in his novel is accepted as fact among Colombians; high school and college history textbooks still teach a version of the strike that frequently quotes García Márquez as a source.[4] For a country that has had numerous other and more violent massacres in the twentieth century and in which many other multinational corporations operated (larger, even, than United Fruit), it is remarkable how the story of the 1928 strike became a symbol of national resistance against American imperialism. García Márquez has admitted he inflated the number of victims to make his novel more spectacular, and he has been surprised to see how many people take his number seriously. In his words, "the legend has been taken as history."[5]

The infamous image of United Fruit as an exploitative corporation is not limited to Colombia. In fact, United Fruit is often regarded as the quintessential representative of American imperialism in Central and South America. "Banana Republics," the pejorative used for the Central American republics, has its origin in the company's operations in the region. United Fruit has been portrayed as controlling most of the economy of the main banana-producing countries in Central America (Costa Rica, Guatemala, Honduras, and Panama). The company is said to have had local dictators in its pocket and have benefited from extremely generous concessions and harsh repression of workers; it was an extension of the U.S. political interests in Latin America, and it had the blessing of a local elite who gained economically from its operations. The classic study of Charles Kepner and Jay Soothill summarizes the commonly accepted view of the company:

> [This] powerful company has throttled competitors, dominated governments, manacled railroads, ruined planters, choked cooperatives, domineered over workers, fought organized labor, and exploited consumers. Such usage of power by a corporation of a strongly industrialized nation in relatively weak foreign countries constitutes a variety of economic imperialism.[6]

The reasons for United Fruit's terrible reputation are numerous. In 1917, Honduras and Guatemala were on the brink of war over the disputed territory along the Montagua river. This territory also was disputed by United Fruit and its rival, the New Orleans-based Cuyamel Fruit Company, and both companies conspired and intrigued in the internal politics of the two countries in order to gain control over that territory. Although Honduras and Guatemala did not go to war, the developments around this dispute made the two countries' political elites seem like puppets of the foreign corporations. Later, in 1923, United Fruit had the strong support of a Guatemalan military government to violently repress a strike by banana workers. The military government took power after a successful coup against a democratically elected president who had antagonized United Fruit.[7] In 1928, Honduras and Guatemala battled over control of the territory along the Montagua river—a conflict encouraged and supported by United Fruit on the Guatemalan side and by Cuyamel Fruit on the Honduran side. As Paul Dosal accurately put it,

> this banana war revealed the nature of politics and the structure of power in the banana lands of Central America. Decisions made in corporate boardrooms in New Orleans and Boston caused armies of poor young soldiers to defend the illusory sovereignty of both Guatemala and Honduras. The battle for Montagua was not much of a war, but it was the best battle two corporate rivals could arrange.[8]

The conflict was eventually settled by the U.S. government, and, in 1930, Cuyamel and United Fruit merged into a single company.

The historical event that further damaged United Fruit's reputation in Latin America was the military coup against Guatemalan president, Jacobo Arbenz, in 1954. Arbenz, a democratically elected president, attempted to implement agrarian reform by expropriating some unused lands owned by United Fruit. Arbenz faced strong opposition from the Guatemalan upper classes, certain sectors of the military, United Fruit, and the U.S. Department of State. In the end, Arbenz was overthrown by a U.S.-backed Guatemalan military force stationed in Honduras, and the agrarian reform was aborted.[9] The coup generated anti-American and anti-United Fruit demonstrations all over Latin America, and, for many, it was nothing more than further evidence that United Fruit served the interests of Washington. Among those opposed to United Fruit's actions was Argentinian Ernesto Guevara (later known as "Ché"), who was in Guatemala at the time of the coup. According to Guevara, the coup against Arbenz exemplified the futility of trying to achieve social changes via democratic means in Latin America, and the only means of change was through armed revolution.

The studies on United Fruit in Colombia portray its operations there as similar to its operations in Central America. This makes sense given that previous scholars focused only on the 1928 strike and the years prior to it. It is difficult to deny that United Fruit created an enclave in Magdalena and had the support of foreign business-friendly national governments that gave it generous concessions and were willing to send in their armies when the company faced a dangerous strike.

The well-researched works of Catherine LeGrand, Judith White, Fernando Botero, and Alvaro Guzmán all provide an understanding of the social dynamics behind the creation of the banana-export economy, the land conflicts between United Fruit and local peasants, and the historical roots of the 1928 strike. However, by focusing only on the labor, land, and class conflicts before the 1930s, these studies have four shortcomings. First, United Fruit has not been analyzed as a business enterprise. The company's behavior and decisions have not been examined in the context of its long-term business strategy, its shareholders' interests, the evolution of its consumer market, or its constant quest for more profitable activities or approaches to business. LeGrand, White, Botero, and Guzmán are certainly aware of the capitalistic nature of United Fruit, but none of them have attempted to use the analytical tools provided by financial accounting or economic theory to understand United Fruit's behavior related to its workers or its host and home governments or how labor and political conflicts affected United Fruit's corporate strategy. Moreover, even though United Fruit is a multinational corporation, its operations in Colombia have not been analyzed in the context of the company's international strategy. None of the studies on United Fruit in Colombia has analyzed how the company's business was evolving in its other divisions, which certainly affected the company's decisions in Colombia. Last, no attention has been given to the fact that the company had owners and shareholders whose wealth was affected by the company's performance in Latin America. The shareholders' interests has not been systematically analyzed in the historical studies on United Fruit, so these studies have not taken into account the differences between the wants of the company's management, its shareholders, potential investors, and the American government. These different interests were complex, especially as seen from Wall Street or in United Fruit's Boston headquarters. When taken into account, these interests provide a better understanding of the company's operations in Colombia and Central America.

The second shortcoming of previous studies is that by focusing solely on the period prior to 1930, these studies neglect the dramatic transformations Colombia underwent during the twentieth century. In the seven decades following 1930, Colombia went through a complex social and political process that affected the way the country related with multinational enterprises and with United Fruit in particular. Colombia witnessed the fall of its foreign business-friendly Conservative Party and the rise of its union-friendly Liberal Party. Unions grew stronger and the government intervened more in economic issues. The relationship between United Fruit and the Colombian government changed as a result of these circumstances. Colombia also went through a long period of violence that shaped its political system after the 1950s—a government shared between Liberals and Conservatives in which there was consensus on how to manage the economy and how to treat multinationals. These political developments affected the long-term strategy of United Fruit, which was forced to adapt to the new political realities.

The third shortcoming of previous studies on United Fruit in Latin America is that they pay little attention to what happened after United Fruit's ships left the Caribbean shores with their cargo. Although all of the studies make the assumption that United Fruit invested in Latin America to profit from selling bananas in European and American markets, no systematic study has analyzed how consumer market behavior may have affected the way the company operated in its tropical divisions and its relationship with local governments and its workers. It is necessary to understand how the demand for bananas evolved to understand why the company accepted the hazards entailed in creating a huge banana production and distribution network.

The fourth shortcoming of previous studies is that the internal archives of the United Fruit Company in Colombia have never been used. The absence of this important source can be a serious flaw in understanding the dynamics of the company's operations in Colombia. In this study, I use several primary sources that have not been used by any other scholars to date. These sources are the documents from the internal archives of the United Fruit Company in Colombia. They include letters from the managers of the company in Colombia to their superiors in Boston and also include the financial information regarding the division's performance. These files are held in the archives of United Fruit's (now Chiquita Brands) offices in Medellín, Colombia. I also used the internal records of Consorcio Bananero, a banana export company from Magdalena. These records are held in the archives of the Colombian national tax office (Dirección de Impuestos y Aduanas Nacionales [DIAN]) in Bogotá, Colombia. The records include financial information, minutes of meetings, and letters between the company's management and governmental officials. As with the United Fruit records, these sources have not been used for any other academic study.[10] I also make use of the information on contracts between United Fruit and the Magdalena planters held in the notary records of Archivo Histórico del Magdalena (in Santa Marta, Colombia), Notaría Primera de Santa Marta, and Notaría Primera de Aracataca. Last, I use a number of government reports from different agencies in Colombia, many of which are not published. Additionally, I conducted interviews with former American and Colombian employees of United Fruit and local export companies, union leaders, banana entrepreneurs, field workers, politicians, and former members of the Colombian guerrillas in plantations, villages, and cities, especially in Santa Marta, Ciénaga, and Aracataca (Magdalena), Apartadó (Urabá), Medellín, and Bogotá. Together, these new data sources—most of them ignored in previous studies—provide material to draw an accurate picture of the general dynamics of the banana business in Colombia from 1899 to 2000.

In this book, I study the operations of the United Fruit Company in Colombia throughout the twentieth century and analyze the company's relationship with the banana workers, local entrepreneurs, and the local government, taking into account the international context in which the company operated and its characteristics as a business enterprise. My study begins in 1899—the year United Fruit started operations in Colombia—and finishes in 2000, when Chiquita Brands (the successor of United Fruit) declared bankruptcy.

## What Was the General Business Strategy of United Fruit during the Twentieth Century?

First, I will look at how the internal structure of the United Fruit Company evolved throughout the twentieth century and how this evolution was affected by political developments in Latin America. Scholars have paid some attention to the process of vertical integration the company followed in the early twentieth century but have not analyzed the divestiture process that it followed after World War II. I will also address the evolution of the company's business strategy in Colombia: Was it unique, or did it correspond to a general strategy for the company on the continent? Last, I will calculate the profitability of the company's operations.

The United Fruit Company followed a process of vertical integration in the first half of the twentieth century because of unfavorable technical limitations and favorable political and social situations in Latin America. Because bananas are perishable goods, integrating all operations (from production to transportation and marketing) under a single company was necessary. This integration coordinated the process and timing needed to minimize the risk of bananas rotting before they reached consumers.

By integrating, United Fruit not only sought to facilitate the production and transportation of bananas, but also sought a monopolization of the banana market, as the U.S. Department of Justice showed in the 1950s. In the years before World War II, United Fruit eliminated its competitors and eventually controlled more than half of the banana market in the United States.

After World War II, however, the vertically integrated system made less sense. Latin American governments became increasingly nationalistic and labor unions grew stronger. Having investments in the Latin American banana producing regions became risky—a fact of which the company's investors were aware. Additionally, technical improvements in the 1950s made it less necessary for United Fruit to control every aspect of the production process. After World War II, the U.S. government also accused the company of violating antitrust legislation and forced it to get rid of some of its assets. So, in the late 1950s and early 1960s, the company decided to divest and leave production in the hands of locals and concentrate its efforts on marketing. United Fruit also showed a decreasing profit rate throughout the 1950s and 1960s. Although United Fruit's divestiture process decreased its profits, it decreased its risk as well, and that was more important for the company's investors.[11]

Several studies on countries other than Colombia have found that a friendly government made it easier for United Fruit to maintain vertical integration. In the case of Ecuador, Steve Striffler found that increasing labor activism in the country discouraged United Fruit's direct production system. In Guatemala, Paul Jaime Dosal found that the more democratic a government was, the harder it was for United Fruit to get generous concessions over national resources, making its vertically integrated system more expensive. In this book, I will show the relationship friendly government-generous concessions was not only true in Ecuador and Guatemala, but also in Colombia and Latin American operations in general. For United Fruit's shareholders, a vertically integrated structure became an investment risk given the rise of nationalistic governments and unionism in all of Latin America, in addition to the risk of the growing hostility of the U.S. government against the company.

Previous studies that focus on the company as a business entity fall short of providing a view of the company's general corporate strategy in relation to the social and political developments of the regions where it operated. The studies that have made a business-historical analysis only pay full attention to the vertical integration the company went through in the first decades of the twentieth century (this is understandable because these studies were written before the 1950s).[12] However, little has been mentioned about United Fruit's process of divestiture after World War II, even among studies written after 1970—the year the divestiture process was completed.

Business historian Robert Read shows how United Fruit's vertical integration was a response to technical difficulties generated by the very nature of the goods—perishable fruit.[13] Even though Read covers through the 1970s in his study, he gives no explanation of why the company divested. Mira Wilkins also included United Fruit in her monumental work on American multinationals, showing it as a textbook example of a company that followed the patterns defined by Alfred Chandler for big American corporations. United Fruit was the most successful agricultural company in the United States in generating a vertically integrated structure that included plantations, transportation facilities, communication networks, and marketing systems.[14] Although Wilkins does not give an explanation of why United Fruit divested, she provides a general hypothesis for why many American multinationals disintegrated in the postwar period. She suggests the main reason for divestiture was political change in the Third World, including nationalism and a rise of the political left. She does not test this hypothesis in general or in the particular case of United Fruit. Alfred Chandler also hypothesizes on the tendency toward divestiture: he claims the technical improvements of the postwar period made the world more globalized and, therefore, decreased the need of vertical integration. My study completes the analysis made by Read but takes into account the divestiture process. I use Wilkins's and Chandler's hypotheses to understand the change that United Fruit went through by including technical improvements and political changes in my analysis.

Bradford Barham wrote the only study on United Fruit that takes into account government action and technical improvements in understanding the company's divestiture process.[15] Barham claims the company owned more than it actually needed (created "excess capacity") to avoid competition. Excess capacity can only be broken by government action or by technical problems. Barham notes the government's antitrust intervention of the 1970s and the technical problems caused by the new banana varieties introduced by Standard Fruit in the late 1960s as examples of breaking United Fruit's excess capacity. As an example of how the company lost ground, he also shows the rise of the private Colombian banana export companies and state-owned Central American companies. Barham, however, does not acknowledge that the political problems and technical improvements that stimulated United Fruit to change were present from the late 1950s. In my analysis, I find in investors' expectations that divestiture began before the late 1960s.[16]

### What Generated the Labor Conflicts of the Colombian Banana Workers with the United Fruit Company in the 1920s?

Labor relations in Magdalena during the 1920s have generated much interest among scholars who study United Fruit in Colombia. The works of Judith White and Catherine LeGrand are the most important studies on United Fruit in Colombia, and both focus on the origins of labor conflicts in the late 1920s.[17] In her study, LeGrand shows the 1928 conflict to be a result of the penetration of foreign capital in a traditional society. The United Fruit Company created a rural proletariat that conflicted with capitalism. Other studies have seen this as an open conflict between capitalism (United Fruit) and a revolutionary working class (the banana workers). This interpretation sees the 1928 strike as the first step of the revolutionary struggle of the Colombian working class against the existing oppressive system.[18]

I believe the 1928 strike was not a revolutionary battle of the workers against the system but rather a fight to modernize existing labor relations. Analysis of the workers' petitions for the strike, as well as their previous petitions, shows their concern for the lack of formal contracts between the company and them. These strikers were fighting for a modernization of unfair and backward labor relations—a fight that was certainly revolutionary but not in the sense some studies have suggested. United Fruit workers wanted to formalize their relationship with the company and be recognized as employees. There was revolutionary rhetoric among those who supported the strike, but there is nothing really revolutionary in the concessions for which the workers were asking. The "revolutionary" character of the strike was argued later by both the Left (they had martyrs in their struggle) and by the Right (the army's open fire against the peaceful and unarmed strikers was "justified" as a battle in the global war against Communism).

### What Happened to Banana Labor Unionism after the 1928 Strike and How Did It Affect United Fruit's Operations?

White's and LeGrand's studies on the labor movement before and during the 1928 strike are extensive. However, they say little of what happened after the strike, and no other author has studied the poststrike period. Any analysis ending with the military repression of workers in Ciénaga can hardly have an optimistic view of the future for labor unionism in the region. The prosecution and repression of the labor movement in the weeks after the massacre were, indeed, extremely hard. However, if we analyze the evolution of labor relations long term, we come to a different view.

First, the strike was not forgotten, as White implies at the end of her study. It did terrible damage to the ruling Conservative Party's reputation and helped the Liberal Party win in the 1930 elections. During the 1930s, the labor movement in the region received strong government endorsement in its conflicts with United Fruit. When United Fruit returned to the country—after the forced interruption of its activities during World War II—it found a much stronger labor movement. During the late 1950s and 1960s, United Fruit ended up giving into almost all of the unions' demands. This stimulated United Fruit to decrease its direct participation in production, and, in the 1960s, it decided to leave all production activities—and, therefore, all the labor problems—in hands of locals. In short, the labor movement had more agency than acknowledged and designed strategies to get what they wanted from United Fruit. In the long run, this success was not beneficial for the workers because it stimulated the company to leave with all the welfare the workers had managed to get from it. In the end, no matter how strong labor unions were, the United Fruit Company managed to adapt to each new situation and kept operating from a distance.

### What Was the Contractual Relationship between United Fruit and Its Local Providers?

White and LeGrand take the local elite of Magdalena into account to show the difficult position of the local bourgeoisie during the labor conflicts of the 1920s. While most planters viewed the rise of unionism with fear, people involved in commerce supported the strikers because they saw United Fruit's stores—selling cheap goods and using tokens given by the company to its workers—as unfair competition for their own businesses. The planters that provided the fruit to the company are portrayed as passive members of a dormant society with the few exceptions of some mavericks that tried to break the company's monopsony in the fruit market. White and LeGrand show United Fruit's unsuccessful challengers as victims of the overwhelming power of United Fruit and the lack of unity among local planters. However, no scholar has studied the specific contractual relations between United Fruit and the local planters. By studying the way these contracts were written and enforced, we can understand why it was difficult for locals to challenge these contracts and even why they were convenient for a number of local planters.

Additionally, in my analysis I find that in the long run, these planters become a dynamic entrepreneurial class. When United Fruit interrupted its activities in Magdalena during World War II, local planters restarted export activities by creating their own companies. When it returned to the area, United Fruit could not stop these companies and, instead, worked alongside them. But, when United Fruit again interrupted its activities in Magdalena in the 1960s, the local entrepreneurs struggled to keep the banana export business alive. Previous studies on the United Fruit Company in Magdalena accept the dependency theory assumption that once a multinational company leaves an enclave, the enclave is destined to die. Here I will show that the locals had agency and designed strategies to keep their businesses running, even though they eventually failed because of destructive weather conditions and disastrous government policies.

In this book I also study the relationship between the planters of Urabá (the region where United Fruit moved in 1963 after halting its operations in Magdalena) and United Fruit. The history of the planters has also received little attention and is limited to official corporate histories or the backgrounds of labor studies. By studying the planters, we can understand how United Fruit operated once it had transformed into a marketing company.[19]

How Did the Relationship between United Fruit
and the Local and National Governments
in Colombia Evolve in the Twentieth Century?

When studying the 1928 strike, White, LeGrand, Hugo Rodríguez, and Gabriel Fonnegra show the Colombian government as submissive in relation to United Fruit. The way the Colombian army repressed the strikers constitutes strong evidence of this. However, one can come to a different conclusion when taking into account a longer period of time. The massacre tremendously weakened the Conservative government, and the opposition Liberal Party took advantage of the massacre to win the 1930 presidential election. The union-friendly Liberal government tightened controls over foreign companies, against which United Fruit had no defense. Here, I also analyze the voting patterns in the banana towns of Magdalena and show that the Liberals got an increasing portion of the votes as time went on, encouraging the government to reward its constituency.[20]

In the postwar period, Colombian import substitution industrialization policies, with all the economic interventionism they included, conflicted with United Fruit. Additionally, the vagueness of the Colombian legislation regarding expropriation of foreign assets by the government made the legislation a constant threat to the company. United Fruit had little political power to change this trend or oppose government policies. These circumstances made United Fruit's divestiture a better option to reduce the company's risk.

In answering the questions I posed, it is clear that during the twentieth century, United Fruit had to adapt its corporate strategy to the changing political conditions of its host countries. Growing nationalism and increasing power of labor unions in both Colombia and Central America forced United Fruit to divest its operations to reduce the risks created by owning producing assets in its host countries. The current literature on United Fruit examines the effects of the corporation on its host countries' polities but not how the local polities affected United Fruit's corporate strategy. This is a common problem in most historical studies of foreign direct investment in Latin America, which assume a unidirectional effect of multinationals on local polities because of their size and economic power and the relative weakness of their host countries. I will show that local political actors had agency and forced United Fruit to change its strategy and internal structure dramatically, so the effect was not unidirectional. Further analyses of how the corporate strategy of other multinationals operating in the region can make an important contribution for our understanding of the political economy of foreign direct investment in Latin America.

## A Long-Term View of the Banana Industry in Colombia

United Fruit started its operations in Colombia in the region of Magdalena in 1899 and started exporting bananas as shown in figure 1.1. United Fruit continued its operations through the following decades until World War II, when it was forced to interrupt its shipments in the Caribbean. The company returned in 1947 and restarted operations in Magdalena. It abandoned the region again in 1966, moving to the region of Urabá, where it had set up operations in 1963. United Fruit operated in Urabá until 1982, when it abandoned the region until 1989, and left again in 2004.

The Colombian banana export industry had two major crises between 1899 and 2000. The first came in 1930 with the Great Depression, and the second, and worst crisis, came in World War II when exports were interrupted. Figure 1.2 shows how exports recovered after each of these crises. Before the 1960s, banana exports came mainly from Magdalena, but after United Fruit moved to Urabá, there is an impressive growth of exports from this region, as shown in figure 1.3. After the 1970s, Urabá became one of the main banana exporting regions in the world.

During the century of operations in Colombia, United Fruit changed its internal structure from a producing company to a marketing company. After the 1950s, the company gradually began to get rid of its producing assets such as plantations and railways and relied more and more on local planters to produce fruit for purchase. Figure 1.4 shows the decreasing importance of land compared to total assets and figure 1.5 shows the increasing importance of loans from United Fruit to local planters. The reasons why the company followed this process of divestiture only can be explained by analyzing the evolution of the labor movement, Colombian national politics, and the international context in which United Fruit operated. These are the main topics of this book.

## The Setting: Magdalena and Urabá

United Fruit began its operations in Colombia in 1899 in the Department of Magdalena and moved in the early 1960s to the zone of Urabá in the Department of Antioquia.[21] The specific areas where bananas were

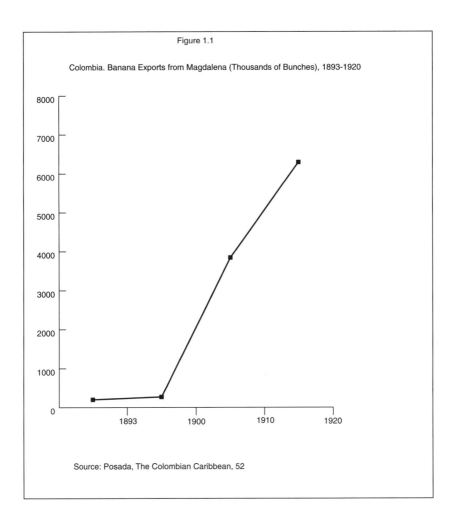

Figure 1.1

Colombia. Banana Exports from Magdalena (Thousands of Bunches), 1893-1920

Source: Posada, The Colombian Caribbean, 52

grown are shown in map 2. These two regions are located in the Llanura del Caribe in northern Colombia—a territory that stretches from the Sierra Nevada de Santa Marta (in Magdalena) on the east to the Serranía de las Palomas (near Urabá) on the west (see map 2). It extends approximately 200 miles from its southwest end to its northeast end and 150 miles from the southeast to the northwest.[22] The region is more humid with more rainfall farther west, and the driest region is located between the cities of Santa Marta and Cartagena.[23]

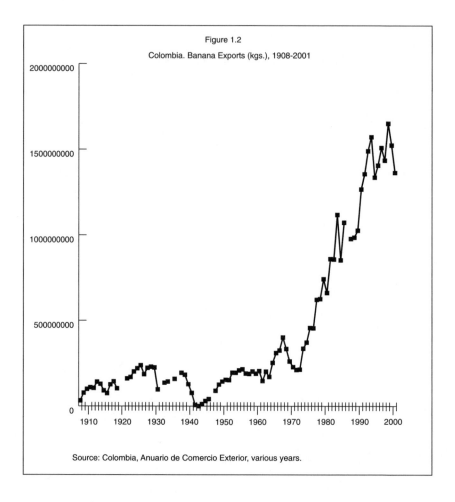

Figure 1.2

Colombia. Banana Exports (kgs.), 1908-2001

Source: Colombia, Anuario de Comercio Exterior, various years.

The Magdalena banana zone (also known as the Santa Marta banana zone) is a plain of about 100,000 acres located between the mountains of the Sierra Nevada de Santa Marta (a huge block of 20,000-foot-high snow-capped mountains less than thirty miles from the Caribbean shore) and a large swampy area known as Ciénaga Grande.[24] Despite being located in the driest region of the Llanura del Caribe, the Magdalena banana zone was blessed with plenty of rain all year due to its closeness to the Sierra Nevada.[25] However, in the 1960s, deforestation of the Sierra changed rainfall patterns, and it became increasingly expensive to transfer water to the banana zone.[26]

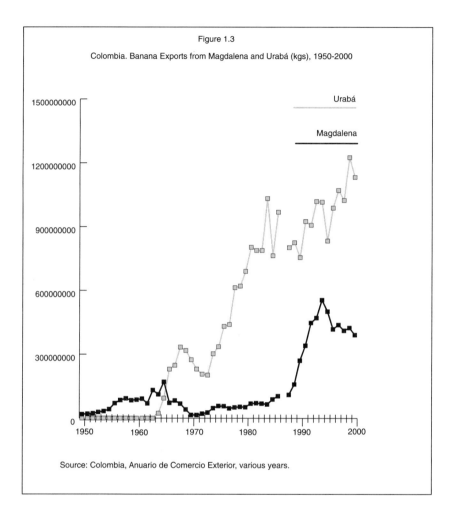

Figure 1.3

Colombia. Banana Exports from Magdalena and Urabá (kgs), 1950-2000

Source: Colombia, Anuario de Comercio Exterior, various years.

The Urabá region is located on the southwest border of the Colombian Caribbean and is known for its rich soil and abundant rainfall.[27] In addition, Urabá has the highest ratio of rivers per kilometer in Colombia, which makes building canals to supply plantations with water unnecessary, but does make it important to drain the soil.

Although both Magdalena and Urabá constituted the first attempts at permanent Spanish settlements in what is now Colombia, both regions were stagnant or decaying prior to the banana export industry. Spanish conquistador Rodrigo de Bastidas established the city of Santa Marta (which is now

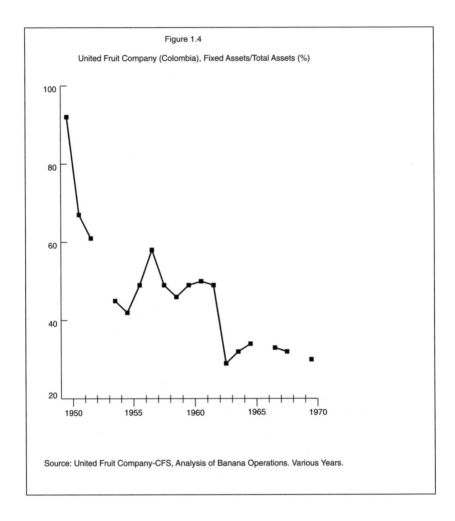

Figure 1.4

United Fruit Company (Colombia), Fixed Assets/Total Assets (%)

Source: United Fruit Company-CFS, Analysis of Banana Operations. Various Years.

the capital of the Magdalena department) in 1524, while Vasco Nuñez de Balboa established Santa María del Darién in Urabá near the same time.[28] Balboa's colony disappeared after a short time because of destructive weather conditions and the constant hostility of the native peoples. Santa María was abandoned and no serious attempts to colonize Urabá were made until the twentieth century. Although Bastidas's Santa Marta survived, its regional importance was overshadowed by the prosperous port city of Cartagena during the colonial period; Cartagena had a protective fortress and its port was used to bring African slaves to the continent.

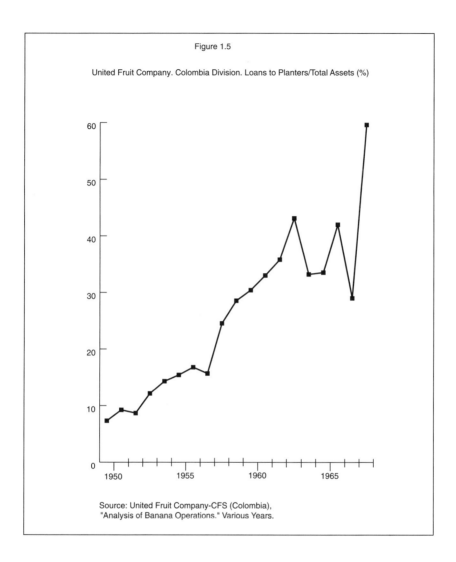

Figure 1.5

United Fruit Company. Colombia Division. Loans to Planters/Total Assets (%)

Source: United Fruit Company-CFS (Colombia),
"Analysis of Banana Operations." Various Years.

Santa Marta's luck did not improve with colonial independence because the city sided with the losers of the war. During the Colombian war
for independence from Spain, the city fought to the end as a loyal bastion
of the Spanish crown, for which it was punished by the succeeding republican governments. During the nineteenth century, Santa Marta was
in a state of abandonment, and the families that owned lands in the surrounding areas had little success in developing any kind of large produc-

tion capacity.[29] These were years of boom and bust exports in Colombia, and the Santa Marta elite tried to join each of these booms but mostly either failed or joined the export too late. Santa Marta also had isolated communities of descendants of runaway slaves or indigenous peoples that lived at a subsistence level and barren fields in which no one showed any interest at all.[30]

While the nineteenth century was a time of stagnation for Magdalena, Urabá was basically forgotten by the rest of the country. The region was an area of conflict between the Dutch, French, Spanish, and native peoples, and this instability was reinforced by Urabá's isolation due to its natural geographic barriers. In fact, the native peoples had managed, to a large extent, to live independently until the nineteenth century despite development aspirations by the province of Antioquia. In those times, Urabá belonged to the province of Córdoba but was the closest access to the sea for the economically prosperous Antioquia. Antioquia lobbied the national government to gain control over what was called the "corridor to the sea," however, the region's harsh geographic characteristics as well as the ongoing civil wars in the area forced Antioquia to postpone its plans to acquire Urabá several times.[31]

## The Effects of the War of the Thousand Days in Magdalena and Urabá: From Oblivion to National Strategic Importance

Between 1899 and 1902, Colombia went through one of the most terrible conflicts in its history—the War of the Thousand Days—a bloody confrontation between Liberals and Conservatives that destroyed the precarious economic infrastructure of the country, causing a national economic recession. Paradoxically, two events that were products of this war contributed to the development of the two forgotten regions of Magdalena and Urabá: the postwar economic policies of President Rafael Reyes and the separation of Panama from the Colombian territory.

During the nineteenth century, Magdalena landowners made several attempts to develop banana exports but always failed to keep their businesses running. Reyes's Conservative government, in its hurry to jump start the national economy, provided incentives for foreign investment such as subsidies and tax exemptions, which the United Fruit Company used for its land purchases and railroad construction.[32] The presence of

United Fruit and its land acquisitions increased the value of real estate, benefiting the sleepy region's upper class. The opening of United Fruit's banana plantations generated a large-scale demand for labor that could not be satisfied with the local population. The scarcity of labor and relatively high salaries offered by the company generated a mass influx of job-seekers from all over the country.[33] The port of Santa Marta restarted operations as the main gate for United Fruit's banana exports, and small towns that had been of little importance, such as Aracataca and Ciénaga, became dynamic urban centers. Santa Marta flourished, while Cartagena, the former economic center of the Colombian Caribbean, slowly decayed due to the end of the slave trade. The rise of the banana business was radically changing the landscape of the Colombian Caribbean.

Colombians began to focus their attention on Urabá after the successful support of the United States for the separation of Panama from Colombian territory, which took advantage of the chaotic situation during the War of the Thousand Days. The painful experience of losing Panama to independence created a consensus among the defeated Liberals and the triumphant Conservatives that a centralization of power was imperative in Colombia to avoid further secessions. Once Panama separated from Colombia, Urabá's strategic importance increased because it bordered the newly created country.

Several studies at that time pointed to Urabá as a potential location for the construction of an interocean canal, so the government feared that the United States would try to create another new country in Urabá to gain control of the canal.[34] This led the central government to rush a formalization of Antioquia's sovereignty of Urabá. With Urabá in its hands, the Antioquian government undertook the infamous construction of a road from Medellín to Urabá (the "Carretera al Mar") during the first decades of the century. The novelistic and epic construction of the road by the Antioquian government was to promote the colonization of the region.[35] The construction, however, took too long and the region's characteristics did not provide enough incentive for colonization.

During the first half of the twentieth century, Urabá did not see the economic development the Antioquian government had wanted. Antioquia's coffee exports continued through the other Caribbean ports of Barranquilla and Santa Marta, leaving Turbo, the main urban center of Urabá, as a small fishing village. The development of the region had to wait until the early 1960s when the United Fruit Company started its operations by financing local entrepreneurs from Medellín to clear the jungle and open plantations. In three short years, Urabá transformed from an unpopulated jungle into one of the main banana producing and export centers in the world.

The rise of Urabá as an export region generated deep and everlasting consequences in the region. Because the region had a low population, the banana export sector had to attract workers from other areas. The first workers came from the surrounding poor Caribbean, but they were joined later by workers from the more developed coffee region of Colombia. The small village of Turbo experienced an incredible increase in population, and other small villages, such as Apartadó, Chigorodó, and Carepa, grew into dynamic urban centers.

The creation of the banana export business in both Urabá and Magdalena broke not only the isolation of these regions from the rest of the world, but also their isolation from the rest of the country. Before the twentieth century, the government's attention was focused on developing other areas of the country, and it neglected these two regions. These regions had never attracted national investors either. Magdalena had an impoverished upper class, while Urabá had not had a large enough population to generate change. These regions had been the first to feel the Spanish sword in Colombia. Both, however, came out of oblivion when a new foreign force—American capital—swept through with what García Márquez called "the leaf storm," and changed them forever.

## Organization

This book is organized as follows: Chapter 2 analyzes the role of demand for bananas in the American market and how it influenced United Fruit operations in Latin America. Chapter 3 discusses the business strategy of United Fruit at the international level. This chapter analyzes the growth of the company and its vertical integration process and the shift of the company from a production company to a marketing company. Chapter 4 studies the evolution of the relationship of United Fruit with the local government of Magdalena and the national Colombian government and how it affected the company's long-term strategy.

Chapter 5 gives a reinterpretation of the origins of the 1928 strike in Magdalena. Chapter 6 studies the evolution of the Colombian banana labor movement after World War II and the effects it had on United Fruit's policies. Chapter 7 analyzes the relationship between United Fruit and local planters in Magdalena and Urabá. Chapter 8 concludes this book.

# 2

# From Hotel Luxury Suites
# to Working-Class Lunchboxes

## Introduction

In the 1880s, Americans had never heard of bananas. A decade later, they were being sold in major American cities in individually wrapped tinfoil packages as luxury goods. By the 1910s, they were considered a cheap fruit—part of the basic diet of the growing American urban working class. After the 1930s, Americans could find bananas in any grocery store or supermarket across the country at any time of year. Bananas were no longer considered an exotic fruit; they became a common part of breakfast with traditional food such as bread and milk. A national mass consumption of bananas was possible because of the production and distribution network created by the United Fruit Company and, to a lesser extent, Standard Fruit.[1]

The U.S. banana imports by United Fruit and Standard Fruit increased long term but experienced three interruptions—World War I, the Great Depression, and World War II. Figures 2.1 and 2.2, which plot the trend of banana imports in stems and tons over the last century, show a steady increase in imports until the 1960s and another increase after the 1970s. In this section I will explain the reasons for that pattern.[2]

United Fruit's management would not have put such tremendous effort into creating a production and distribution network (described in chapter 3), if the year-round demand for fresh fruit did not exist. The first decade of the twentieth century witnessed a clear change in the way American consumers perceived bananas—from a luxury good into a part of their basic diet.

## From Luxury Good to Basic Staple: The Evolution of Mass Banana Consumption, 1880s to World War I

With the exception of a few shipments in the 1860s, bananas were imported to the United States on a regular basis only after the mid-1880s.

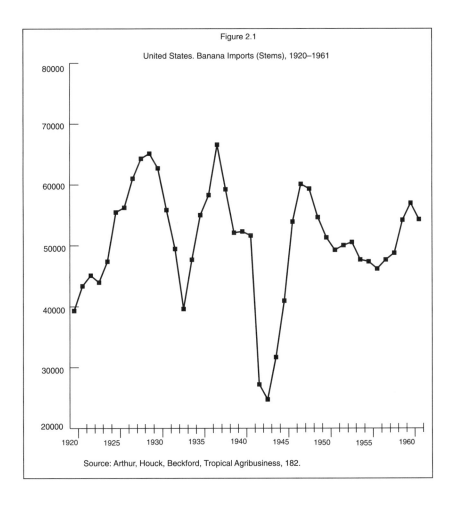

Figure 2.1

United States. Banana Imports (Stems), 1920–1961

Source: Arthur, Houck, Beckford, Tropical Agribusiness, 182.

Figure 2.3 shows a constant increase in banana imports measured in dollars from 1884 to the 1900s. Unfortunately, American customs offices did not record the number of stems of bananas or the weight of the imports before 1908, so there is no way to calculate the quantity of bananas actually imported before that year. However, a rise from zero dollars before 1884 to more than ten million dollars in 1906 shows undeniably impressive growth. The steady growth of the 1880s coincides with the creation of the Boston Fruit Company. After experiencing a slight decline during the 1890s, there was a new push to import bananas after 1899—that is, after the creation of United Fruit and Standard Fruit.

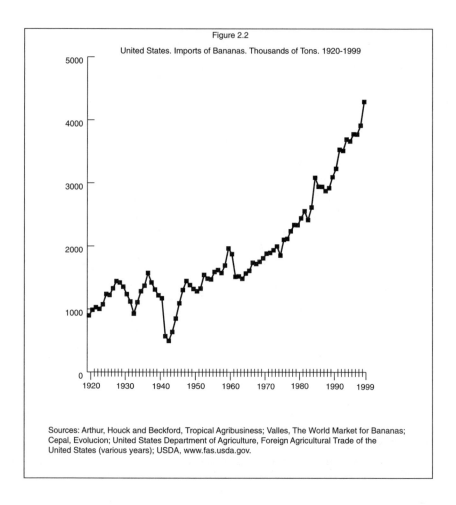

Figure 2.2

United States. Imports of Bananas. Thousands of Tons. 1920-1999

Sources: Arthur, Houck and Beckford, Tropical Agribusiness; Valles, The World Market for Bananas; Cepal, Evolucion; United States Department of Agriculture, Foreign Agricultural Trade of the United States (various years); USDA, www.fas.usda.gov.

In its first annual report, United Fruit told its stockholders the company was making gains as a result of the growing demand for bananas in the American market. The numbers mentioned by president Andrew Preston in the 1901 annual report demonstrate the dramatic changes of this market:

> Through its distributing department, the Fruit Dispatch Company, your company has organized a most thorough and systematic method of disposing of its products throughout the United States, agencies for marketing of the fruit having been established in all of the principal cities of the country. While only a short time has elapsed since its organization was

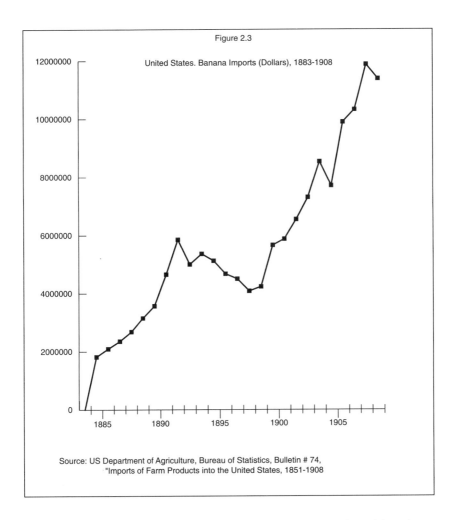

Figure 2.3

United States. Banana Imports (Dollars), 1883-1908

Source: US Department of Agriculture, Bureau of Statistics, Bulletin # 74,
"Imports of Farm Products into the United States, 1851-1908

perfected, the results have been extremely gratifying, not only enabling the consumer to purchase bananas at less cost than ever before, but largely increasing the consumption of the fruit. During the year 1901 the Fruit Dispatch Company distributed 18,906 carloads of tropical products, against 16,197 the preceding year, an increase of 2,709 carloads, or nearly 16%.[3]

The impressive figures continued over the next several years until World War I. In 1902, the company reported an increase of 12% in banana sales and a significant reduction in transportation costs.[4] The company marketed aggressively, increasing the number of branches of Fruit Dispatch by 50% in 1905 alone[5] and reporting an increase in sales of 17% from this subsidiary for 1906.[6] The company reported the increase in demand was not only in the United States but also in Europe, its next target.

The change in consumption patterns can be linked to the way people perceived bananas. In her study of the evolution of bananas in American society, Virginia Jenkins reveals that in the late nineteenth century, bananas were advertised as items to be tasted in upscale hotels and restaurants, but by the early twentieth century, widely read magazines began publishing recipes that required bananas as an ingredient. Bananas gradually disappeared from the menus of expensive restaurants and were increasingly mentioned in popular songs and in newspaper cartoons. Late into the first decade of the 1900s and early into the second, bananas were even shown in magazines and silent films as a food of the poor. In fact, bananas were offered to European immigrants who came through Ellis Island as their first taste of the United States.[7]

Import companies tried to increase demand even more by distributing books and pamphlets that highlighted the benefits of bananas. Their main target was housewives, who were taught banana recipes, the nutritional value of the fruit, and the advantages of using it as baby food because of its texture. Import companies even tried to change cultural perceptions of the American population, such as the perception that a respectable lady would not eat a banana in public. The attempts were so successful that, in time, people considered bananas a fruit for women and children.[8]

Evidence of the changing status of bananas in the United States became a political debate in the second decade of the 1900s. In July 1913, the Senate Finance Committee included bananas in the proposed Underwood-Simmons Tariff. Bananas would be taxed five cents per bunch in order to raise one million dollars a year. This proposal faced strong opposition from many sectors. The Atlantic Fruit Company argued this tax would hurt them and other small companies and favor United Fruit, turning it into a monopoly. Byron W. Holt, chairman of the Tariff Reform Committee of the Reform Club called the tax regressive. According to Holt, bananas not only were the "poor man's luxury," but also, more important, they were the only fresh fruit Americans could count on finding in grocery stores year long at affordable prices. Additionally, Holt praised the high nutritional value of bananas and highlighted that they were one of the few products that had not increased in price over the last decade. In a widely publicized letter to the *New York Times*, Holt wrote, "the consumption [of bananas] is greater in the poorer districts of large cities than any other fruit. Its sale is rapidly increasing—from 18,000,000 bunches in 1900 to 42,000,000 in 1912."[9]

Protests against the banana tariff were numerous. In 1913, the Banana Buyers' Protective Association held a public meeting in New York City to demand that President Woodrow Wilson reject the banana tax proposal. During the meeting, the president of the Housewives' League, Sophie Loeb, claimed the current cost of five cents for four large bananas would increase to five cents per banana under the tariff, severely hurting working-class families. During his speech, the president of the Buyers' Association, Harry Weinberger, said,

> The only fruit that comes every day in the year, year in and year out, almost unvarying in price, within the reach of all, nutritious, healthy in its germ-proof coat, is the golden ranks of the incoming tide of bananas, 40,000,000 bunches a year, two to four billion golden satisfiers of American desires. Does Congress expect to cheapen the banana for the poor man by a tariff?[10]

Consumer organizations were soon joined by larger import firms and the media in their protest. Joseph DiGiorgio, a banana importer from New York, brought over foreign delegations of producers to lobby the American government against the tariff. Senator Williams, one of the proponents of the tariff, defended it by saying it would hurt the quasi-monopolistic power of United Fruit more than the final consumers. The *New York Times* immediately attacked his view by arguing that United Fruit was not exactly a "bad trust" because it was benefiting the poor. "Never were bananas cheaper, better or more plenty" than in that year, argued the *Times*.[11]

The lobby against the tariff included diplomatic delegations and international organizations. The ambassadors of Costa Rica, Panama, Guatemala, and Nicaragua appealed to President Wilson to oppose the tariff. The director general of the Pan-American Union expressed that the banana business had done more for the development of producing countries in a short time than anything before. The economic prosperity of Central America and the Caribbean and their political stability would be at stake if the tariff was approved. The debate continued for several months until November 1913, when the banana tax was dropped from the Underwood-Simmons Bill tax list. The defeat was announced joyfully by the *New York Times*.[12]

Were the opponents of the tariff correct? One way to test their argument is by analyzing the per capita consumption of bananas in that period. Between 1909 (the first year this information was available) and 1914, the consumption of bananas per person climbed from 17 pounds to 18.1 pounds. This increase is significant when comparing the weight of bananas with the consumption of all fresh fruits. The results are shown in table 2.1.

Table 2.1 shows that by the mid-1910s, bananas were important in the diet of American consumers. By taxing bananas, authorities would have affected the prices of more than a quarter of the fresh fruit consumed by Americans. At that time, no other fruit could be found in stores year round, and fruit processing had not yet been developed in a way that could satisfy existing demand. The tax also would have affected an important subset of consumers—babies—because canned baby foods with fruit were not produced until the mid-1930s. Table 2.2 shows the percentage of processed food consumption for the same period as a total of all processed and fresh fruits consumed.

TABLE 2.1

*Per-capita consumption of bananas in retail weights vs.*
*percentage of per-capita consumption of bananas of total fresh fruits*

| Year | Bananas (pounds) | % Bananas/ Total Fresh Fruits |
|------|------------------|-------------------------------|
| 1909 | 17               | 20.9                          |
| 1910 | 16.9             | 20.7                          |
| 1911 | 18.8             | 26.1                          |
| 1912 | 17.1             | 24.3                          |
| 1913 | 18.4             | 21.9                          |
| 1914 | 18.1             | 26.5                          |

Source: Author's calculations with information from US Department of Agriculture, Economic Research Service, *U.S. Food Consumption*, Statistical Bulletin # 364 (Washington: USDA, 1965: 35)

TABLE 2.2

*Per-capita consumption of processed foods:*
*Percentage on total fruits (fresh and processed)*

| Year | % Processed fruits/Total Fruits |
|------|----------------------------------|
| 1909 | 9.3                              |
| 1910 | 9.9                              |
| 1911 | 12.4                             |
| 1912 | 13.9                             |
| 1913 | 10.4                             |
| 1914 | 15.4                             |

Source: Author's calculations with information from US Department of Agriculture, Economic Research Service, *U.S. Food Consumption*, Statistical Bulletin # 364 (Washington: USDA, 1965: 18-19)

The quantitative and anecdotal evidence shows that before World War I, bananas became an important staple of the American diet. During a time of rapid urbanization, industrialization, and a growing population, this fruit came to satisfy a demand for fresh fruit not met by local production or processed food.

## The Boost of the 1920s and the Effects of the Depression on Banana Consumption

World War I caused a downturn in the banana market. Trade in the Caribbean basin was interrupted as the U.S. government required both United Fruit and Standard Fruit to provide ships to support the war effort. This caused a dramatic decrease in the amount of imports, but as figures 2.1 and 2.2 show, the banana market recovered remarkably after the conflict. In fact, United Fruit's management was so confident the demand would continue rising that it announced to its shareholders it would increase significantly the amount of land for cultivation in the following months.[13]

The exceptional increase in imports for the period after World War I can be attributed to the increasing demand of a nonsaturated market. As figure 2.4 shows, the per capita consumption of bananas jumped during the 1920s, stimulating import companies to increase their shipments. In order to maintain a growing demand, United Fruit advertised new ways to eat bananas. In 1924, the Fruit Dispatch Company, a subsidiary of United Fruit, distributed a recipe book promoting the consumption of bananas with corn flakes and milk for breakfast. This was such a success that in the years following, the company made deals with cereal companies in order to mutually promote their products.[14] Fruit Dispatch also embarked on a campaign to show the health benefits of bananas for working-class Americans. In 1927, the company published a book that provided scientific evidence proving bananas contained most of individuals' necessary vitamins, calories, and proteins in greater quantities than other fruits and at a much cheaper price.[15] By 1929, United Fruit decided to form an advertising department at Fruit Dispatch in order to have a full-time staff create new ideas for marketing bananas.

The constant growth of demand for bananas in the United States constituted an enormous incentive for United Fruit not only to increase its production in Latin America, but also to eliminate its weaker competitors in the lucrative market. In chapter 3 I will show how this period of

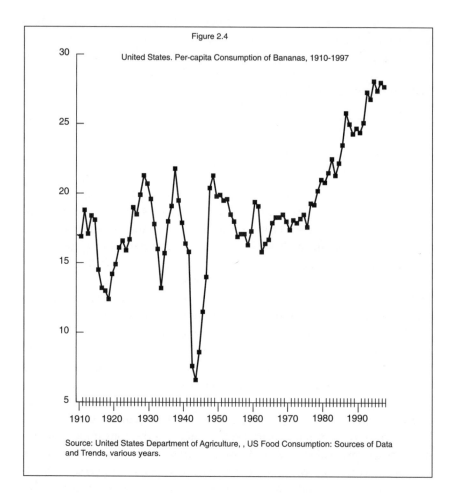

Figure 2.4

United States. Per-capita Consumption of Bananas, 1910-1997

Source: United States Department of Agriculture, , US Food Consumption: Sources of Data and Trends, various years.

growth in the banana market coincides with the process of vertical integration of the company's operations and the aggressive war it made against other firms importing bananas to the United States and creating a monopolistic market. Over the twentieth century, the banana market in the United States was less and less competitive, gradually falling under United Fruit's control.

The stock market crash of 1929 affected the banana sector as it did the rest of the economy. Import companies faced difficulties keeping imports afloat while per capita consumption fell. It is worth highlighting that as per capita consumption of all fresh fruit in general declined during the

TABLE 2.3
*Per-capita Consumption of Fresh Fruits vs. Bananas, 1928-1938 (Pounds)*

| Year | Bananas | Total Fresh Fruit | % Bananas of Total Fresh Fruit |
|------|---------|-------------------|-------------------------------|
| 1928 | 21.3 | 133.7 | 28.5 |
| 1929 | 20.7 | 128.1 | 26.5 |
| 1930 | 19.6 | 119.3 | 23.4 |
| 1931 | 17.8 | 147 | 26.1 |
| 1932 | 16 | 115.9 | 18.5 |
| 1933 | 13.2 | 114.8 | 15.1 |
| 1934 | 15.7 | 115 | 18.0 |
| 1935 | 18 | 134.2 | 24.1 |
| 1936 | 19.1 | 124.1 | 23.7 |
| 1937 | 21.8 | 142.7 | 31.1 |
| 1938 | 19.5 | 131 | 25.5 |
| 1939 | 17.9 | 148.6 | 26.6 |

Source: Author's calculations with information from US Department of Agriculture, Economic Research Service, *U.S. Food Consumption*, Statistical Bulletin # 364 (Washington: USDA, 1965: 18-19)

first four years of the Great Depression, the amount of bananas consumed as a percentage of all fresh fruit shrank accordingly. This may be a result of the rising price of bananas due to the decrease in imports. Bananas reached their lowest point of consumption in 1933—the same year as the lowest per capita consumption of fresh fruit in the pre–World War II period, as shown in table 2.3.

The recovery of fresh fruit and banana consumption in the late 1930s, along with the revival of the American economy, was interrupted once again with the outbreak of World War II in 1939. As seen in figures 2.1 and 2.2, banana imports fell to their lowest historical levels, severely affecting the per capita demand for the fruit. Once the war ended, the import companies were ready to resupply the market as they did after World War I. However, the postwar period presented a different scenario. Bananas, and fresh fruit in general, had to compete with a substitute that affected demand patterns for several decades.

## The Development of Processed Food and Its Impact on the Demand for Bananas

The Buyers' Association protested the federal government's tariff on banana imports arguing the tariff would negatively impact the American working class. This was true when American consumers depended on the fruit of the season to get the nutrients needed from fruits. However, the post–World War II period witnessed technological innovations that permitted better preservation of fruit and led to a loss in market share by fresh fruits.

By the time World War II ended, Americans had been living without one of their favorite prewar fruits for almost four years and welcomed the return of bananas. Imports of bananas increased as never before, as shown in figure 2.2, and reached their highest levels in the late 1950s. This huge increase in imports, however, responded more to changes on the supply side of the industry than on the demand side. This is evident from the fall of per capita consumption after the war; a simultaneous fall in retail prices for bananas; a new market for processed fruit; and a boost in imports from more productive banana plantations in Latin America.

After imports returned, the per capita consumption of bananas reached its then-highest historical level—an average 21.8 pounds of bananas per person—in 1948. This level was slightly higher than before the war in 1937, when per capita consumption was 21.3 pounds. Import companies could not keep up with the demand for bananas. However, as figure 2.4 shows, per capita consumption gradually began to fall during the 1950s.

This decrease and skyrocketing imports caused a drop in real retail price. In figure 2.5 I have calculated the real retail price of bananas for the period between 1947 and 1963 using the consumer price index provided by the Department of Agriculture. My calculation of the banana real retail price is based on the consumer price index for food calculated by the USDA (1958=100). Unfortunately for the marketing and producing companies, this tendency was not unique to the United States. The calculations made by Jean-Paul Valles show a similar trend in Europe, sinking United Fruit's hopes for postwar demand there.[16]

The fall in per capita consumption of bananas was similar to all fresh fruit. What happened to demand? What was replacing the nutritional value of fresh fruit? Processed foods. After World War II, the technological developments in processed foods made various types of fruit available year round and ended the banana's nonseasonal advantage. Figure 2.6 shows how per capita consumption of fresh fruit declined in the postwar period while processed fruit increased during the same period. While, in 1909, processed fruit represented only around 5% of all fruit consumed

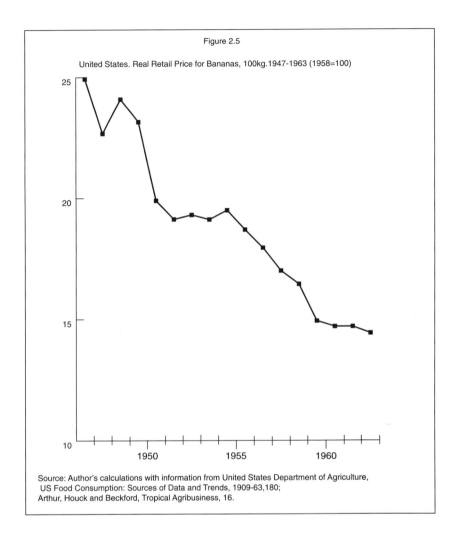

Figure 2.5

United States. Real Retail Price for Bananas, 100kg.1947-1963 (1958=100)

Source: Author's calculations with information from United States Department of Agriculture,
US Food Consumption: Sources of Data and Trends, 1909-63,180;
Arthur, Houck and Beckford, Tropical Agribusiness, 16.

in the United States, by the early 1960s it had reached levels above 40% (see figure 2.7).

One specific industry that replaced bananas was the processed baby food industry. In 1934 the total supply of canned baby food was twenty-one million pounds, but by 1956 it was one billion pounds (see figure 2.8). The per capita consumption increased dramatically, as seen in figure 2.9. The banana industry had lost one of its early target consumers—babies.

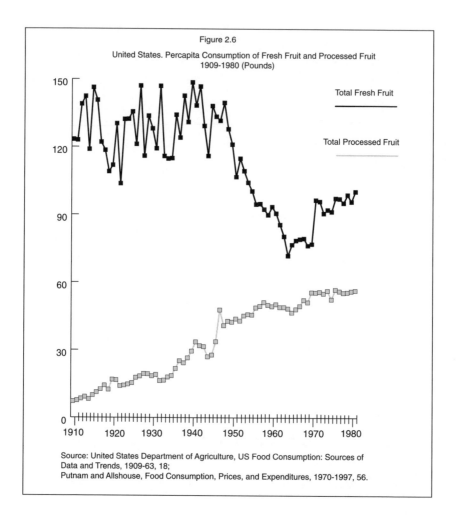

Figure 2.6

United States. Percapita Consumption of Fresh Fruit and Processed Fruit
1909-1980 (Pounds)

Total Fresh Fruit

Total Processed Fruit

Source: United States Department of Agriculture, US Food Consumption: Sources of
Data and Trends, 1909-63, 18;
Putnam and Allshouse, Food Consumption, Prices, and Expenditures, 1970-1997, 56.

The shift in consumer preferences paralleled an increase in productivity by Latin American producers. During the second half of the 1950s,
Standard Fruit and United Fruit experimented with a new kind of banana
plant that had a higher yield and was more resistant to diseases and
strong winds. This higher productivity, along with a fall in demand,
helped to push down the price of bananas.[17] The banana companies decided to join the growing processed food industry and began to diversify
their operations in the mid-1960s. In 1970, United Fruit merged with

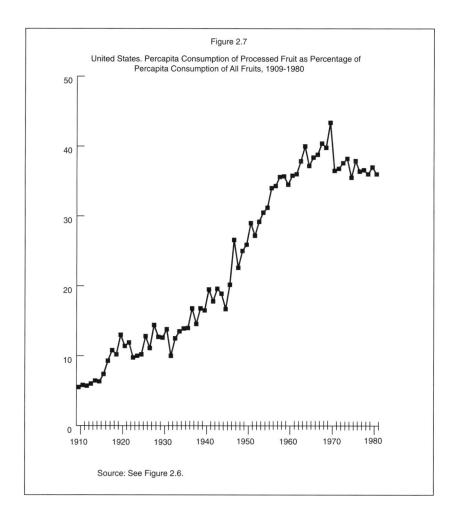

Figure 2.7

United States. Percapita Consumption of Processed Fruit as Percentage of Percapita Consumption of All Fruits, 1909-1980

Source: See Figure 2.6.

AMK-John Morrell, a meat packing company, and created a new company called United Brands. United Brands continued a strong marketing campaign for bananas, promoting the Chiquita brand, while expanding into a wide range of processed foods.

The changes in banana consumption paralleled another series of political and labor problems for United Fruit in the 1960s that I describe in chapter 3. The combination of these political events, together with changes in banana demand patterns, stimulated the company to decrease

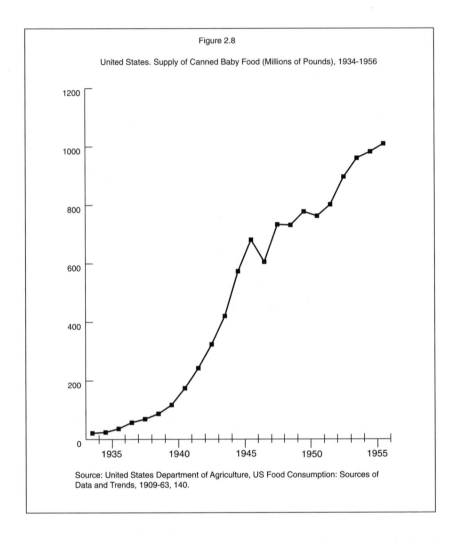

Figure 2.8

United States. Supply of Canned Baby Food (Millions of Pounds), 1934-1956

Source: United States Department of Agriculture, US Food Consumption: Sources of Data and Trends, 1909-63, 140.

its participation in direct production of bananas in Latin America and concentrate its efforts on marketing bananas and processed fruit. The changes in banana supply after the 1950s were also affected by a wider participation of other banana producing companies after the American government forced United Fruit to sell some of its participation in the banana market to other companies—a move that permitted the rise of the Dole and Del Monte companies and created a more competitive market (see chapter 3).

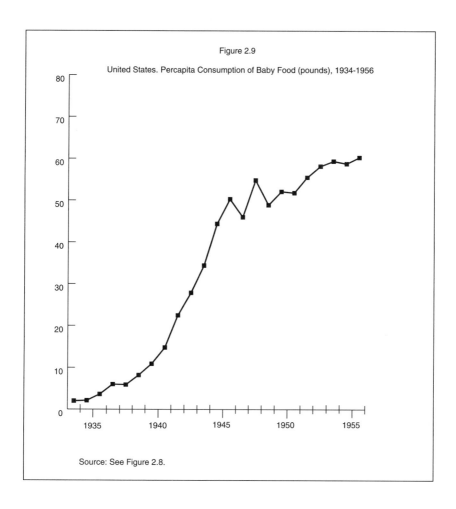

Figure 2.9

United States. Percapita Consumption of Baby Food (pounds), 1934-1956

Source: See Figure 2.8.

## A Nation Obsessed with Weight and the Revival of Banana Consumption after the 1970s

Processed fruit did not eliminate fresh fruit from the diets of American consumers. The displacement of fresh fruit by processed fruit stabilized in the second half of the 1960s and recovered during the latter half of the 1970s. Demand for bananas skyrocketed in the 1980s, surpassing the 1939 record of 21.8 pounds per capita in 1984 and reaching 27.7 pounds in 1997 (see figure 2.4).

The increase in consumption was in response to a general trend of fashion and health. After World War II, an increasing number of Americans worked sedentary jobs and used cars as their main mode of transportation more frequently than previous generations. This lifestyle, together with a high sugar and high fat diet, created an overweight population with serious and costly health problems. During the 1970s, Americans became aware of this problem. Dieting became trendy, and the market was flooded by books, magazines, and products to lose weight.

In the 1970s, Americans also began to worry about the risks of cancer and heart disease. Various government and medical reports began to associate the risks of cancer with an unhealthy diet. The government funded a campaign to educate the public on the need to change eating habits to reduce health risks. Thus, led by fashion trends and health concerns, more than ever before, Americans began to exercise regularly, and being "on a diet" became a household expression.

The awareness of obesity in the 1970s had a huge impact on American food consumption. Between 1970 and 1997, the American per capita consumption of fruits and vegetables increased by 24%. At the same time, vegetarianism was no longer considered an exotic hippie, Buddhist, or counterculture practice, and red meat consumption decreased by 16%.[18] By 1997, Americans reduced their consumption of flour and cereal products by 100 pounds per person compared to 1909.

In the 1980s, there was a consensus among Americans that eating fruits and vegetables was better than eating fatty foods. Both the consumption and price of fruits and vegetables increased between 1982 and 1997. According to USDA calculations, fruits and vegetables led to food retail price increases in this period. The price of fresh fruit increased dramatically (by 138%) compared to an increase of 107% for fresh vegetables, 54% for processed fruit, and 50% for processed vegetables. During this period, the consumption of fresh fruit increased by 24% while processed fruit increased by only 5%.[19]

United Brands responded to the changes in demand by reversing the process initiated by Eli Black, who tried to expand the processed food branch of the company. When Carl Lindner took over the company in the 1980s, he decided to refocus on the banana business and got rid of some of the processed fruit subsidiaries. Although the analyses made by the Food and Agriculture Organization [FAO] in 1986 stated that the U.S. and European markets had reached saturation and forecasted a decrease in demand in the years to come, Lindner embarked the company on long-term plans to increase world banana supply (which included investing again in plantations as the company did before the 1960s). Contrary to the FAO's forecast, the market did not saturate in the 1980s. In the late 1980s and early 1990s, Lindner decided to bet on the promising unified European market. The enlargement of the European Union and the opening of former Communist economies was seen by United Brands (now renamed Chiquita) as a place where it would find a larger demand to satisfy. Unfortunately for Chiquita, E.U. regulations and the way the Eastern European economies evolved did not permit the company to gain from this promising market and cost the company dearly (see chapter 3).

In the 1990s, some American consumers were not only more concerned about eating bananas and fresh fruit in general, but also about how the fruit was grown, popularizing the consumption of organic food among a certain segment of the American population. Even though organic bananas represent just 0.5% of total consumption, the growth of organic banana imports to the United States in the late 1990s was impressive: 1999 showed an increase of 25% from 1998, and the year 2000 showed an increase of 50% from the previous year.[20] The producing countries, aware of the growing demand for organic bananas, have made an effort to supply this market: the Dominican Republic increased its exports by 80% from 1999 to 2000, and Colombia and Ecuador increased organic production by 115% and 80%, respectively, in the same period.[21]

Though the market for organic bananas was still small in 2000, the rapid growth of their demand was incentive enough for Chiquita to work on supplying the U.S. market with organic bananas. In 2001, the FAO forecasted good prospects for growth in the organic food market in the E.U. and the U.S., and in that year, Chiquita began to promote its organic bananas heavily. Although it will take time before organic bananas become mainstream, Chiquita, despite its recent declaration of bankruptcy, has begun to think ahead and prepare for the twenty-first-century changes in the fruit market.

## Conclusion

The literature on the history of the United Fruit Company ignores a crucial aspect of the company's operations. United Fruit developed its production and distribution network in order to satisfy an existing demand for bananas in the United States. Varying demand patterns influenced the company's operations in Latin America. Therefore, in order to understand the company's behavior in Latin America, it is crucial to understand the changes in the consumer market. As long as Americans wanted to eat bananas, United Fruit justified its investments in Latin America.

The international banana industry developed by United Fruit in the early twentieth century was created to satisfy an existing demand for fresh fruit in the United States. During the first half of the century, this demand could not be satisfied by other local fruits because their availability depended on seasonal changes, while bananas were available year round.

The effort made by multinational corporations to make the fruit available for American consumers helped bananas evolve from being a luxury and exotic fruit in the late nineteenth century to becoming a mass-consumed good and part of the basic diet of the American population. The shift was due to a realization by banana companies that bananas could supply the American market with a fresh fruit that did not depend on seasonal changes. The banana companies made large investments in Latin America and provided the fruit in large quantities. Despite an ever-increasing supply, the American per capita consumption of the fruit continued to grow through World War II, with the exception of the economic crisis of the Great Depression and international conflicts that did not permit trade in the Caribbean Basin (World War I and World War II).

Per capita consumption—which for so many years looked like it would never stop growing—began to decrease in the 1950s. The developments in food processing permitted Americans to have other options to satisfy their demand for fruits out of season. Demand for processed fruit increased dramatically, while demand for fresh fruit decreased in absolute terms. This trend caused multinational corporations to change their internal structure, diversify, and reorient their operations toward the processed fruit industry.

In the 1970s, however, American demand reversed. People began to consume more fruits and vegetables, and the per capita consumption of bananas increased steadily until the end of the century. This encouraged United Brands (and Chiquita Brands) to refocus its efforts on the banana trade and to reinvest in banana production after several decades of a marketing emphasis.

In short, there is a direct correlation between the evolution of the American demand for bananas and the way United Fruit operated in its producing regions. The company specialized in bananas as long as bananas faced little competition in the consumer market. The rising demand for bananas in the first half of the century justified the company's huge investments in Central America and the Caribbean. This demand also justified United Brand's schemes to eliminate competition and gain monopoly power. Once consumers found a substitute for bananas, the company changed its focus and began producing the substitute—processed foods. This change came when the company was facing increasing political problems in its producing countries and in the United States, so it had many incentives to decrease its participation in direct production. However, after the 1970s, and especially during the 1980s and 1990s, the demand for bananas rose again due to the new dieting patterns of the American people, and the company again refocused on bananas.

In the case of United Fruit, as in the case of other multinational corporations operating in Latin America, we can not have a complete and accurate understanding of the actions taken by the company in a host country without taking into account what was going on in the consumer market. Multinational corporations operate in their host country because they want to sell their products to a consumer market and generate profits for their shareholders.

# 3

# The United Fruit Company in Latin America

*Business Strategies in a Changing Environment*

This chapter examines the evolution of the United Fruit Company's business strategies throughout the twentieth century. The company had to adapt to the changing political environment in Latin America; these changes were facilitated by technical improvements in the banana industry. Prior to World War II, the company built its production and distribution empire following vertical integration. This system ensured the coordinated flow of highly perishable bananas to their final markets. United Fruit had good relationships with most of the governments of the countries in which it operated, so its huge investments were safe from any threat. Additionally, United Fruit used its growing power to eliminate its competitors either by absorbing them or by forcing them out of the market through price wars. In this way, the company eventually managed to control more than half of the international banana market. Because of this, United Fruit was repeatedly accused of creating a monopoly.

After World War II, however, the situation changed. In the decades following the war, the company was faced with a different political-economic environment—one characterized by increased labor union activity, higher taxes on exports, growing nationalism, competition from independent producers in Ecuador, and a technological transformation that made vertical integration less important. In addition, United Fruit faced the growing hostility of the U.S. government itself, which accused the company of violating antimonopoly legislation. Well aware of these changes, the company slowly transformed its operations from being a direct producer of bananas into a marketer of tropical fruit. This change was made with the support of the company's shareholders and American institutional investors.

In this way, during the 1960s the United Fruit Company got rid of its fixed assets—its main source of risk. In the decades after 1970, United Fruit faced new political problems in Latin America that reinforced its decision to stay out of the direct production of bananas. Later, in the 1990s, United Fruit faced new kinds of problems in the policies followed by European banana importers, which created high costs for United Fruit and eventually made it file for bankruptcy in 2001.[1]

## The Creation of the Banana Empire

Marketing bananas in the United States existed before the United Fruit Company was created. Between 1860 and 1870, several companies attempted to create a banana market in the United States, but they failed to keep a constant flow of the fruit going to final markets. This was because some of them did not have boats fast enough or with adequate enough refrigeration systems to keep the fruit fresh until it reached U.S. ports. According to Robert Read, 114 banana import companies were created between 1870 and 1899, but only 22 had survived by 1899.[2] These companies did not have their own plantations, but bought their fruit from unreliable Central American and Caribbean producers. Therefore, before 1870, no large banana import company existed in the United States.

The challenges of the banana business were resolved in 1870 when Boston ship captain Lorenzo Dow Baker imported some of the fruit from Jamaica to Boston. Baker sold his fruit to Andrew Preston, a local businessman, who then sold the fruit to consumers at reasonable prices. After their initial success, Preston and Baker organized more shipments, which initially came in irregular intervals. However, by 1885, they accumulated enough capital to create a company specialized in banana imports—the Boston Fruit Company. Preston and Baker were aware that developing a reliable transportation system consisting of a large number of ships was crucial for business success. With this in mind, they made their first big investment and created what would be later known as the Great White Fleet—a fleet of ships conditioned solely for banana transportation, which later also operated as passenger ships.[3]

Around the same time, another Boston entrepreneur, Minor C. Keith was developing a railway network in Central America. Keith was the nephew of Henry Meiggs, a legendary entrepreneur who built several railways in South America. In 1871, Meiggs invited Keith to work with him to build a railroad in Costa Rica, contracted by the Costa Rican government. The railroad was to stretch from San José to the port of Limón on the Caribbean coast, and Meiggs had already successfully built the

Callao-Lima and the Oreja railroads in Peru some years before. Keith accepted the invitation and went to Costa Rica with his two brothers to work on the railroad project.

During the construction of the first twenty-five miles of the railroad, Meiggs and the Keith brothers faced incredible odds. Building in the jungle was much harder than they had calculated because disease and difficult working conditions cost them greatly; around five thousand men died during the construction, including Meiggs and Minor Keith's two brothers. In 1874, Keith was left in charge of the project and stubbornly continued with it despite the odds. The large number of deaths made it hard for him to recruit new workers in Central America, so one source of labor was prisoners from the jails of New Orleans. With the seven hundred convicts Keith began with, it is said only twenty-five survived the end of the construction. When Keith brought in two thousand Italian immigrants from Louisiana by boat, many of them rose in rebellion when they discovered the miserable working conditions. Many ran away, and sixty were lost in the jungle.

By 1882, Keith had carried the construction of the railroad seventy miles—from the coast to Río Sucio—but he was running out of money and had received no help from the Costa Rican government, which had defaulted on promised payments. The situation was so difficult that at one point, Keith encouraged banana trees to be planted along the railroad tracks to feed the workers. With time, Keith began using the train to export the bananas he planted, and, by 1883, he owned three banana export companies. Keith's financial situation, however, did not improve, and he was obliged to obtain a loan of 1.2 million pounds that permitted him to finish the railroad to San José in 1890.

Once the railroad was finished, however, Keith faced a new problem—there were not enough passengers to travel on it. Neither operating costs nor Keith's debts could be paid. But Keith quickly found that he could keep his business alive by exporting the bananas he had planted for the railroad workers. His experiment proved successful, and, by 1890, the train was used solely to transport bananas, and the new plantations surpassed the value of the train.

During a business trip to London, Keith organized the Tropical Trading and Transport Company to coordinate his banana business and to provide transportation for his increasing shipments to the United States. In addition, his new company managed a chain of stores he established along the Costa Rican coasts to trade local produce. He also expanded his banana business to the region of Magdalena, Colombia, through the

Colombian Land Company and made a deal to export fruit to the United States with the Snyder Banana Company of Panama (at that time Colombian territory). With these deals, by 1899, Keith dominated the banana business in Central America. But new problems for Keith were not slow to arrive. In 1899, Hoadley and Company, a New York brokerage firm against which Keith held $1.5 million in drawn bills, declared bankruptcy, and Keith lost all of his money. The Costa Rican government and several members of the local elite tried to help him, but Keith's financial situation did not improve.[4] He was forced to go to Boston and talk with Andrew Preston and Lorenzo Baker of the Boston Fruit Company, Keith's rivals. Keith hoped a merger of his Tropical Trading and Transport Company and the Boston Fruit Company would end his debt. They all agreed to the deal, and the United Fruit Company was born on March 30, 1899.

The United Fruit Company was led by Preston with Keith as vice-president. Their diverse interests and skills complemented each other. Keith had his railroad network and plantations in Central America and an established market in the southeastern United States, and Preston grew bananas in the West Indies, ran the Great White Fleet of steamships, and sold to the northeastern United States. As the company grew, Keith continued with his railroad projects in Central America.[5]

The United Fruit Company needed to ensure a steady output of bananas to its consumer market in the United States. This was a difficult task because of the nature of bananas—unlike other goods, bananas rot quickly and easily. Given that bananas could not be produced in U.S. consumer markets, it was necessary to develop a production and distribution network between the Caribbean and the United States. This required the United Fruit Company to closely coordinate the whole banana production process from beginning to end.

Before the integration of the independent banana companies into the single United Fruit Company, most of the difficulties and losses these companies faced resided in problems of coordination between the production centers, the transporters, and the final distribution in the United States.[6] When a shipment was lost it was usually for the same reason—the fruit perished quickly. The invention of the closely coordinated vertically integrated structure of the company included plantations (with health and housing infrastructure), railways, ports, telegraph lines, and steamships. Most of the lands the company owned were given as concessions by the producing countries' governments, which were eager to promote foreign investment as a way to modernize their economies.

Shortly after the merger, the new United Fruit Company continued its expansion to other sectors in order to have under its roof most of the stages of banana production. United Fruit established the Fruit Dispatch Company—a subsidiary in charge of distributing bananas in the United States. United Fruit became a major shareholder of the Hamburg Line, a German shipping company, and also bought 85% of the shares of the British banana import and shipping company, Elders and Fyffes, with which United Fruit was assured a privileged position in the British market. (By 1928, United Fruit had bought 99% of Elders and Fyffes's shares.) In 1913, United Fruit created the Tropical Radio and Telegraph Company to keep in constant communication with its ships and plantations.[7] Additionally, the company owned newly developed steamships that permitted faster trips between the plantations and the final markets than the older sailing vessels.[8] With these operations, United Fruit was successfully monopolizing the banana market.

In the second decade of the 1900s, United Fruit saw its monopoly challenged by a newcomer—maverick Samuel Zemurray. A Jewish Russian-born New Orleans entrepreneur, Zemurray established the Hubbard-Zemurray Fruit Company in 1910 with his plantations in Honduras. Zemurray financed and organized a military coup against Honduran president, Miguel Dávila, replacing him with Manuel Bonilla. Once in power, Bonilla granted the Hubbard-Zemurray Fruit Company generous tax concessions and grants. For a time, Zemurray's business continued to operate and expand up the Honduran coast and created a new banana export corporation—the Cuyamel Fruit Company.

However, as Cuyamel Fruit grew, the competition between Cuyamel and United Fruit grew as well. To improve the size and quality of his bananas, Zemurray built an expensive irrigation system, and, in 1922, he acquired the Bluefields Fruit and Steamship Company. By 1929, the Cuyamel Fruit Company had thirteen steamships running between ports in Honduras and Nicaragua and New Orleans. Cuyamel Fruit also had a sugar plantation and refinery, and, in 1929, Cuyamel's stock rose while United Fruit's fell. The two companies went into a fierce price war that included a short armed conflict between Honduras and Guatemala until United Fruit decided its best option was to acquire Cuyamel. In 1930, Zemurray sold Cuyamel to United Fruit for 300,000 shares of the latter's stock, making him United Fruit's largest shareholder. He was also given a seat on the board of directors. The acquisition of Cuyamel meant 250,000 more acres of land in Honduras, fifteen more steamships, port facilities, and the concession on the Honduran national railway for United Fruit. With Cuyamel out of the way, United Fruit continued as the biggest and most powerful banana producing and marketing corporation in the world, reinforcing the monopolistic nature of the banana market in the decades to come.[9]

United Fruit maintained its vertical integration in the years after the acquisition of Cuyamel. Early studies viewed United Fruit's move toward vertical integration as either a triumph of civilization over nature[10] or as an example of what Lenin called "the latest stage of imperialism."[11] More recent scholarship sees the company's shift as part of a broader trend toward vertical integration within corporate America during the late nineteenth and early twentieth centuries.[12] In this argument, the reasons behind vertical integration were purely technical—ships were not fast enough, agriculture was uncertain, and bananas are a perishable fruit that can not be grown in the principal places they are marketed. Companies that marketed bananas had to ensure a smooth flow of fruit from production sites in Latin American to consumers in Europe and the United States. The best way to reduce uncertainties was to control all stages of the production process from plantation to market. By so doing, United Fruit was able (during the first half of the twentieth century) to coordinate the entire process.

This vertical integration was done under particular political circumstances. Central American and Caribbean countries were gradually falling under the United States–dominated economic sphere. The United States paid some of the debt of these countries' to European powers, changing the debtors' creditors to private American banks or to the American government. This debt payment was at the same time as what Mira Wilkins calls the United States' "spill-over" into the Caribbean. According to Wilkins, in the late nineteenth century, American companies considered Mexico and the Caribbean natural extensions of U.S. territory, and they expanded in these regions to open new markets and ensure their control of raw materials. While this spill-over covered the mining and oil sectors of countries like Chile, Mexico, Peru, and Venezuela, the effect was concentrated in the agricultural sector in Central America. These Central American countries were relatively young because they all had belonged to the short-lived United Provinces of Central America in the nineteenth century and had gone through several civil wars when this federation collapsed. The republics were ruled by military *caudillos* who had little affection for democratic institutions. In the early twentieth century, the Central American republics were ruled by infamous, grotesque, and corrupt dictators such as the Somozas, Ubico, Estrada, and Trujillo, who ruled their countries like their personal fiefs.

The Central American military dictators were initially friendly toward foreign investors. Because they ruled by decree, it was easy for them to grant concessions to foreign corporations without opposition. Political scientist Paul Dosal has found that in pre–World War II Guatemala, it was much easier for United Fruit to get concessions from military dictators than from the few and short-lived elected presidents. Some of these dictators ruled in countries extremely dependent on banana exports, such as Panama, Guatemala, and Honduras, which each depended on bananas for more than half of their total exports.[13]

Additionally, there was strong American intervention in the region in the period before World War II. Using the guise of protecting American interests (or American lives), the United States invaded Honduras, the Dominican Republic, Cuba, Nicaragua, Panama, Haiti, Guatemala, and El Salvador during this time, and some were invaded more than once. These invasions helped to perpetuate the dictatorial systems in these countries.

In summary, in the period before World War II, the United Fruit Company followed a vertical integration process both because of a need for a closely coordinated system and because of a friendly political environment. The need for coordination in production and distribution made it more advantageous to vertically integrate. Furthermore, the political reality of Central America and the Caribbean before World War II created a situation in which foreign investors, especially American investors, could feel secure operating in the region. Not only did the investors know the Central American governments would not bother them, but they also knew that if they did try to intervene, the American government would back the foreign investor with force. This scenario, however, changed with time (especially during the 1950s), and United Fruit had to adapt.

### The Octopus Loses Its Arms: United Fruit's Vertical Disintegration

The vertical disintegration of the United Fruit Company has not been studied. Scholars have focused their attention either on United Fruit's vertical integration process in the first decades of the twentieth century or on the political conflicts the company faced in post–World War II. However,

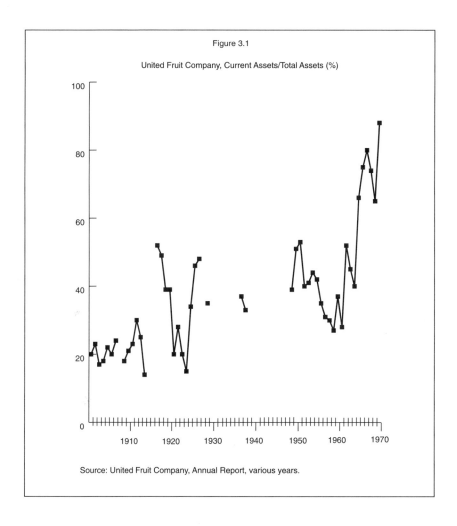

Figure 3.1

United Fruit Company, Current Assets/Total Assets (%)

Source: United Fruit Company, Annual Report, various years.

no one has tried to see any relationship between the disintegration of United Fruit and the political changes in Latin America. In this section I will show that the company faced increasing political uncertainties in the 1950s that led to its divestiture in the 1960s.

Three different sources indicate United Fruit's internal shift from a production company to a marketing company in the decades after World War II: the relation of current assets and total assets, land ownership, and steamship ownership. One way to see this shift is by tracing the evolution of the company's current assets in relation to its total assets. Total assets

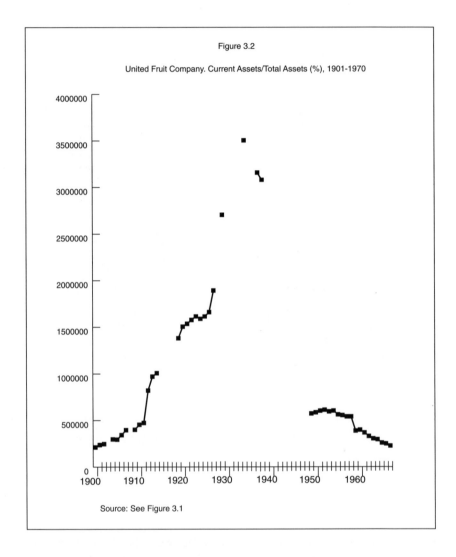

Figure 3.2

United Fruit Company. Current Assets/Total Assets (%), 1901-1970

Source: See Figure 3.1

include current assets and fixed assets. United Fruit's current assets were the wealth the company had in financial securities, cash, and future sources of income, like accounts receivable. Its fixed assets included the company's physical wealth, such as buildings, ships, cars, trucks, lands, furniture, and other wealth. Service companies, such as banks, tend to have a larger percentage of their assets in current assets than in fixed assets. Production companies, on the other hand, tend to have a significant

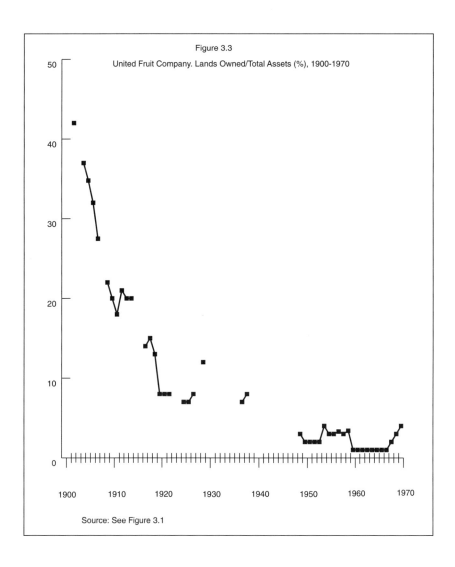

Figure 3.3

United Fruit Company. Lands Owned/Total Assets (%), 1900-1970

Source: See Figure 3.1

portion of their assets in fixed assets. If United Fruit's current assets are weighed in relation to its total assets, a clear tendency toward service is seen after 1961 (see figure 3.1). This tendency becomes clearer when we analyze the behavior of the most important asset United Fruit owned to produce its product—land. Figure 3.2 shows that after World War II, United Fruit decreased its landholdings dramatically, and it did so much more aggressively after 1960.[14] Figure 3.3 shows how land also decreased

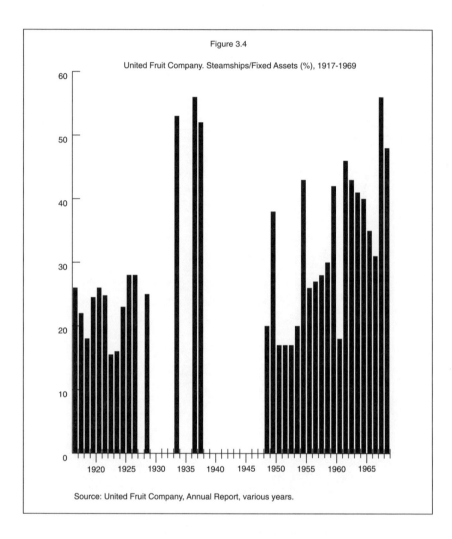

Figure 3.4

United Fruit Company. Steamships/Fixed Assets (%), 1917-1969

Source: United Fruit Company, Annual Report, various years.

in importance as a proportion of United Fruit's total assets. Figure 3.3 also shows that after 1960, lands decreased in proportion to total assets even more. United Fruit did not get rid of all its fixed assets, however; ships remained an important fixed asset (figure 3.4), because the company still needed them to effectively focus on marketing.

The evolution of United Fruit's assets shows that in the late 1950s and 1960s there was a clear change in the company's strategy; its internal structure began to resemble more that of a marketing company than a production company. One way to understand why the company changed is to see the evolution of its profit rate in the long term.

## Profitability of United Fruit's Operations

Given the company's image throughout Latin America as *El Pulpo* (the Octopus), one would expect United Fruit to have exorbitantly high profit rates. Indeed, in some years, especially early in its history, the company did well. However, if we examine the company's return on equity and return on as-

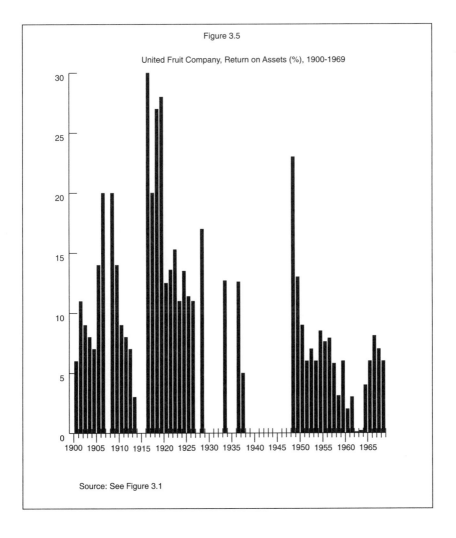

Figure 3.5

United Fruit Company, Return on Assets (%), 1900-1969

Source: See Figure 3.1

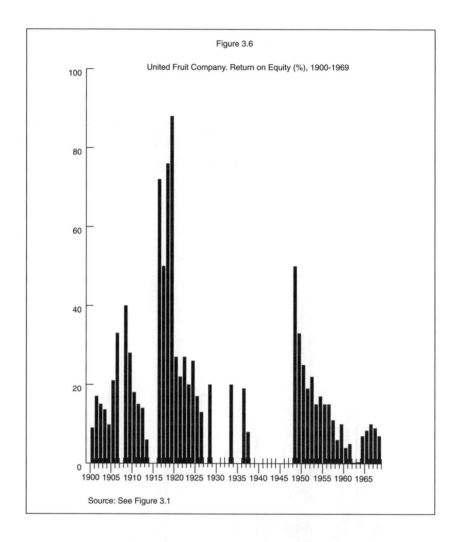

Figure 3.6

United Fruit Company. Return on Equity (%), 1900-1969

Source: See Figure 3.1

sets, we get a somewhat more complicated picture characterized by declining profits, especially after World War II. Return on equity is how much income the company brought in from the amount of capital it received from its investors. Return on assets establishes the relationship between net income and total assets; it is how much profit the company earns from its assets. The higher each of these ratios is, the better the company is doing.[15]

The return on assets shows a variable rate for the pre–World War II period, but a decreasing tendency in the post–World War II period. Late in the second decade of the 1900s, it reached levels of 30%, falling to around 5% just prior to World War II. After the war, the return on assets began at levels around 25% and then fell below 5% in the early 1960s. In short, United Fruit's return on assets peaked in the 1920s and declined dramatically in the postwar period (see figure 3.5).

The return on equity ratio shows a similar pattern. Figure 3.6 shows how this ratio reached levels over 20% in the early 1920s and then de-creased. During the postwar period, it fell dramatically, actually having a negative value in 1970.[16]

One potential counter-argument to United Fruit's declining profits is that the fall in United Fruit's profit rate came from one of the other busi-nesses in which the company was involved. Although United Fruit is rec-ognized for its banana business, it was not their only line of operation. After World War II, the company's management showed an increasing in-terest in diversifying its operations. United Fruit began an aggressive di-versification program in 1960, with businesses in sugar, transportation, processed foods, fast food products, communications, and others. How-ever, despite a strong effort to decrease the company's dependence on ba-nanas, this remained the most important of the company's businesses, and banana marketing always represented more than half of all of United Fruit's other businesses combined (see table 3.1).[17] Therefore, even in times of diversification, the business that counted was bananas.[18]

United Fruit's profitability ratios suggest the earlier period of the com-pany's history—the one defined by vertical integration—was actually more profitable. Why, then, did the multinational choose switch to a sys-

TABLE 3.1
*United Fruit Company: Sales of Products and Services.*
*Percentage of participation, bananas vs. other businesses*

| Year | Bananas (%) | Sugar, transportation, communications, processed food, and others combined (%) |
|---|---|---|
| 1962 | 63 | 37 |
| 1963 | 60.4 | 39.6 |
| 1964 | 60.8 | 39.2 |
| 1965 | 65 | 35 |
| 1966 | 65 | 35 |
| 1967 | 63.8 | 36 |
| 1968 | 63 | 37 |

Source: Author's calculations, made with information taken from United Fruit Company, *Annual Report to the Stockholders* (Boston: Various Years)

tem that appears to have been less profitable in the long run? Was this decision a strategic miscalculation or were there other factors that compelled the company to divest itself of landholdings and production?

## United Fruit's Risks and Shareholders Fears

Why did the company continue to divest (that is, pull out of direct production and switch its resources into marketing), despite the fact that the strategy resulted in decreased profit rates? Part of the explanation has to do with the expectations of United Fruit's investors. What was the perception the investors had of the company? What did financial analysts think? What was the risk perception related to the company's internal structure? Two ways to answer these questions are by analyzing the company's own views of what their problems were (such as, by looking at their annual reports) and by looking at the perception of independent financial analysts such as Moody's Investors Service. Moody's is one of the two most important analysts in the United States. Because negative evaluations from Moody's can prove fatal to a company's share prices, no publicly traded American corporation can afford to ignore Moody's recommendations. This was especially true during this time period, when the stock market was dominated by major institutional investors.

Before 1949, Moody's considered United Fruit a fairly good investment option. As late as 1946, the company was even included among Moody's "Recommended Investment Stocks." By 1949, however, doubt about the company's activities emerged. Although Moody's still considered United Fruit a good option, it attributed the company's decreasing profits to rising social and political problems in Central America. Moody's warned, "future political developments remain an uncertainty."[19] This warning coincided with a gloomy letter from United Fruit's president to its stockholders. Whereas at the beginning of 1949, the company had expectations of exceeding the prior year both in tonnage of bananas marketed and in sales volume, conditions arose that made this impossible. Labor trouble in Guatemala interrupted shipments from that country for six weeks; labor troubles in Colombia and Costa Rica of shorter duration also resulted in the loss of fruit from these countries.[20] The market reacted to the company's situation by raising its risk ratio, as shown in figure 3.9. Moody's overall concern emanated from labor unrest in United Fruit's Central American divisions. These concerns were highlighted in the opening statements of three analyses from 1950 and 1951: "The lower earnings last year were caused by abnormal weather conditions and labor troubles in several important Latin American areas."[21]

In 1950 and 1951, Moody's saw conflicts with the Guatemalan labor movement as an important issue affecting the company's stock:

> Outcome of the company's wage dispute with Guatemalan labor could have longer term effects than the mere reduction in earnings this year. If United Fruit were to abandon production there, other companies would probably move in and develop a competitive position. Or, if the company compromises the issue, labor in other countries would probably demand similar concessions.[22]

The 25% price decline of this stock from its 1951 all-time high can be attributed primarily to the impact upon earnings of a hurricane and a six month work stoppage at the company's Guatemala plantations.[23]

The company's report to its stockholders was not more optimistic:

> During recent years banana production in Guatemala has been declining due to frequent windstorms, inroads of disease, and the absence of conditions conducive to the planting of new cultivations. At the same time labor costs have been rising sharply. The company has always paid wages far greater than those paid by others in Guatemala for similar work, and up to the last few years its labor relations have been most satisfactory. During recent years, however, extremists who are not employees of the Company have kept the laborers in a constant state of unrest. . . . To date the Company's offer to negotiate participation contracts with Guatemala similar to those negotiated with other countries has not been accepted.[24]

Moody's suggested the problems in Central America were not limited to labor but to potential difficulties United Fruit could have with local governments. Moody's proved prophetic. United Fruit faced its most infamous problem in 1951 when Jacobo Arbenz was elected president of Guatemala. With United Fruit in mind, in 1953, Arbenz developed an agrarian reform law and expropriated some of the company's uncultivated lands.[25] The company saw its conflict with Arbenz as serious and gave a long explanation of the conflict in its annual report, but United

Fruit president Kenneth Redmond was nonetheless unable to assure shareholders the company would prevail:

> The Company has filed with the Department of State, for presentation to the Government of Guatemala, a claim for just compensation for the expropriation including the appraised present value of the lands and improvements expropriated, and the damage caused to the Company by depriving it of its reserve banana lands and greatly shortening the useful life of its expensive facilities on the west coast. Since the lands have actually been expropriated, the acreage has been dropped from the records. . . . Under the present conditions the Company is not planting additional acreage in Guatemala, and the acreage of banana cultivations in production will become less each year. As long as the political atmosphere remains inimical to American enterprise, the Company must of necessity follow a policy of retrenchment.[26]

But Moody's was worried about the broader implications: "This is not a question of immediate crucial importance to the company's earning power. More important is whether Guatemalan events are indicative of what may happen elsewhere in Latin America where United Fruit operates."[27]

Arbenz was eventually ousted by opposition from certain sectors of the Guatemalan army, the U.S. Department of State, the Organization of American States, and Guatemalan large land owners. Colonel Castillo Armas, who took power after the coup, overturned Arbenz's social reforms and returned the expropriated lands to United Fruit. The twenty-five-year-old Argentinian, Ernesto Guevara (later known as "El Ché"), who had previously applied for a position as a medical doctor with United Fruit, witnessed the coup. He was living in Guatemala at the time as a doctor and bookseller and organized resistance militias against Castillo's army. Facing an inevitable defeat, he escaped to Mexico where he met another political refugee who would become one of his closest friends—Cuban Fidel Castro.[28]

The United Fruit Company reported the change of government with great relief to its shareholders and emphasized the negotiations it was holding with other Central American governments regarding land, labor, taxes, and welfare: "The overthrow of the Communist-dominated government of Guatemala, while causing a cessation of shipments from that country for a period of about three weeks, was a decidedly favorable development which will have far-reaching effects in the future."[29]

United Fruit also reported its cooperation with the new Guatemalan government in land distribution and welfare policies. However, despite the company's optimism, Moody's was skeptical. In 1954, Moody's published an article—"United Fruit's Prospects under Political Pressures"—that suggested the problems in Guatemala reflected United Fruit's general inability to manipulate Latin American governments in the postwar period (which an unfavorable tax policy in Costa Rica quickly confirmed). Three years after the ouster of Arbenz, Moody's still warned, "Further political disturbances in the Caribbean area can never be ruled out."[30] Similarly, in 1956, Moody's reported, "United Fruit has finances that are proportionately among the strongest of any United States corporation. . . . Unfortunately, however, the company's operations are subject to natural and foreign political hazards beyond its control."[31]

United Fruit's political risks were not limited to Central America; it also had to face the hostility of the U.S. government. In 1954, the U.S. Department of Justice filed a lawsuit against United Fruit for violating antitrust legislation. As a result, in 1956, the company had to sell its holdings of the International Railways of Central America (IRCA), as well as the lands in its Guatemalan division (an obligation the company eventually met in 1972 when Del Monte acquired these lands). Three years later, in 1959, United Fruit reported bad news from the Caribbean. First, the Cuban revolutionary government was expropriating Cuban land.[32] Second, in Costa Rica (a country with a very different political regime), United Fruit clashed with the government on labor legislation. For United Fruit's efforts, it was rewarded with a massive strike by its workers.

In November 1959, the Costa Rican congress passed (over the president's veto) a law requiring all employers to pay laborers a year-end bonus. As some of the terms of the law were clearly discriminatory and in direct violation of United Fruit's operating contracts with the government, United Fruit refused to comply with the improper and discriminatory provisions. United Fruit's refusal was used as a means to provoke an illegal strike and, by threats and intimidation, prevented laborers from working.[33]

Following these events, Moody's began to advise investors to look elsewhere: "United Fruit has been hurt by political troubles in several Latin American countries and periodic weather damage to its banana crops. . . . Management is currently attempting to combat its problems . . . but any appreciable effect will be far in the future. . . . We therefore see no reason to hold the stock, and would switch into U.S. Rubber for better prospects."[34]

The changing situation in the 1950s for United Fruit was not limited to Central America; United Fruit also faced competition from the emergence of a fairly independent banana industry in Ecuador. Table 3.2 shows the rapid emergence of Ecuador as the world's largest banana producer by the mid-1950s.[35] Ecuador was unique in the sense that its government helped keep the industry in the hands of domestic planters. The dramatic increase in exports from Ecuador threatened United Fruit by leading to a general decrease in international banana prices.[36] Ecuador had a tremendous competitive advantage in terms of production costs, as summarized in table 3.3, and was seen as a problem by United Fruit's president:

[In Ecuador] the local growers were not required to furnish housing, schools, hospitals, the necessary access roads, port facilities, as United Fruit had to as its own cost [in Central America]. . . . Wages of banana workers in these areas were also far less than United Fruit paid its workers in other producing countries. The small compensatory tax put on export bananas in Ecuador was insignificant compared with the costs to United Fruit elsewhere. . . . Large quantities of bananas became available at costs less than United Fruit's costs.[37]

In Ecuador, United Fruit was in a different situation than in Central America. United Fruit never had a significant share in banana production, producing just 2% of the national total banana crop.[38] Additionally, no associate producer program existed in Ecuador, so United Fruit had to compete with other marketing companies in the open market.[39] By the late 1950s, the company's lands in Ecuador suffered from the banana destroying disease Sigatoka and peasant activism, which encouraged the company to get rid of these minor plantations.[40]

United Fruit also faced difficulties when its main rival, Standard Fruit, dramatically increased its productivity and decreased the risks inherent to banana production by pursuing the biggest technological change in the banana industry since the 1900s. In 1956, Standard Fruit began conducting experiments to develop a new kind of banana resistant to the Panama Disease that had destroyed many of its (and United Fruit's) plantations in Central America.[41] Before the 1950s, all bananas traded worldwide were from the Gros Michel family, which had a thick skin that made them easy to export in bunches, but were not resistant to the Panama Disease. The fruit developed by Standard, known as Valery, was smaller, less tasty, and had a weaker skin, but it was resistant to the disease and pro-

TABLE 3.2
*Banana Exports by Country (thousand of tons), 1950-1970*

| Year | Colombia | Costa Rica | Ecuador | Guatemala | Honduras | Panamá |
|------|----------|------------|---------|-----------|----------|--------|
| 1950 | 143.8 | 222.0 | 169.6 | 160.2 | 262.1 | 145.6 |
| 1951 | 154.5 | 216.0 | 246.5 | 124.1 | 241.7 | 142.2 |
| 1952 | 152.6 | 412.0 | 429.8 | 95.1 | 261.7 | 118.9 |
| 1953 | 196.2 | 355.0 | 406.4 | 170 | 248.4 | 184.6 |
| 1954 | 195.7 | 355.3 | 492.2 | 153 | 221.6 | 221.7 |
| 1955 | 209.6 | 329.4 | 612.6 | 134.5 | 133.8 | 275.1 |
| 1956 | 215.9 | 232.0 | 578.9 | 124.8 | 181.4 | 247.8 |
| 1957 | 191.2 | 315.4 | 677.6 | 129.8 | 261.5 | 289.6 |
| 1958 | 189.0 | 302.4 | 742.2 | 112.9 | 398.2 | 273.2 |
| 1959 | 203.3 | 213.4 | 885.6 | 146.2 | 359.6 | 291.5 |
| 1960 | 190.7 | 272.8 | 897.4 | 197.6 | 363.0 | 263.3 |
| 1961 | 205.6 | 230.9 | 842.3 | 153.5 | 430.4 | 271.5 |
| 1962 | 147.1 | 287.3 | 656.8 | 81.3 | 334.5 | 262.3 |
| 1963 | 202.6 | 323.6 | 632.3 | 118.5 | 290.7 | 308.7 |
| 1964 | 171.6 | 347.8 | 624.9 | 92.6 | 306.6 | 377.0 |
| 1965 | 253.5 | 402.2 | 531.2 | 32.7 | 489.8 | 483.6 |
| 1966 | 310.9 | 293.3 | 653.1 | 60.9 | 668.9 | 543.7 |
| 1967 | 325.6 | 453.0 | 505.9 | 42.7 | 723.8 | 595.8 |
| 1968 | 401.5 | 711.8 | 556.5 | 66.4 | 787.8 | 682.3 |
| 1969 | 334.5 | 944.8 | 518.5 | 20.1 | 715.1 | 833.5 |
| 1970 | 261.8 | 839.5 | 540.1 | 28.0 | 737.2 | 825.3 |

Source: Table made with information taken from Colombia, Departamento Administrativo Nacional de Estadística, *Anuario de Comercio Exterior* (Bogota: various years); Economic Commission for Latin America (ECLA), *Boletín Económico para América Latina* (Santiago: 1950-1959); International Monetary Fund, *International Financial Statistics* (Washington: September 1968, September 1970)

TABLE 3.3
*Comparative costs of banana production.*
*Ecuador vs. Central America*

|  | Ecuador | Central America |
|--|---------|-----------------|
| Cost of opening a banana plantation ($/hectare) [1958] | 120 | 2000–3100 |
| Workers/hectare [1964] | 0.5 | 0.60–0.75 |
| Cost of harvested bananas [1958] | 1.16 cents | 1.98 cents |
| Share of total freight plus unloading of the CIF Price [1964] | 36% | 32% |

Source: Table made with information taken from Valles, Jean-Paul, *The World Market for Bananas, 1964–72: Outlook for Demand, Supply, and Prices* (London: Praeger, 1968) 115, 117, 119, 123, 136, 137.

duced more fruit per acre. This resistance was enough incentive for Standard to begin a gradual change from Gros Michel to Valery bananas. Despite the advantages of Valery bananas over Gros Michel bananas, United Fruit did not change its crop immediately but waited until 1962. As a result of the delay, Standard Fruit increased its participation in the international market dramatically, from 8.9% in 1950 to 31% in 1965.[42]

Shifting from Gros Michel to Valery required huge changes. Valery's fragility made it necessary to change the entire transportation process of the bananas from the time they were harvested at the plantation until they reached the last consumer. United Fruit developed a system of "air wires" inside its plantations to avoid damaging the bunches. The air wires consisted of poles connected to each other with a moving wire going from the banana trees to the packing plant where the fruit was selected and packed. When the workers cut the banana bunch off the tree, they hung the bunch on a hook on the moving wire; in this way, the bananas were transported to the packing plant with minimum damage because they were not hit by anything. The stems of the bananas were then cut from the bunch, and they were packed in cardboard boxes. But, although the fruit was resistant to the Panama Disease it was not resistant to insects, so the company also had to cover the bunches with plastic bags while they were growing. All of these new processes required extensive changes; the company installed the air wire system, cardboard and plastic manufacturing plants, and packing plants.

A study by the Harvard Business School also pointed to the rise of Ecuadoran production as one of the most worrisome issues faced by United Fruit in the early 1960s. According to the study, the company had just two options: to get rid of all of its Central American production and associate producers and buy only from Ecuadoran producers in the open market or drastically reduce its costs and increase its productivity in the areas in which it operated.[43] United Fruit could survive only if a radical change was made.

## The Banana Empire Strikes Back: Changes and Adaptations in the 1960s

It was under these circumstances that United Fruit appointed Thomas Sunderland as president of the company. In his 1960 letter to shareholders, Sunderland announced that the company was going through a long-range readjustment program. The main transformations included a switch from the Gros Michel to Valery banana variety, a growing reliance on contract producers, an increase in purchases from Ecuador, and a general diversification of operations.[44] Indeed, a number of factors reflected the company's withdrawal from direct production. Total income from the sale of tropical properties increased dramatically from \$2,871,094 in 1960 to \$16,483,492 in 1961.[45] Indeed, the Harvard Business School study noted that although United Fruit could produce bananas more cheaply on its own, it made sense to get out of direct production for a number of reasons that were not strictly economic in nature:

> By encouraging the nationals to enter the banana industry, Mr. Sunderland believed United Fruit could contribute to the development of stable conditions in the tropics (i.e., aid in the creation of a growing middle class), gain partners who would be valuable allies in the development of joint interests, and reduce the frequent attacks by "trouble makers" against United Fruit as a large land owner and employer. . . . as a straight matter of production United Fruit could probably produce bananas at less cost on its own.[46]

Despite United Fruit's positive outlook, Moody's remained only cautiously optimistic about the company's prospects:

> Symbolic of management's innovations is its policy of selling Latin American land holdings to local interests while contracting to take their produce. This defense against possible expropriations has had mixed success, but it has aided in a 37% cut in the number of 'tropical' employees in the last four years.[47]

A year later, in 1962, Moody's maintained a similar attitude:

> Fourth quarter earnings were hurt by windstorm damage last summer, and the continuing longshoremen's strike. This may cool near-by investor enthusiasm for the stock, but with the price still well below book value, and the longer range outlook brighter, we would hold it.[48]

However, in spite of these transformations, United Fruit had not solved its remaining political problem—its unfinished antitrust trial—and Moody's reminded investors of this looming issue.[49] In fact, the only year

United Fruit's yield was again above the average yield of the top 200 companies traded on Wall Street was in 1965, when it informed its shareholders that the following year's earnings would fall by 15% of the gross revenue when the antitrust legislation consent would be implemented.[50] After the company presented a plan in 1966 to be implemented in 1968, both the market perceptions calculated in the yield and Moody's analyses improved. After having mentioned little about the company in its stock survey for two years, in 1967, Moody's saw United Fruit with optimism and advised investors to hold the stock because of its future growth perspectives.

The replacement of the Gros Michel strain of banana with the Valery also proved successful, improving productivity (now mostly under the associate producers' control) and return on equity (after 1966). The increase in Central American productivity due to Valery was enough to counterweigh the low production costs in Ecuador in such a way that by the late 1960s, Ecuador had lost its comparative advantage.[51] Central American production increased after 1965, quickly reaching levels similar to those of Ecuador, as shown in table 3.4.

In the late 1960s, United Fruit's management made it clear to shareholders it was aware of the social and political changes in Latin America and the company had no other choice than to adapt. In a retrospective analysis of United Fruit's operations, company president Herbert Cornuelle wrote, "No matter how successful we are in this process, we still will be perceived, however, I am sure, as a threat to national independence and sovereignty. The fact that we are domiciled in a foreign country and that we are big assures that."[52]

In 1970, United Fruit merged with the AMK Corporation to create a new company, United Brands. This event marked the end of United Fruit's transformation process. The company became part of a giant food conglomerate that included processed foods and meat packing. In his initial letter to shareholders, Eli Black, the first president of the conglomerate, again emphasized the political issues the company had to deal with:

> While these operations are in stable countries with enlightened governments, the fact is that all Latin American countries are being swept by strong winds of nationalist aspiration. [The company] knows that it must adjust to change in Latin America. It is adjusting. . . . One of the most sensitive areas is that of land use policies. . . . Since 1952 the Company has divested itself of 65% of its holdings in the four countries. Many thousand acres have been given to the governments for distribu-

TABLE 3.4

*Productivity of the Central American Banana Industry.*
*Tons per hectare, 1947-1970*

| Year | Costa Rica | Guatemala | Panama | Honduras |
|------|-----------|-----------|--------|----------|
| 1947 | 622 | 870 | 940 | 870 |
| 1948 | 762 | 860 | 1163 | 860 |
| 1949 | 957 | 513 | 1196 | 513 |
| 1950 | 879 | 712 | 1051 | 712 |
| 1951 | 841 | 515 | 1030 | 515 |
| 1952 | 955 | 252 | 810 | 252 |
| 1953 | 849 | 796 | 825 | 796 |
| 1954 | 919 | 811 | 904 | 811 |
| 1955 | 878 | 647 | 1043 | 646 |
| 1956 | 663 | 664 | 909 | 663 |
| 1957 | 1045 | 627 | 1071 | 627 |
| 1958 | 1111 | 528 | 930 | 528 |
| 1959 | 756 | 595 | 985 | 595 |
| 1960 | 965 | 829 | 839 | 829 |
| 1961 | 757 | 830 | 917 | 830 |
| 1962 | 843 | 552 | 867 | 552 |
| 1963 | 764 | 948 | 852 | 948 |
| 1964 | 929 | 1734 | 984 | 1734 |
| 1965 | 1083 | 738 | 1082 | 739 |
| 1966 | 1253 | 1275 | 1262 | 1275 |
| 1967 | 1339 | 1763 | 1598 | 1763 |
| 1968 | 1547 | 2330 | 1652 | 2330 |
| 1969 | 1982 | 2351 | 1952 | 2351 |
| 1970 | 2203 | 2561 | 2386 | 2561 |

Source: Ellis, *Las transnacionales del banano*, 410.

tion; the remainder has been sold to individuals and firms. . . . In several countries land has been given to unions to build low-cost housing financed by the company.[53]

The change in risk perception by the company's shareholders and potential investors can be quantified by calculating the yield on common stock. This is a widely accepted measure of risk and can show how the market perceives a certain stock in relation to other alternatives. The higher the yield, the riskier the investment is considered.

I calculated the yield on common stock for United Fruit and compared it with the average yield calculated by Moody's Investors Service for the top 200 companies traded on Wall Street.[54] If the company's ratio is higher than those of the top 200 companies, its stock is riskier than the average stock of the top 200 companies traded in the stock market. If its risk ratio is lower than the top 200, investing in United Fruit faces a lower risk than investing in the average company. Figure 3.7 displays the results of this calculation and clearly shows that before 1949, the company was considered less risky by investors than after that year. Perceived risk increased from 1950 to 1959. From 1960 on, however, United Fruit was seen as a less risky investment because it announced it would pull out of direct production and depend more heavily on contract producers.[55]

These events and their relationship to investors' perceptions of the company are summarized in table 3.5. This table compares yields on the company's common stock with the average yield calculated by Moody's for the top 200 companies traded on Wall Street.[56] The yield on common stock measures how risky an investment is perceived by the market—the higher the yield, the higher the risk perception.[57] A calculation of the yield in itself does not say much, as investors need to know if a stock is more or less risky than other stocks. When United Fruit's yield is compared with that of the top 200 companies, it can be seen whether the company was considered more or less risky than other investments.[58] The data show the risk perception of United Fruit decreased when the company diminished its direct operations in Latin America and, therefore, reduced its labor and political problems in the region.

As labor unions grew more powerful, governments sought more revenue from exports and local elite became less reliable agents of foreign capital, the company witnessed an erosion of the political and economic control on which its vertical integration rested. Simultaneously, the company could no longer count on the unconditional support of the American government, at least where direct military intervention was concerned. All of these developments contributed to a perception among investors that because of the political and social environment in Latin America, it was an increasingly risky place to do business.

Examination of the data presented in this chapter shows how United Fruit adapted to these perceptions, eventually choosing to withdraw from direct production and become a marketing company. These changes were made possible, in part, by the technical improvements of the post–World

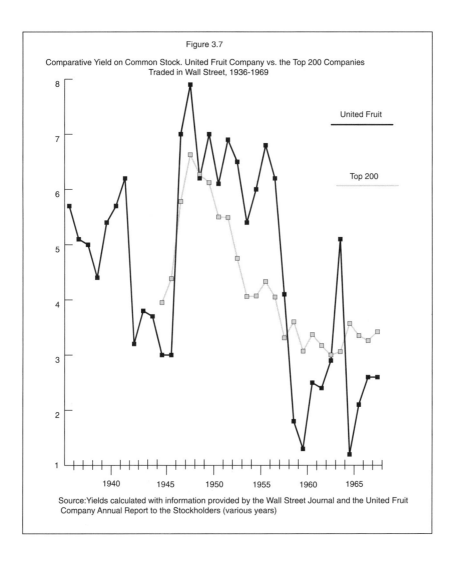

Figure 3.7

Comparative Yield on Common Stock. United Fruit Company vs. the Top 200 Companies Traded in Wall Street, 1936-1969

Source: Yields calculated with information provided by the Wall Street Journal and the United Fruit Company Annual Report to the Stockholders (various years)

War II period in the banana industry. Despite nationalist politicians and labor leaders creating the conditions leading to the company's divestiture from Latin America, these corporate policies were intended not as concessions to company adversaries but as strategies to please both financial analysts and investors. The "octopus" of the "Banana Empire" in the early twentieth century consciously dismantled itself in later years, largely to insure a continued place on top of the banana world.

TABLE 3.5

*Comparison of the Yield on Common Stock for United Fruit,
Yield for the top 200 Companies, and Issues Affecting Earnings
from United Fruit Annual Reports*

| Year | Yield: United Fruit | Yield: Top 200 Companies | Issues having significant impact on earnings in the Annual Reports |
|---|---|---|---|
| 1946 | 3 | 3.95 | |
| 1947 | 3 | 4.38 | |
| 1948 | 7 | 5.98 | |
| 1949 | 7.9 | 6.62 | Labor problems in Guatemala, Colombia, and Costa Rica decrease production and interrupt shipments |
| 1950 | 6.2 | 6.27 | |
| 1951 | 7 | 6.12 | Labor unrest in Guatemala plantations. United Fruit has problems at solving the conflict. |
| 1952 | 6.1 | 5.5 | Slow recovery of Guatemalan operations after strike. |
| 1953 | 6.9 | 5.49 | Expropriation of some company lands in Guatemala under Arbenz. The company reports problems in the negotiations. |
| 1954 | 6.5 | 4.75 | The U.S. Department of Justice files antitrust suit against United Fruit. The company faces ten-week strike in Honduras. |
| 1955 | 5.4 | 4.06 | Big losses from weather problems. |
| 1956 | 6 | 4.07 | Heavy windstorms provoke new losses. |
| 1957 | 6.8 | 4.33 | Company losses lawsuit from International Railways of Central America's (IRCA) shareholders. |
| 1958 | 6.2 | 4.05 | Company announces change of banana from Gros Michel to Valery to decrease potential losses from windstorms and Panama Disease. |
| 1959 | 4.1 | 3.31 | Conflict with Costa Rican government for "discriminatory" labor legislation followed by strike by workers. The Cuban Agrarian Reform Law makes almost all company's lands subject to expropriation. Little hope of succeeding in a conflict with revolutionary government. |
| 1960 | 1.8 | 3.6 | United Fruit announces long-term plan to restructure the company that includes larger role of the associate producers. |
| 1961 | 1.3 | 3.07 | The company reports no labor problems with larger participation of associate producers. |
| 1962 | 2.5 | 3.37 | Losses due to windstorms. |
| 1963 | 2.4 | 3.17 | |
| 1964 | 2.9 | 3 | |
| 1965 | 5.1 | 3.06 | The company announces it will lose about 15% of gross revenue when antitrust legislation consent is implemented. |
| 1966 | 1.2 | 3.57 | |
| 1967 | 2.1 | 3.35 | |
| 1968 | 2.3 | 3.25 | |
| 1969 | 2.6 | 3.42 | |

Source: Yields calculated with information taken from The *Wall Street Journal* and the United Fruit Company annual reports. Information on issues taken from United Fruit Company annual reports various years.

## The Banana Republics Rebel: United Brands and the Creation of the Unión de Países Exportadores de Banano [UPEB]

The structure of the international banana market witnessed radical changes in the 1970s. First, United Brands began to lose ground to rival, Standard Fruit, after Standard Fruit merged with Castle and Cook in 1972. Second, when Del Monte merged with the West Indies Fruit Company and purchased United Brands's banana plantations in Guatemala (as a result of the antitrust action against United Brands), it made Del Monte a stronger and more aggressive competitor in the banana market. Third, hurricane Fifi destroyed most of United Brands's production areas in Honduras in 1974. Last, United Brands had to confront the challenge of the creation of the Unión de Países Exportadores de Banano [UPEB] by the Central American governments in 1974 to control banana exports.

When Eli Black took over United Brands, he wanted to transform the company's image in Latin America and the United States. The company awarded several Central American students with scholarships and made significant improvements in the health and housing services of its employees. In his letter to the company's shareholders in 1973, Eli Black proudly presented the company's social programs in the opening letters of the 1972 and 1973 annual reports. In 1972, he said,

> [There] was a dramatic change in the image of our company. It is a reflection of many years of effort to improve the working and social conditions of our employees, especially in Latin America. Our changing image was exemplified in numerous articles in the *New York Times*, the *Chicago Daily News*, the *Boston Globe*, etc., in which it was said of the company, "It may well be the most socially conscious American company in the hemisphere."[59]

In another section of the same report, the company quoted the *New York Times*: "What emerges from talks with labor, management and government is a picture of a company that anticipated the changes that have swept Latin America and has quietly set about to adjusting them."[60] To show how things had changed, United Brands gave a detailed description of the economic and social aid it provided Nicaraguans after the devastating earthquake the country had in 1972.[61]

In spite of these changes, Black faced new political problems in Latin America in 1974.

In March 1974, the governments of Costa Rica, Guatemala, Honduras, Panama, and Colombia signed the Panama Agreement, forbear of the Unión de Países Exportadores de Banano. The agreement's main goals were to increase taxation on banana multinationals, control supply to manipulate prices, and modify the tax and land concessions granted to the multinationals decades earlier. This was a response to the steady decline of the international price of bananas and the hardships of these countries due to an international oil crisis and hurricane Fifi, which destroyed hundreds of Central American banana plantations.[62]

The founders of the UPEB claimed producing countries were getting an unfair share of banana export profits. According to the founders, Central American countries were getting 11% of the income generated in the banana market, while the multinationals received 37%, and the retailers in consuming countries earned 19%.[63] The export taxes the producing countries wanted to impose violated what had been originally agreed on in the concessions given to the multinationals. These concessions had been granted for long periods of time (between fifty-eight and ninety-nine years, and sometimes with an indefinite deadline) and established an average tax of 2 cents per bunch, which is equivalent to 80 cents per ton. In order to increase the tax to 55 dollars per ton, the governments of Costa Rica, Honduras, and Panama passed laws that nullified the previous contracts between their governments and the multinationals in 1974, 1975, and 1976, respectively. These laws not only increased taxes but also eliminated many of the generous concessions the foreign corporations had enjoyed.[64]

The multinational corporations did not remain passive and protested by interrupting shipments and threatening the countries with export strikes and layoffs. Standard Fruit interrupted its exports from Honduras, and United Brands reduced its Costa Rican exports by 30%.[65] In response, the Central American governments began to use harsher language against the multinationals, and strong mutual accusations began. The situation reached a tense point in June 1974 when two high-ranking officials of the Panamanian government accused Standard Fruit and United Brands of conspiracy to murder Panama's president, Omar Torrijos, and of supporting military coups in the region.[66] In the meantime, banana workers in Costa Rica went on several strikes supporting the creation of the UPEB. Torrijos, a charismatic president known for his strong nationalism, anti-imperialistic discourse, and close friendship with Fidel Castro, refused to give in to United Brands, saying he would "take the war to its last consequences," and showed the conflict as a war for national sovereignty. United Brands continued its boycott by destroying around $1 million worth of bananas and refusing to continue exporting. Torrijos promised United Brand's 15,000 banana workers he would pay their wages as long as the conflict continued, and Castro offered to buy the Panamanian bananas.[67]

The conflict was settled in September 1974, when UPEB was formally created with strong resistance from Torrijos and no help from the U.S. government, United Brands accepted the new policies of the Panamanian government, which also meant accepting the UPEB and the new political environment in Central America. Shortly afterward, the company restarted its operations.

The year of these conflicts was not a profitable one for United Brands. That year alone, the company reported a net loss of $43,607,000, for which they blamed weather problems and the conflict with the Central American republics.[68] Figure 3.8 shows United Brands's dip in net revenues in 1974. In that year's report, the company informed its shareholders the new agreements with the local governments were going to mean higher taxes and fees and less property in Central America, but added the company

is proud of the long working relationships it has had with the nations of Latin America. We look forward to continued associations which are mutually beneficial both to our company and to the peoples of the nations in which we work. We further have pledged to those nations our support as a responsible corporate citizen.[69]

The conflict around the creation of the UPEB revealed the new political realities of the region. On one hand, local governments stubbornly insisted on pushing ahead with their new policies despite strong opposition from the largest two banana corporations. On the other hand, it was clear that the U.S. government distanced itself from what was going on in the banana producing regions despite pleas made by both United Brands and Standard Fruit.

Under the UPEB, the producing countries increased their participation in the banana market via tax income. Central American producers increased their earnings from banana export taxes from $25.4 million in 1974 to $44.5 million in 1975 to $51.4 million in 1976. This growth continued steadily to a peak of $102.1 million in 1981. The UPEB countries

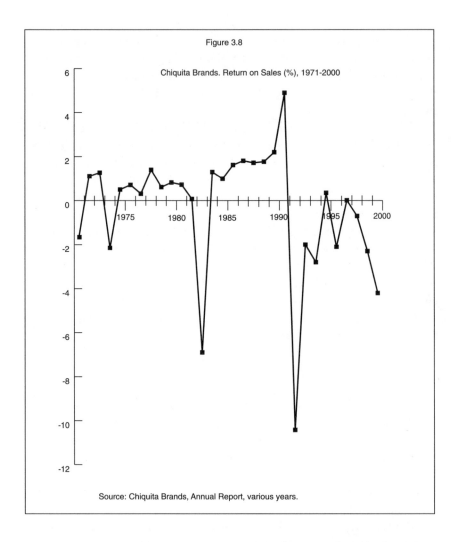

Figure 3.8

Chiquita Brands. Return on Sales (%), 1971-2000

Source: Chiquita Brands, Annual Report, various years.

also attempted to participate in the international marketing of bananas by creating Comunbana, their own export corporation, in 1977. This enterprise was owned jointly by the governments (with 80% of the shares) and local entrepreneurs of each Central American country, and it exported to Eastern Europe and the United States in the early 1980s. Comunbana was a short-lived effort and was never a real competitor for the traditional multinationals, which actually increased their international market participation from 58% in 1973 to 70% in 1981.[70]

The multinational corporations adapted to the political changes in Central America by using the mechanisms created by the UPEB to expand their share in the banana industry. In the 1970s, the Central American governments channeled loans provided by multilateral agencies (such as the World Bank or the Inter-American Development Bank) to local producers in order to stimulate local production to gain more independence from the multinational corporations. According to José Roberto Lopez's calculations, from the twelve Costa Rican farms that received subsidized governmental loans in 1980, United Brands had a stake of more than 40% in five of them; similar results could be observed in Honduras.[71] At the same time, the multinational corporations gradually increased their participation in Ecuador.[72]

### Eli Black's Suicide: United Brands at the Center of Scandal

The creation of the UPEB not only cost United Brands financially, but it also damaged their reputation. In February 1975, president Eli Black committed suicide by jumping from the 44th floor of his office building. The investigations by the Securities Exchange Commission uncovered a corrupt scheme by the company to negotiate a reduction in the UPEB's export tax in Central America. Black was at the center of a bribery case involving several high-ranking officials of the Honduran government, including Honduran president, Oswaldo López Arellano. When the results of the investigation became public, United Brands admitted it had paid $1.25 million in bribes to Honduran officials through the company's subsidiaries, whose books were falsified to cover up these transactions. According to United Brands, the whole scheme had been authorized by Black. The deeper the investigations went, the worse the situation became for the company. The Securities Exchange Commission also discovered United Brands had paid $750,000 in bribes in Italy to get favorable business opportunities in Europe.[73]

In the 1974 annual report, Wallace W. Booth, Black's replacement as president of the company, claimed the bribes had been made without the knowledge of the board of directors.[74] The company's new management made a huge effort (with some success) to recover the company's reputation, but by 1974 analysts still described United Brands as a "case of corporate calamity."[75]

## Chiquita versus Europe:
## A New Era of Political Conflict in the 1990s

United Brands began the 1980s precariously. It was losing market share to Standard Fruit (renamed Dole) and Del Monte; a new Ecuadoran enterprise (Noboa) was on the rise; and the diversification process started by Black did not seem to help the company regain its prior domination of the banana market. The importance of banana sales in the company's operations had gradually decreased in the 1970s to a point where, in 1979, the company reported that meat represented 62% of its sales, while bananas and related products represented only 27%.[76] The diversification process had been successful, but United Brands lost a substantial share of the banana market to its competitors during the second half of the 1970s. It was during those years that a high school dropout (but successful businessman) named Carl Lindner began to acquire shares of United Brands and became its largest shareholder and CEO in 1984.[77] Lindner's strategy was to follow a divestiture process selling several subsidiaries (the sale of Elders and Fyffes being the most significant) and nonagriculture related business, refocusing the company's attention on bananas. In 1989, Lindner changed the name of the company to Chiquita Brands International, Inc., emphasizing the company's best-known brand.

During the first seven years of Lindner's management, it looked like his strategy was successful. Between 1984 and 1991, the company's profitability improved (see figure 3.8), its dividends per share increased from 2 cents to 55 cents, its earnings per share increased from 27 cents to $2.52, and its market value per share increased remarkably from $3.58 to $40.[78] Lindner's luck, however, radically changed in the 1990s—one the worst decades in the company's history.

Chiquita's problems in the 1990s stemmed from the way the European banana market evolved during that decade. One of Lindner's greatest ambitions was to take advantage of the promising European market due to the establishment of the European Union (EU) and the fall of Communism in Eastern Europe in the late 1980s. Particularly, Lindner had enormous hopes for the reunified Germany market. Germany was the largest importer of bananas in Europe with the highest level of per capita consumption, so Lindner's strategy anticipated a much larger market with Germany and the former Communist countries.[79]

To prepare for a larger market, Chiquita focused its efforts on banana production and shipping.[80] During the late 1980s and early 1990s the company again began to buy lands in Latin America and purchased and conditioned more ships, all at a cost of around $1 billion, most of it financed with debt.[81] However, Lindner's optimistic calculations proved wrong for two reasons. First, the Eastern European market did not grow as much as Chiquita anticipated, which hurt all the companies that invested in increasing their production capabilities. And second, in the early 1990s the European Union decided to establish a quota system on banana imports that favored the producers of Africa, the Caribbean, and the Pacific (the ACP countries) and left out Latin American producers—the main providers of bananas for Chiquita. Lindner challenged the European Union through his high-level political connections and started what became the most serious economic conflict between the European Union and the United States.

The predicted large consumer market in the former Communist countries was a disappointment for banana companies that anticipated a market in Eastern Europe. According to the Food and Agriculture Organization [FAO], the deep economic crisis Russia suffered in the late 1990s made bananas more expensive for Russian consumers and many of the distribution companies and supermarkets that distributed them went bankrupt. An FAO study reported that the sudden impoverishment of Russian consumers made them choose locally grown fruits instead of bananas. This created problems for Chiquita, which had heavily invested in increasing their production infrastructure.[82]

In addition to the miscalculation of the Eastern European market, the import system instituted by the European Union took Chiquita by surprise (although the roots of the import system can be traced back to the creation of the European Economic Community [EEC] in 1957).[83] From the beginning, the founding nations of the EEC had different views on how to deal with the banana market. While Germany wanted free market imports, France wanted a quota system that favored its former colonies. As long as a common external tariff existed, the two countries would never agree on how to include bananas in their common agricultural policy. In the end, bananas enjoyed a particular status among agricultural goods imported in Europe—the French imported only from its former colonies under a quota system and the Germans imported freely, mostly from Latin America.[84] The fruit coming into France was shipped from Africa and the Caribbean by French companies, while that imported into Germany was shipped from Latin America by United Brands and Standard Fruit.

The expansion of the EEC in the 1960s and early 1970s created more differences surrounding the policies on banana imports. Italy wanted a quota to protect Somalian producers; the United Kingdom wanted a quota for its former colonies in the Caribbean; Spain wanted to protect its production in the Canary Islands; Greece its production in Crete; and Portugal its production in Madeira. On the other hand, Denmark, Ireland, and the Benelux countries joined the Germans in advocating a free market. As a result, bananas continued to be imported into Europe under a different system for each country. The bananas imported into France and Britain were brought in by French and British corporations, while the American multinationals still were selling their Latin American fruit mostly in the German market.[85]

With the reunification of Germany in 1989 and its subsequent expansion of markets, the European Union considered it imperative to create a common policy toward banana imports. After the reunification, consumption in the former East Germany jumped from "3.1 kg in 1987–88 to 22.5 kg in 1991, more than 50% above the level in Western Germany,"[86] which reinforced the German preference for a free market system. In the early 1990s, the European Union began to look for a solution to the banana import disagreements that would not only be consistent with its commitments to some African and Caribbean producers under the treaties of the Lomé Convention, but also would be consistent with the negotiations with the General Agreement on Tariffs and Trade (GATT).[87] As a member of the GATT, the European Union could not simply raise the tariffs of Latin American bananas in order to protect their former colonies' production. Between 1992 and 1993, two crucial votes took place among European Union members in order to define a common policy toward bananas. With the opposition of Germany, the Netherlands, and Belgium, but the support of all the other members, the European Union approved a quota system that favored Caribbean and African producers.[88] The agreement became effective in July 1993.

The new European policy was a blow for Chiquita. The company already had suffered losses of $284 million in 1992, generated mostly by reduced production and decreased quality of bananas due to unusual weather patterns created by El Niño, so the new quota system was a disaster. Between 1992 and 1997, Chiquita's share in the world market fell from 32% to 26%, in the EU market it fell from 30% to 19%, and in

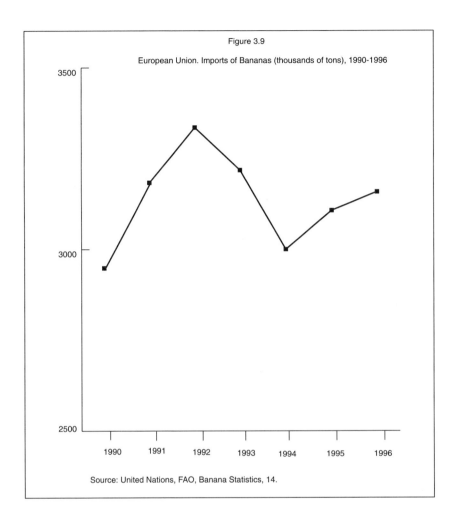

Figure 3.9

European Union. Imports of Bananas (thousands of tons), 1990-1996

Source: United Nations, FAO, Banana Statistics, 14.

Germany, its largest customer, its share fell from 40% to 20%.[89] During this period, and as a result of the new quota system, European consumption of bananas decreased as a whole, as shown in figure 3.9.
While Chiquita was facing these difficulties, its rival, Dole, was doing
better because it had prepared itself for the possibility of a regulated
market in Europe by investing in African production, reducing its dependence on bananas, and focusing its marketing on Asian markets.[90]
In a desperate attempt to survive, Chiquita belatedly tried to diversify

its operations. This was not enough, and the company announced in January 2001 it was unable to meet its public debt obligations of $862 million.[91]

During the early stages of the European banana dispute in the 1990s, the U.S. government did not intervene because it felt the issue was not important to the American economy. However, this attitude changed when Lindner approached high-ranking politicians, especially Republican Senator Bob Dole.[92] Dole was beginning his presidential campaign and received a sizable donation of $1.5 million from Lindner plus an airplane owned by Chiquita for his campaign tour. Even though Lindner was closer to the Republicans than to the Democrats, he donated $5 million to both parties between 1993 and 1999 and became a frequent visitor at the White House, holding meetings with President Clinton and U.S. Trade Secretary Mickey Kantor.[93]

By August 1994, a group of twelve senators, including Dole, wrote a document urging President Clinton to intervene in what they considered an "illegal" measure by the European Union against American corporations. In January 1995, the U.S. government made its first official complaints to Europe, threatening with retaliation if the European Union did not drop the quota system. The Europeans rejected the U.S.'s complaints.[94] In response, the United States brought the case to the newly formed World Trade Organization [WTO] in September 1995.

Chiquita gained several new allies in its struggle against the European Union in the first months of the conflict with the EU quota system. It could count on the support of the Clinton administration and the Republican Party. Ecuador, the world's largest producer of bananas, brought the case to the WTO shortly afterward. Additionally, American beef producers requested help from the U.S. government to overturn the European ban on hormone beef, expanding the case against the European Union in the WTO to include both beef and bananas.

Senator Dole not only targeted the European Union but also the governments of Costa Rica and Colombia. In 1993, the two countries signed the Framework Agreement with the European Union, which gave them access to the European market under a quota system similar to the ACP countries' system. Although this meant Chiquita bananas produced in these two countries would reach the European Union, Chiquita complained to the U.S. government, accusing the two Latin American countries of unfair trade practices and cooperation with the restrictive European system. Even with some access to Europe for the Costa Rican and

Colombian bananas, Chiquita still could not export its bananas produced in the rest of its Latin American divisions.

In September 1994, Chiquita Brands and Senator Dole requested that the U.S. trade representative investigate the Colombian and Costa Rican banana exports to find out whether or not these countries were following discriminatory practices against U.S. corporations and to impose economic sanctions if they were.[95] In late 1995, the U.S. government threatened Colombia and Costa Rica with sanctions unless they abandoned the Framework Agreement. But the Clinton administration eventually dropped this threat, despite Senator Dole's strong opposition and let the two countries continue with the agreements they had previously signed with the European Union. In exchange, both Colombia and Costa Rica promised to fully cooperate with the WTO's final ruling in this matter.[96]

In May 1997, the WTO ruled in favor of the United States, but the policies followed by the European Union after January 1998 did not show that the Europeans were willing to comply with the decision. This marked the beginning of what the media called the "Banana War."[97]

The "Banana War" was the WTO's first serious issue, and it tested the organization's ability to settle differences. By January 1999, the United States established the first sanctions against some luxury European imports valued at $191 million as a retaliation for not complying with WTO regulations. The conflict continued throughout the year 2000—the last year of the Clinton administration. The administration rejected any EU proposal that would not benefit Chiquita by claiming the proposals were not compatible with WTO rules. Simultaneously, the Republican-dominated Congress continued pressuring the president to impose tougher sanctions on Europe.[98] Clinton finished his term without resolving the problem and passed it on to his successor, George W. Bush.

President Bush was also close to Lindner, who donated $1.03 million to his campaign (plus $677,000 to Democratic candidate Al Gore).[99] The Bush administration continued negotiations and reached a final agreement with the involved European countries (approved by the WTO) in April 2001. The new agreement established import licenses distributed based on past trade, which gave Chiquita the possibility of importing into Europe a volume of bananas similar to that it had in the early 1990s. The European Union and the United States agreed this system would last until 2006, when a new "tariff only" system would be established instead of per-country quotas.[100] Chiquita had won the "Banana War" but at a high cost.

## *The Fall of a Giant: Chiquita Files for Bankruptcy*

At the end of the "Banana War" with the European Union, Chiquita was in a terrible financial situation. According to the company, before the imposition of the quota system by the European Union, 70% of the bananas consumed in Europe came from Latin America, and Chiquita imported 40% of them, giving the company control of 22% of the European market. This market share was reduced by half during the quota system, costing Chiquita around $200 million.[101] During the period that Chiquita concentrated its efforts and resources in its conflict with the Eu-

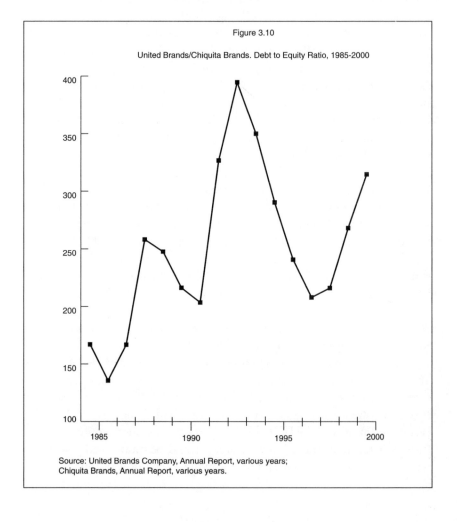

Figure 3.10

United Brands/Chiquita Brands. Debt to Equity Ratio, 1985-2000

Source: United Brands Company, Annual Report, various years;
Chiquita Brands, Annual Report, various years.

ropean Union, its closest rival, Dole, was adapting to Europe's regulations by investing in African production and diversifying its operations. Additionally, during this period Chiquita lost market share in the Japanese market when it withdrew from the Philippines as a result of agrarian reform.[102]

Chiquita finished the century with enormous debt and high losses. As figure 3.10 shows, the debt on equity ratio of the company increased from 167% in 1985 to a peak of 394% in 1993 and decreased to a still high 315% in 2000. The company made a huge effort to recover by restructuring itself—strengthening its nonbanana and vegetable businesses, diversifying into other products (the opposite process Lindner originally followed), and selling many of its subsidiaries to repay its debt. The company's management, however, could not save Chiquita, and, in 2001, the company filed for bankruptcy. Exactly one century after it started operations with Minor Keith and Andrew Preston as heads of United Fruit, the company began the twenty-first century in its worst financial condition ever, trying to recover from bankruptcy.


## Conclusion

The ever-expanding banana empire that Kepner and Soothill described in their 1930s classic has had its counterparts in the political and literary imaginations of Latin Americans throughout the twentieth century. From the leaf storm that swept through García Márquez's Macondo to the sinister interests that installed Asturias's Green Pope, United Fruit has been seen by scholars, activists, and writers alike as an implacable and overwhelming force throughout the hemisphere. Yet even as these images were being fixed in the minds of United Fruit's opponents, the conditions that had given rise to United Fruit's unrivaled control over land and national governments were rapidly changing.

By the mid-twentieth century, altered conditions in Latin America obliged the company to transform itself or lose significant terrain. In Central America, where national governments once had nearly surrendered sovereignty over the company's areas of operation, United Fruit found itself confronting increasingly assertive workers, less compliant national officials, and growing demands from would-be landowners. More ominous for the company, by mid-century, similar pressures were growing throughout the hemisphere, all of which threatened United Fruit's ability to marshal the quantities of land and labor necessary to maintain production on a large scale.

Until now studies have cared only about United Fruit's vertical integration process and the political conflicts the company faced in the countries in which it operated. United Fruit needed to vertically integrate in the first decades of the twentieth century because of technological constraints in banana production and marketing. Vertical integration was facilitated by the favorable political conditions in the area. In the 1950s, the company faced political uncertainties that made it change its internal structure once again, the changes this time facilitated by the technical innovations at the time.

The dynamics after 1970 must be seen under a different light because United Brands was more than just United Fruit with a different name. The new conglomerate had a more diversified structure and, therefore, did not depend on bananas as did the pre-1970 company. United Brands faced new political conflicts in Latin America with the creation of the UPEB and a lack of much U.S. government support, but the company adapted itself by reinforcing its marketing activities and its business in processed foods.

The conflict over European quotas in the 1990s did not begin as a political issue but became one when Chiquita decided to use its political connections to change the EU's policy. This strategy proved extremely costly for the company and was one of the main reasons for its bankruptcy in the year 2000. After a century of operations, Chiquita began the twenty-first century still with powerful market control but with weak finances and an uncertain future.

## *Appendix*

The risk ratio of United Fruit is measured by calculating the yield on common stock, a widely accepted ratio. The ratio is calculated by dividing the share's dividend earnings by its market price and tells how much of a return investors would have if they purchased a share of the company. The higher this ratio is, the riskier an investment is considered. The calculation was made in the following way: first, I took the information on the stock price and dividends from the *Wall Street Journal* as published on the last day of each month for the years 1936 to 1970. Though this information is published daily, this method is considered a good proxy. Second, I calculated the year's average stock price and dividend using the monthly information. Third, I calculated the company's annual yield using those averages. Fourth, I compared these yields with the annual yields calculated by Moody's Investors Service for the top 200 companies traded on Wall Street. Moody's did not publish an annual yield for the top 200 in 1947, 1949, and 1968, but published a monthly yield. For those three years, I calculated the yearly average with the monthly information.

# 4

# The United Fruit Company and Local Politics in Colombia

## Introduction

The United Fruit company did not wield the same kind of political and economic influence in Colombia that it wielded in Central America.[1] Chapter 3 described how the evolution of Latin American politics forced the company to change the way it operated throughout the region. This was even more true for Colombia, where United Fruit was more affected by the changes in the national political environment. Eventually, Colombia's political and economic development through the century encouraged United Fruit to divest its operations in Colombia earlier than in its Central American divisions.

United Fruit's relationship with the Colombian government was different in the pre–World War II than in the postwar period. During the first half of the twentieth century, the fate of United Fruit was in the hands of the party in power. The company benefited from a business-friendly Conservative Party in the period prior to 1930, whereas it had to deal with a union-friendly Liberal Party from 1930 until World War II. When United Fruit returned to Colombia after the forced interruption of its operations during the war, its relationship with the government changed—United Fruit depended on the lobbying power of the local politicians of the regions in which United Fruit operated.

## Falling into a Downward Spiral of Violence: Liberals, Conservatives, Church, and Coffee in the Nineteenth Century

When United Fruit's founder, Minor C. Keith, arrived in Colombia during the early 1890s to buy land in Magdalena on the Colombian Caribbean, he found a country falling into a downward spiral of violence between Conservatives and Liberals. Three main issues polarized the Liberals and the Conservatives—the role of the church, a centralist versus a federalist government, and the direction of economic policies. Simply put, the Liberals supported a total separation of state and church, a federal government, and laissez-faire economics. The Conservatives promoted a close relationship with the church, a centralized political system, and a protectionist and interventionist state. The Liberals had been in power for more than thirty years during the Liberal Republic (1849–85) and had implemented an extreme version of the policies they supported. The result was a fiasco—the extreme political and economic independence of each region led to a chaotic and unmanageable situation that included no unified monetary system and a series of civil wars. The Catholic Church felt threatened by what they considered an atheist policy from the Liberal government and began to openly support the Conservative Party and oppose the Liberal government. Last, with the international fluctuation of coffee prices, businesses from various economic sectors endorsed government intervention in order to protect the national economy.

When the Conservatives took power in 1885, tensions between both parties increased. The Conservative government was just as extreme as the Liberal one. It did everything to centralize power in Bogotá and return the church to a privileged position. It attempted to increase taxes on coffee exports and regulate the industry through government agencies. The Conservative government wrote a new constitution to assure that its principles ruled Colombia into perpetuity and to end any vestiges of Liberal federalism. These policies were achieved with a parallel decrease in individual liberties and an increase in harassment against the Liberal opposition. The final outcome of this strife was a break between Liberals and Conservatives in 1899. This break was called the War of the Thousand Days (1899–1902).

## The Conservative Hegemony: Tax Grants, Concessions, and a Foreign Business-Friendly Government

The War of the Thousand Days was the most destructive conflict in Colombian history. Not only did this war cost the country an innumerable number of human lives, it also destroyed the national infrastructure and permitted the separation of Panama from the rest of the country—an event still remembered by Colombians as the hardest historical lesson of what can happen with a lack of national unity.

By defeating the Liberals in the bloody Palo Negro battle in 1902, the Conservatives assured their rule over the country for the next thirty years. This period, known as the Conservative Hegemony, is characterized by a government that was closely linked with the church, allowed few civil liberties, sought to both protect local industry and promote national exports, and concentrated all political power in the city of Bogotá, in detriment of the provinces. The Conservative Hegemony marked the age in which Colombia took off as the world's second largest coffee producer and developed a relatively important industrial sector by Latin American standards. This was also a time of little political violence, which set the stage for the country's remarkable economic growth.

It was during the Conservative Hegemony when United Fruit created the banana export infrastructure in the region of Magdalena. It was also at this time that the 1928 strike occurred. In this section I will show how the Conservative government created a friendly environment for the company, going so far as to use the army to repress the 1928 strikers. The company enjoyed many of the privileges multinational corporations had in the underdeveloped world in the first decades of the twentieth century, such as land concessions and tax exemptions. The good times, however, only lasted as long as the Conservatives remained in power.

### Rafael Reyes and the End of the War of the Thousand Days: Incentives for Foreign Investors and Export Promotion

The War of the Thousand Days had a paradoxical outcome. Although it destroyed the national economy and left a traumatic legacy of hate between Liberals and Conservatives, it forced the national government to pay attention to the neglected regions of Magdalena and Urabá. Magdalena had the potential to fuel a national economic recovery. Meanwhile, Urabá rose to importance as a border zone after Panama declared its independence from Colombia.

In 1904, after having signed a peace treaty following the War of the Thousand Days, Colombia elected General Rafael Reyes as president. Reyes ran against another Conservative candidate, Marceliano Vélez, in an election without a Liberal candidate. Despite the Liberal Party's weakened state, Reyes appointed several influential and important Liberals to his government as a way to initiate a new era of tolerance between the two parties and thereby to cool the political struggle. Among those appointed to government was Rafael Uribe Uribe, the defeated general of the Liberal army and a strong supporter of free markets and agricultural export specialization.[2] The promotion of banana exports provided common ground for these political rivals.

Rafael Reyes was a strong admirer of Mexican President Porfirio Díaz and tried to imitate his policies. Nicknamed by his contemporaries as *el modernizador,* Reyes believed that economic development was key to avoiding future internal conflicts. For Reyes, this kind of development depended on a strong central state that ensured order, peace, and a clear national legal system. Although he agreed with the Liberals that economic development would only occur if Colombia joined the international economic system, Reyes believed entering the world economy could only be done under strong government support.

Reyes's administration was among the most foreign business-friendly governments in Colombian history. Reyes encouraged foreign direct investment as a key development policy. He created tax incentives for companies involved in the expansion of electric infrastructure, railways, and telegraphs. Additionally, he gave concessions and grants to companies involved in the oil and banana export industries. This generated conditions that facilitated United Fruit's investments in Magdalena in the first decades of the twentieth century. Reyes, a native of the Caribbean, had always shown strong interest in developing an industry that could boost the region out of its historical stagnation.

### Reyes and the Magdalena Banana Zone

Paradoxically, the War of the Thousand Days, which caused an economic recession in all of Colombia, contributed to the rise of two forgotten regions with two events: the postwar economic policies of President Rafael Reyes and the secession of Panama from Colombia. During the nineteenth century, Magdalena landowners made several attempts to develop banana exports but failed to keep the business running. Reyes's Conservative government, in its hurry to jump start the national economy, provided major incentives for foreign investment in subsidies and tax exemptions, which were used by United Fruit for its land purchases and railroad construction.[3]

The most influential members of both parties strongly endorsed the development of the banana export industry in Magdalena. In 1904, Reyes toured the Magdalena banana zone and reinforced the incentives for foreign companies to invest in the country. For the banana sector, in particular, he gave loans of $15 (Colombian pesos) per hectare cultivated with bananas.[4] At the same time, Uribe praised the virtues and potential of the fruit for this region in a speech given at the Sociedad de Agricultores. In 1908, Uribe also wrote an influential article encouraging and endorsing the cultivation of bananas in the Caribbean in the *Revista Nacional de Agricultura*, the sector's main journal.[5]

Reyes created several incentives by decree for the banana export sector.[6] He granted tax exemption on exports to bananas until 1929. He also granted government owned lands (*baldíos*) to those who used them for banana cultivation—a policy that United Fruit used to purchase 13,078 hectares of land around the town of Aracataca. In 1909, the government granted a tax exemption to the Santa Marta Railway for the following twenty years, subject to a commitment by the company to build a new line per thousand hectares cultivated with bananas on request of the local planters.[7] These generous incentives continued until 1911 when government began to impose restrictions starting with the halting of land grants.[8]

These concessions for the banana industry were not as generous compared to the ones United Fruit received in Central America. In fact, in Colombia the exemptions and concessions were for anyone who wanted to export bananas. In Central America, on the other hand, they were exclusively awarded to United Fruit. While banana exports in Colombia never reached levels above 5% of total exports, countries like Guatemala depended on banana exports for almost half of its exports, and Panama and Honduras depended on them for more than 40%.[9] The Central American governments, therefore, had more incentive to attract United Fruit. Inevitably, this gave United Fruit more bargaining power in those countries.

The presence of the company and its land acquisitions increased the value of real estate in the formerly sleepy region of the Colombian Caribbean, benefiting a new upper class as well as the existing upper class. The opening of the banana plantations generated a large-scale demand for labor that could not be satisfied with the local population. The scarcity of labor in the region along with the relatively high salaries offered by the company to attract new workers generated a mass influx of workers, both Colombian and foreign.[10] The foreign workers included Italians, Spaniards, Syrians, Lebanese, and Central Americans. The port of Santa Marta restarted operations as the main gate for United Fruit's banana exports, and small towns such as Aracataca and Ciénaga, became dynamic urban centers. As Santa Marta flourished, Cartagena, the previously foremost Colombian Caribbean city, began to decay due to the end of the slave trade. The rise of the banana business was changing the landscape of the Colombian Caribbean. While the rest of the country was still licking the wounds of the War of the Thousand Days, Magdalena was experiencing unprecedented social, political, and economic changes.

### Conflicts on Taxation in the 1920s: United Fruit, the Regional Government, and the Colombian National Government

The Colombian tax concession system had a flaw that generated conflicts between the central and regional governments—tax concessions granted by the national government precluded the regional government from taxing banana exports and reaping any benefit from the local industry. For the banana growing regions, bananas were the only thing that could be taxed efficiently. In a pioneering study on the political economy of the banana export sector from 1925 to 1930, Adriana Corso shows the centralist system created by the Conservatives generated a competition for rents between the national and local governments.[11]

Since the nineteenth century, the Department of Magdalena has been one of the poorest in the country. The Magdalena local government had little income compared with other regions. The situation worsened when the national government took over the administration of a growing number of taxes previously administered by individual local governments. This was part of a larger process of political centralization. Once United Fruit began to export bananas from the region, many of Magdalena's local politicians saw it as a potential source of tax revenue. There was a problem, however. Reyes had granted tax exemptions to the banana export companies for twenty years as part of his incentives to attract foreign capital.

Magdalena politicians tried to change this situation with measures that conflicted with the central government's policies. During the 1920s, when banana exports were at their highest, Magdalena's local politicians approved resolutions to tax banana exports. These resolutions created conflicts from 1925 to 1930 between the national government and the Magdalena Departmental Assembly (the regional congress). The national government declared unconstitutional every attempt of the departmental assembly to tax banana exports. The case ultimately went to the Colombian Supreme Court, which declared the departmental assembly had no right to tax exports as long as the national government exemption was in effect.[12]

The opposition to the Magdalena assembly's initiatives came not only from the national government, but also from local planters. They feared that United Fruit would pass the extra cost of any new tax to them. Such pass-alongs were, in fact, stipulated in the purchase contracts between the growers and the company.

The Magdalena assembly also tried to take advantage of the fact that the Santa Marta Railway Company had not fulfilled its promises under the terms of its concession. In 1928, the Magdalena assembly proposed that the national government nationalize or tax the Santa Marta Railway Company operations because the company did not complete the railway branches to the Magdalena river that were specified in the company's concession. The branches were supposed to have been constructed by 1911, but as late as 1928 the company had only built branches to the banana plantations. The national government, however, opposed both nationalization and taxation.

## Liberal Opposition to United Fruit Concessions during the Conservative Hegemony

The strongest criticisms against tax and railway concessions came from members of the liberal party. At the regional level, the harshest critic was Juan B. Calderón, a representative for the liberal party in the Ciénaga municipal council. After having criticized the railway concessions in local newspapers, Calderón decided to create a lobbying group called the Sociedad de Agricultores de Ciénaga y Santa Marta in 1927. One of his main partners was Julio Charris who, in 1928, became the first liberal president of the departmental assembly in many years.[13]

The opposition to United Fruit was represented by the opinions of the Liberal newspapers. Starting in 1923, several local Liberal newspapers harshly criticized the concessions and supported that year's workers' strike. The newspapers also criticized the terms of the contracts with the local producers, especially the *pactos de retroventa*—purchase contracts in which loans were secured with the planter's property. Also in 1923, the national government established in Bogotá the Banco Agrícola Hipotecario (Agrarian Mortgage Bank). A year later, the Santa Marta and Ciénaga producers asked the government to open a local branch of the bank to compete with United Fruit's loans. In spite of the pressure from local groups, the national government took much longer than expected to open the branch. The office was open only until 1927 and was a disappointment—the loan requirements were even more stringent than those of United Fruit.[14]

The pressure groups—the Sociedad de Agricultores de Ciénaga y Santa Marta and the press—were mostly Liberal and were concentrated more in Ciénaga than in Santa Marta. In the banana region, Ciénaga was home to Liberal *mestizo* small landholders, whereas Santa Marta was home to Conservative, white, large landholders. White's interpretation of this demographic is that the Liberals represented the self-made small entrepreneurs of Ciénaga more so than the Santa Marta aristocracy. However, further research is needed to assure this affirmation.[15]

The year the local Banco Agrícola Hipotecario branch opened, United Fruit "rewarded" those planters that did not join the anti-United Fruit pressure group by issuing an unprecedented amount of loans. For the month of July, the company loaned $331,671—almost half of what it loaned for all of 1924. The loan recipients were mainly Conservative landowners of Santa Marta and were the same ones that later created the Sociedad de Agricultores de Magdalena, a different organization from the Sociedad de Agricultores de Ciénaga y Santa Marta.[16]

Around the time the departmental assembly was trying to create a banana export tax, the protests against United Fruit loans reached a higher level. In 1927, it was not a lobbying group but the departmental assembly itself that protested. That year, the assembly ordered an investigation of the way United Fruit acquired some *baldíos* (public lands) because some people suspected the company did not follow normal procedures. The Medellín Liberal newspaper, *El Espectador*, led a campaign at the national level to force the central government to intervene in this conflict.[17] The problem, however, was difficult to solve because the legislation on land property was not clear.

## The Growing Opposition from the Liberal Party and the Voting Behavior in Magdalena

In the early twentieth century, most of the country voted Conservative, and Magdalena was not an exception. However, the Caribbean region always leaned more toward either the Liberals or the less conservative faction of the Conservatives. In 1918, the Liberal Party was in crisis and could not efficiently organize to compete against the Conservative candidate in the presidential election. That year, the country had to choose between two Conservatives in the election. The Liberal press encouraged its followers to vote for the less conservative candidate who was more willing to accept Liberals in his government. The Liberals' favorite Conservative candidate was Guillermo Valencia who ran against Marco Fidel Suárez. Suárez won the elections at the national level getting 52% of the votes, while in Magdalena, Suárez got 49.4%, and in the entire Caribbean region he got 59% of the vote.[18]

Although the Conservatives won the Magdalena votes in the presidential election four years later, the Liberal vote in this region was higher than in the rest of the country. In that year's presidential election, Conservative Mariano Ospina received 62% of the votes at the national level, while Liberal Benjamín Herrera received 37%. In Magdalena, Ospina won with 55.5% of the vote. In 1926, the Conservatives won again by default with Miguel Abadía Méndez because the Liberals refused to participate in the presidential election.

On the eve of Abadía's Conservative administration, the government had to deal with an event that was highly exploited by the Liberal opposition—the massacre of the United Fruit banana workers demonstrating in the plaza of Ciénaga in December 1928. This was the biggest strike seen in Colombia and was harshly repressed by the army, as explained in more detail in chapter 5. The massacre was used by the young Liberal politician Jorge Eliécer Gaitán against the conservative government and proved fatal for the government's reputation.

### The Political Consequences of the 1928 Massacre

After the 1928 massacre, the Liberals mounted an intense campaign against the Conservative government and managed to win the 1930 presidential election with Enrique Olaya Herrera. The 1930 election was a watershed in Colombian history, in which the Liberals put an end to the Conservative Hegemony. The Liberals benefited from the internal division of the Conservative Party. Olaya won a plurality with 45% of the votes at the national level against the two Conservative candidates who had 29% and 26%, respectively.[19]

Some studies point to the 1928 massacre in Ciénaga as one of the main causes of the Conservative's defeat in 1930.[20] A more detailed look at voting behavior, however, does not give such a clear casualty. Although it is clear the national Liberal vote increased over time, the Conservatives got 55% of the votes in that election. Had they been united under a single candidate, they could have won the 1930 election. More significant, in Magdalena, the Conservative candidate Guillermo Valencia defeated Olaya. Valencia got 58.5% of the vote against 38% for Olaya.[21]

One important political fact undeniably linked to the army's intervention in Ciénaga was the rise of Jorge Eliécer Gaitán as a national figure. Gaitán was a young and radical Liberal who considered himself outside the traditional Liberal establishment. At the time of the massacre he had recently returned from Italy, where he had studied law and become an admirer of Mussolini's rhetoric and populist policies. The Liberal establishment never accepted Gaitán, and he always faced their hostility. Nevertheless, he had the increasing support of the most radical wing of the Liberal Party and some sectors of the Socialist and Communist parties. He also had a close relationship with the national unions, which was viewed by the Liberal establishment with suspicion.

Gaitán used the radio as a political tool in a way that had never been done in Colombia. He called attention to the 1928 massacre and blamed the Conservative government. He openly supported the strikers in congress, and he also toured the Caribbean region after the massacre, giving dramatic speeches in which he accused the Conservative government of putting the interests of a foreign multinational above the interests of the people. In short, although it is difficult to affirm the 1928 massacre was crucial to the defeat of the Conservatives, it certainly helped the Liberals in their opposition to the government. It is possible that the Conservatives may have lost due to their lack of unity and the country's economic crisis at the time.

## The Liberal Administrations: Union-Friendly Governments and Tighter Control of Multinationals

The Liberal period from 1930 to 1946 saw deep changes in Colombian society. During this time, the country sowed the seeds of the violence that erupted in the 1950s. The government introduced unprecedented social reforms and backed labor organizations. These were also times of increased individual liberties and the rise of the organized Left. This did not mean, however, all Liberal governments were radical reformists, or that the Liberal elite wanted to change the status quo.

The years of the Liberal republic had two important characteristics. First, the more liberally Magdalena voted in the presidential elections, the more stringent the policies of the national government toward United Fruit were. This indicates that national politicians were "rewarding" their constituency in this region, and the way to reward regional support was by being less tolerant of the multinational. This policy made sense at the time after the 1928 strike. Second, despite the fact that the country had a Liberal president, the Magdalena assembly could not ensure they would get the revenues of banana exports or the Santa Marta Railway. The Liberals in the national government maintained the centralization of taxation.

### Olaya's Transition: Disappointments for the Radicals and the Magdalena Assembly

Despite the expectations of many of his followers, Olaya's administration did not bring dramatic change. Before the 1930 election, the Liberal Party witnessed the growth of a radical wing closely connected with the Socialist and Communist parties. This wing played an important role during Olaya's election and expected to be rewarded when he took power. But once in power, Olaya did everything possible to keep his distance from this faction. Olaya's lack of energy in instituting labor and social reforms backed by the radical Liberals exasperated them and caused them to grow increasingly militant.

One of Olaya's main goals was to improve the country's relationship with the United States. Olaya, the Colombian ambassador in Washington, D.C., before running in the 1930 elections, wanted to assure Americans that Colombia was a safe place to invest and that his government did not sympathize with the growing European fascist movement. One of the ways he demonstrated this was in his policy toward United Fruit. Despite the strong expectations for change, especially after the 1928 massacre, Olaya did not give the unions the support they expected during their conflicts with the company. Although the country did not see additional military repression, the unions did not find in Olaya the ally they thought they would. Over time, the unions grew more sympathetic to the more radical Gaitán.

The Magdalena departmental assembly also grew disappointed with Olaya. He approved the extension of the Santa Marta Railway lease to United Fruit for an additional thirty years (the original concession ended in 1930). This extension approval came right after United Fruit gave a loan to the national government for one million dollars.[22] The extension faced strong opposition from the local and national media, including Liberal newspapers. Nevertheless, Olaya could not be swayed and the local authorities had no choice but to drop the possibility of receiving tax revenue from the Santa Marta Railway. The taxes the company paid for this lease did not go to the local government but to the national one.[23] And because the central government granted the concession, only the central government could change it.

The third disappointment was Olaya's policy regarding the taxation of banana exports. In 1930, the Kemmerer mission came to Colombia to advise the new government on economic policies.[24] Kemmerer proposed ending the banana export tax exemption and imposing instead a tax of two cents per stem. The departmental assembly had been waiting for 1930 because that was the year the tax exemption granted by Reyes was to end. Kemmerer's suggestion, therefore, came as a great boon to the assembly's position. The Magdalena congressmen supported the abolition of the exemption and the creation of an export tax to finance the local banana industry because the Banco Agrícola Hipotecario had proven useless.[25]

It is worth highlighting, however, that not all the local Liberal politicians supported the creation of the export tax. An antitax lobby was created by José Vives, who represented Liberal planters who did not want to be taxed.[26] In addition, Vives was a major United Fruit grower and remained close to the company until the early 1960s when it halted its activities in the region. Vives eventually took over the business and many of the company's lands.[27]

In October 1930, the Tax Commission of the House of Representatives approved Kemmerer's project to tax banana exports. It looked like the ideal law the Magalena politicians had been looking for because it did not tax the producers, only the export companies. This meant local producers would still be exempt but United Fruit would have to pay. The new law, however, faced a big problem: at the same time it was approved, Olaya reinforced the central tax administration to prevent the Department of Magdalena from getting any of this tax revenue directly. In 1931, Olaya raised the tax to three cents a stem but, again, these benefits went straight to the central government in Bogotá.[28]

The members of the radical wing of the Liberal Party waited for the 1934 election. A government whose leader called it *La Revolución en*

*Marcha* was elected, bringing with it the most extensive social changes in twentieth-century Colombia.

### The *Revolución en Marcha* and United Fruit

The Liberal Party nominated Alfonso López Pumarejo as its candidate for the 1934 elections. López was a successful businessman who had made remarkable contributions to the Colombian financial sector. He belonged to a traditional upper-class family of Bogotá and had been educated mostly in London. This gentleman politician had been more involved in the business world than in politics and was well known for his contributions introducing elegant English-style sports among the Bogotá elite. An admirer of Franklin D. Roosevelt, López ran for president on an aggressive social change platform. He won the elections easily because the Conservatives could not get organized or agree on who their nominee should be. The reforms López had in mind had no precedent in Colombian history, and they were so radical for their time that, as historian David Bushnell put it, "after López Colombia would not be the same again."[29] Among other social issues, López's program included agrarian reform, official support for labor unions, and tighter controls on foreign investment. He worked closely with members of the Communist and Socialist parties, as well as with union leaders. In fact, López has been the only president in Colombian history to have invited the leader of the Communist Party to give a speech from the presidential balcony.

Some of the most important conflicts in Magdalena between United Fruit and local peasants regarded the lack of clarity in property rights. After the 1928 massacre, several politicians pushed for clearer legislation on this matter. López proposed the country's first agrarian reform law in 1936. The goal of the reform was not to expropriate existing large properties, rather it was intended to define the country's loose property rights, especially those of small tenants. The new law established possession as "nine-tenths of the land" for landless peasants who had moved on to the unused outer fringes of large private estates. The law also imposed higher taxes on lands not being used efficiently for productive purposes, and, in some areas, the law moved to purchase private properties for subdivision and distribution among farmers.[30] Although he was not attacking directly the large landowners, López's law had a clear goal of redistribution.

While López tried to make property rights clearer for peasant masses, he also made some constitutional amendments that made these rights more ambiguous for multinationals. In 1936, the congress approved his amendment regarding the right of expropriation. By saying that property rights had social duties and obligations, the constitutional amendment gave the government the right to expropriate, without compensation, any property if the initiative was "reasons of social interest." An analysis by the U.S. Library of Congress for American investors interpreted this Colombian legislation as a potential threat but emphasized that the technical legal requirements for expropriation made it difficult to carry out.[31] In general, though the study advised investors to take the reforms of the López administration seriously, it also suggested not to overestimate their impact because expropriation required the approval of the Colombian Congress.

López also gave official support to labor unions. He provided them with financial aid and sided with them during strikes. His government also created agencies to educate unions on how to organize effectively and use reform laws to their benefit. In 1936, the first nationwide labor federation—the Confederación de Trabajadores de Colombia [CTC]— was created with the close help of radical Liberals and members of the Communist Party, and with the help of government funding. During López's administration, the eight-hour labor day was introduced in Colombia, as well as employer obligations on welfare and social security.

López also sought for a way to increase the income taxes paid by corporations. While campaigning, he criticized the Conservative tax system, considering it obsolete, and proposed a tax increase. Once in power López increased corporate income taxes for both national and foreign corporations. During the first year of tax reform, the foreign petroleum corporation Tropical Oil Company paid in that one year as much as it had paid over the past eight years.[32]

López had specific measures in mind for United Fruit. Once he was in power, he explicitly told the banana workers that they now could count on the government's support in their struggles against United Fruit. His government even initiated an investigation of the company's labor policies, holding United Fruit's manager in jail for several days. Even though the charges against the manager were dismissed, this sent a strong signal to the banana worker unions.[33]

The aggressive reforms of López and his close relationship with Communists and radical Liberals worried some sectors of the Liberal establishment. In addition, López's plans to reform the education system faced opposition by the church and the Conservative Party. All these factors led the Liberals to nominate a more moderate candidate for the 1938 election. This candidate, Eduardo Santos, won with virtually no opposition because the Conservatives, once again, did not participate.

### Slowing Down the Reforms: Santos's Administration and United Fruit's Withdrawal

Eduardo Santos's administration is known as "The Great Pause" in contrast to the times of radical changes during López's rule. Although Santos did not set back any of the reforms made by López, he did not go further either. During his administration, unlike López, he sought to distance himself from the radical Liberals and the Communists. During this time, the Conservatives succeeded in organizing themselves under the leadership of ultraconservative and charismatic Laureano Gómez and his closest ally, the Catholic Church. Their goal was to roll back the reforms that had taken place under the López administration.

Problems in the banana sector rose during Santos's administration. The Magdalena banana zone began to suffer an attack of the Sigatoka disease on the banana trees. Even though the government proposed a joint plan to fight the disease, United Fruit refused to participate, alleging that the uncertainty created during López's administration did not encourage the company to make the necessary investment in improvement to their properties. The differences between the Colombian government and United Fruit reached a point at which the American ambassador volunteered to work as a mediator. According to Fernando Cepeda and Rodrigo Pardo, an agreement on fighting Sigatoka was reached only after the Colombian Supreme Court declared some of López's policies toward multinationals unconstitutional. The agreement was signed in 1941, but the campaign was subsequently delayed several times.[34] Once World War II broke out, the project was postponed indefinitely. The company interrupted all its operations in Colombia; it had become dangerous to sail in the Caribbean and many of the company's ships had been requisitioned by the U.S. government for military transport.

### The Evolution of Local Politics during United Fruit's Temporary Withdrawal: The Return of the Conservatives to Power and the Rise of Gaitán's Popularity

Just before United Fruit interrupted its operations in Magdalena, Colombia went through a new presidential election. The Liberal Party nominated Alfonso López again, who ran against the Conservative Carlos Arango. López was still popular among labor unions, and both the Communists and the Socialists openly endorsed his candidacy. He won the elections with 58.6% of the vote at the national level. He was even more popular in Magdalena, where he won with 64.6% of the vote.[35]

Despite his broad popular support, López's second administration was not as radical as his first. He faced a better organized opposition, which tempered his ability to advance a program of social reforms. In addition, moderate Liberals sought to limit the influence of the Communists in the lower and radical flanks of their party. López's reform program faced obstacles from his fellow Liberals, the Conservatives, certain sectors of the army, and the radical opposition led by Gaitán. Conservative leader Laureano Gómez torpedoed López's popular support by creating Conservative labor unions that competed with the left-wing unions created during López's first administration. López's opposition reached its highest point in 1944 when, during a political tour in the city of Pasto, he faced a military coup attempt. During the brief time he was arrested by the rebel military, massive demonstrations were held in major cities in support of López. The demonstrations were primarily led and organized by the Communist Party. Even though these demonstrations forced the rebels to free López, the coup demonstrated that López faced an implacable opposition. A few months later he resigned and appointed his close advisor, Alberto Lleras, as president.

The Conservative opposition grew in parallel to the rise of Gaitán's radical movement. Gaitán's rise during the first three Liberal administrations had been impressive. His organizational capabilities and his rhetoric made him increasingly popular among the lower classes. Moreover, he had undertaken remarkable reforms as mayor of Bogotá and as minister of labor, contributing to his popularity. The Liberal establishment, however, disliked his ascent. Even though he proposed reforms that differed only slightly from those proposed by López, the Liberal elite trusted López—a blond, blue-eyed, upper-class gentleman—over Gaitán—a dark-skinned, self-made man of humble origin, who they pejoratively nicknamed *El Negro* (the black one). Gaitán also showed his distrust of López, whom he considered just another member of the ruling bourgeoisie (or what he called *el país político*), in contrast to *el país nacional*—the real country of the average citizen.

The situation between Gaitán and the Liberal establishment deteriorated after López's resignation. Gaitán declared himself a presidential candidate in the 1946 election, but the party's machinery decided to choose the moderate Gabriel Turbay instead. Gaitán refused to accept the party's decision and decided to run on his own. The Liberal electorate was therefore divided between Gaitán and Turbay. The Liberal party machinery managed to keep small towns loyal to the official candidate, but could do little to oppose the immense popularity of Gaitán in major cities. Even union leaders dithered on whom to support. Those loyal to the radical reforms initiated by López supported Turbay, while others willing to go further with social change endorsed Gaitán.

The Conservatives, on the other hand, were solidly united under the strong leadership of Gómez. They nominated Mariano Ospina, a successful industrialist from Medellín, as their candidate and could count on the Catholic Church's open support.

Under these circumstances, the results of the 1946 elections were not surprising—the unified Conservative Party won against the divided Liberals. Mariano Ospina won with 41.4% of the votes; Gabriel Turbay was second with 32.3%, and Gaitán was third with 26.3%.[36] In Magdalena, the results were different—Gaitán was first with 35.7%, Ospina was second with 33.4%, and Turbay was third with 30.9%. Although the two extremes of the political spectrum received a similar amount of votes in Magdalena, the Liberals still held two-thirds of the electorate—a similar majority to the one they had in the 1942 election with López, who received 64.6% of the vote.

The electoral behavior during the Liberal administrations shows that although it is not conclusive that the massacre gave immediate popularity to the Liberals in Magdalena, the people of that department eventually gave support to the politician that most used the massacre as a political tool—Gaitán.

## The Comeback of the Conservatives and the Beginning of La Violencia

Although certain sectors of the Conservative Party wanted to turn back the clock to the 1920s, the new Conservative president, Mariano Ospina, was more pragmatic. He sought a smooth transition of power and even included several Liberals in his cabinet. He also shared with the Liberal Party a fear of the increasing popularity of Gaitán, who aspired to run again in the 1950 election.

The Liberal Party's fate changed dramatically on April 9, 1948—the day Gaitán was assassinated in downtown Bogotá. His death was followed by a popular riot in the city that spread throughout the country. Gaitán's assassination marks the beginning of the era known as *La Violencia*. This period is said to have lasted until 1957, when the military intervened, although the actual political violence in the countryside began a few years before and continues until the present day.

Contrary to the War of the Thousand Days, La Violencia was not a conventional war between two armies. Rather, it was a war among neighbors in little towns, guerrillas, and paramilitary death squads. The countryside was heavily affected, encouraging a mass migration of *campesinos*, or peasants, to Bogotá, Medellín, and Cali, dramatically increasing the size of these cities. The Liberals financed guerrilla groups in the Llanos region of Colombia in a war that eventually spiraled out of control in the 1950s.

The violence and chaos that erupted after Gaitán's assassination was taken by the Conservative government as an excuse to blame and harass the members of the radical Left. Thus began the decay of the labor movement and the Communist and Socialist parties, a process reinforced by the 1950 election when radical Conservative Laureano Gómez came to power.

## The Return of United Fruit to Colombia under Different Political Conditions

When United Fruit returned to Colombia it found a different place from the one it had left at the beginning of World War II. The Liberals were not in power, and the labor movement had been weakened. The new administration did not support the radical workers' organizations, as the López administration had, but rather supported the church-led right-wing unions. However, even though the company did not have to deal with these annoyances anymore, it had returned to a country that was falling into a chaotic spiral of violence.

United Fruit was not directly affected by the conflicts of La Violencia. In fact, in the first report submitted to the central offices in Boston, the local manager of United Fruit reported that the Magdalena banana zone remained peaceful after Gaitán's assassination.[37] The outburst of violence that followed Gaitán's assassination affected more the prosperous coffee regions of Antioquia, Santander, and Tolima.

During the last two years of the 1940s, United Fruit did not report many political issues affecting it. The problems were limited to some property taxes the company had to pay to the *municipio* of Ciénaga[38] and some new import restrictions on cheap rice to feed its workers.[39] The Colombian government did increasingly restrict imports in order to protect national industry. These restrictions were a growing annoyance to United Fruit because it imported most of the goods it sold to its workers in the *comisariatos* (the company stores). The company finally negotiated with the government and obtained a special import permit in 1950.[40]

The Conservatives became more powerful after 1950. That year, the country went to the polls again and elected Conservative Laureano Gómez. Gómez won without opposition because the Liberals withdrew from the election, claiming the violent climate of the country was not safe for them or for their voters. Although his government was officially democratic under the constitution, Gómez's administration was a virtual dictatorship. He declared a state of siege, justified by the increasing violence in the countryside and used it to repress the Liberal opposition. During his administration, several right-wing paramilitary groups were created, terrorizing civilians with extreme cruelty. In addition, Gómez restricted free speech in a way never seen in Colombia.

Gómez was a friend of big business, and, during his administration, he endorsed the industrial sector and encouraged foreign investment. Paradoxically, during the height of La Violencia, the country witnessed spectacular economic growth. Between 1945 and 1955, economic growth reached an average rate of 5% with industrial output at 9%.[41]

Not surprising, during the Gómez administration, United Fruit reported business as usual in the banana region. In fact, there was a remarkable absence of conflict with the government during Gómez's administration.

### The Military Dictatorship's Economic Policies

In 1953, a military group led by General Gustavo Rojas put an end to Gómez's government. The military justified their coup as a response to the violence in the country. Rojas's dictatorship did not exclude the traditional parties' politicians. An assembly of both Liberals and Conservatives approved his rule for a four-year period. Although Rojas appointed members of both parties in his government, it was heavily dominated by Conservatives.

Rojas engaged in a four-part strategy to end La Violencia: he offered amnesty to the guerrillas; backed the right-wing labor unions; repressed the opposition; and made impressive investments in welfare and infrastructure. His approach was successful; an important faction of the Liberal guerrillas signed a peace treaty, opposition activists "disappeared," and Rojas's welfare policies made him popular among the working class.

The banana sector began to see benefits of Rojas's government in 1956 when it established a system of open currency exchange for the banana industry, a measure that was gratefully received both by local growers and United Fruit. Until 1956, Colombia had a system of differential exchange rates for coffee and other exports. Francisco Dávila, president of the Consorcio Bananero, the regional association of banana planters, stated in the March 1957 edition of *Economía Colombiana*[42] that the introduction of this measure saved Colombian exporters because it allowed them to increase internal investment. Nonetheless, Dávila recognized that rather than creating boom conditions for the industry, the measure merely served to avoid its collapse in the face of Ecuadoran competition. Dávila stated, "Without free currency exchange, industry would have remained static and most probably, the independent producers and exporters would have disappeared." Manager Eustace Hall informed United Fruit in Boston of a reduction in his operating costs thanks to this legal reform.[43]

Although Rojas did not stop the import substitution industrialization process, the industrial sector disliked his approach to the working class. Some of his policies were seen as populist, such as the introduction of a stock dividend tax and the establishment of welfare institutions. Rojas also attempted to debilitate the Conservative union federation, the Unión de Trabajadores de Colombia [UTC], by creating the Confederación Nacional de Trabajadores [CNT]. Even though Rojas made some remarkable reforms, such as giving total civil rights to women and investing in substantial public works, Rojas did not succeed in what he said he was there for—to end the violence. The violence, in fact, did decrease but did not end. Despite this, Rojas experienced increasing popularity that made him want to stay in power longer than he had initially promised, but this was something the Liberal and Conservative elite could not permit. Thus, the army, the Conservatives, and the Liberals suggested that he withdraw, which Rojas did in 1957.

## The Frente Nacional: United Fruit in a New Age of Bipartisan Politics and Protectionism

After Rojas, Colombian politics took a dramatically different turn. The Liberals and Conservatives decided to settle their differences for the sake of national peace and created a transitional system known as the *Frente Nacional*. The Frente Nacional allowed both parties to share power over the next sixteen years; there would be elections every four years, but Liberal candidates and Conservative candidates would alternate participation. Once in power, the president, regardless of his or her party affiliation, committed to sharing the government with the other party on a 50-50 basis. The Frente Nacional would last for four elections (sixteen years), after which, open political competition would be restored.

Although the Frente Nacional sought to end internal political conflicts, it gained enemies among those who felt excluded from this new system, such as the Communists. The existing guerrillas used their exclusion to justify the continuation of their struggle (in their view, the oligarchs had arranged the political system in an exclusive way, forcing them into armed opposition). This hardened the Colombian Revolutionary Armed Forces' (Fuerzas Armadas Revolucionarias de Colombia [FARC]) position and led to the creation of new guerrilla groups such as urban M-19, the People's Liberation Army [EPL], and the National Liberation Army [ELN]. The EPL eventually operated in the region of Urabá, where United Fruit had operations starting in the early 1960s. One of the EPL's main goals was to create a revolutionary cell among the banana workers, which heavily affected the industry's development and the labor relations in the region.[44]

The Frente Nacional was business-friendly and protectionist. During this period, the industrial sectors of Medellín, Cali, and Bogotá flourished with government-supported import substitution industrialization. The government also strongly endorsed export industries, including the banana sector. The beginning of the Frente Nacional coincided with Urabá's beginning as an export region. The rise of the Urabá banana exports was brought about by local planters with the financial support of United Fruit. These local planters came from the industrial sector of Medellín and had close links to the Sindicato Antioqueño, a group of the largest industrial firms in Medellín that had strong lobbying power in Bogotá.

In the early 1960s, the government showed an interest in intervening in the banana export economy. Their interest included issues such as workers' services and plant disease control, which up to this point had been in the hands of United Fruit. The government proposed the creation of the Magdalena Banana Fund, an entity in charge of workers' services and disease control and financed with a 9% reimbursement tax.[45] Thus, the Magdalena Banana Fund would arrange contracts with shipping lines for the transport of the fruit around the world, as well as negotiate their sale price. Negotiation of sale price was viewed by United Fruit officials as prejudicial because it implied state control over marketing. During the 1960s, the company began transferring certain sectors, such as its clinic and hospital, to social security to be managed by the banana fund.

The first services provided by the government were drainage and irrigation services in the Magdalena region. However, this type of action did not bring any great advantage to United Fruit because the debts the government created in these works were classified at various times as "bad debts."[46] These services were provided as part of the transfer of operations in the region from United Fruit to the government.

In 1963, members of the Colombian Congress debated proposed economic policies affecting United Fruit. In July, the minister of finance, Carlos Sanz de Santamaría, defended plans to raise taxes.[47] In response to his opponent's argument that a tax increase would create industrial fatigue, Sanz de Santamaría believed the national development plan was not feasible under the current tax budget; it required reform.[48] As part of this reform, the reduction of certain transport subsidies was proposed, and the minister singled out the Magdalena railway among those that were unprofitable and had labor problems. United Fruit's concession over the Magdalena railway had ended in 1963, and it can be assumed that the railway's situation was not much better when owned by United Fruit just a few months before. In fact, United Fruit reported that when the concession period ended, it had not been able to give the railway back to the government on the designated date because of the many maintenance jobs it still needed to complete.[49] United Fruit's manager also reported that the government's transport taxes, together with reports of unjustified maintenance costs, caused heavy increases in the costs of banana shipments.[50]

The coming of the first Frente Nacional Liberal administration did not stop tax increases. With Carlos Lleras Restrepo taking power as president of Colombia in 1966, United Fruit officials reported a strong increase in the costs of imported goods as a result of the new economic policies. The rate on certain preferential imported articles increased from $9.00 to $13.00, and others with free rates, from $13.00 up. United

Fruit manager Victor MacMillan stated, with obvious dismay in a report to United Fruit in Boston, "The new President of Colombia, Carlos Lleras Restrepo, lost no time in strongly devaluating the peso." At the same time, MacMillan reported poor banana exports with low prices from Magdalena, while mentioning better prices and better quality fruit in the Turbo (Urabá) region.[51]

In April 1967, the Colombian Congress passed one of the most important economic measures in the country's history, containing several ideas Sanz de Santamaría had requested years earlier. Decree 444 of 1967, which regulated Colombian foreign trade until the 1990s and that created, for the first time, a legal system for the clear and effective control of foreign investment.[52] The decree announced that export exemptions were terminated (which bananas enjoyed only to a limited extent) and that free currency exchange for certain exports, as well as the free exchange between these goods and bananas, were eliminated. The decree maintained refunds for exports, consisting of the return of the tax paid on the export after a predetermined time had elapsed. According to the data, the refunds increased between 1963 and 1964 and maintained high levels until 1970.[53] This may be explained by the fact that it was during this period that Urabá started exporting bananas.

During the Frente Nacional, the government also intervened in agrarian structure by creating the National Institute for Agrarian Reform (Instituto Colombiano para la Reforma Agraria, or Incora). Incora was in charge of land redistribution. The government was aware that most of the violent conflicts in the country were rooted in vague property rights for land ownership and in the structure of land distribution. The creation of Incora was also part of the continentwide Alliance for Progress reforms that attempted to counterbalance the increasing popularity of Fidel Castro's revolution in Cuba.

Contrary to what might be expected, the creation of Incora was not prejudiced against United Fruit but beneficial in that it facilitated the company's withdrawal from Magdalena. In 1967, United Fruit had reported difficulties leaving the region because it could not get rid of its assets profitably. Some of the assets could not be sold at good prices, and others, which had already been sold, were not being paid for by the buyers.[54] By the middle of 1967, United Fruit began negotiations with Incora in the hope that Incora would buy the remaining United Fruit assets and also pay the debts to United Fruit on the properties in default.[55] The company reported that Incora probably would not be inclined to pay the prices it proposed, but it was the best alternative available.[56] Incora was the second government entity to receive goods from United Fruit following its withdrawal after the Colombian Social Security Institute (Instituto Colombiano de Seguro Social [ICSS]) had received the hospital facilities. The negotiations with Incora continued until April 1968, when a preliminary agreement was signed.[57] Under the terms of this agreement, Incora would cover the balances of loans made to plantation owners, current accounts, and sale of the remaining United Fruit farms.

This was a much better outcome than what the United Fruit officials had originally hoped to achieve. With this agreement, by the end of 1969, United Fruit managed to report a major decrease in costs compared with the previous year due to the transfer of obligations to Incora, which paid United Fruit with government bonds.[58] Thus, after nearly sixty years in the Magdalena region, United Fruit managed to withdraw without financial problems in only a few short months because a state institution, charged with carrying out agrarian reform, purchased its properties.

The economic interventionism Colombia witnessed during the Frente Nacional along with Colombian legislation on foreign investment were seen by United Fruit as sources of risk and uncertainty. In 1965, a seminar titled "Rights and Duties of Private Investors Abroad" was held in Dallas, Texas. The vice-president and general counsel of United Fruit, Victor C. Folsom, presented a paper in which he reported on the vagueness of the laws on foreign investment in Latin America.[59] Folsom asserted that any obligation on a multinational company should not normally be different from the duty of a good citizen, but that United Fruit's experience showed that, in general, the Latin American laws required more from multinational companies than from domestic companies because of the greater earnings generated by the multinationals. Latin Americans expected behavior from the multinational that Folsom characterized as similar to a good parenting, instead of the behavior of a good capitalist enterprise. Folsom also recommended abandoning the concession system because this was generally seen as a privilege given to the multinational and could easily be canceled by the host state from one moment to the next. As an alternative, Folsom proposed contracts that would give both parties rights and obligations and would be more difficult to act on arbitrarily by the host government.

Folsom described Colombia as a place where the local legislation generated uncertainties for the foreign investor. He indicated that under the Colombian constitution, foreigners clearly had the same rights and obligations under the law as nationals. However, with regard to the concept of property, Folsom noted certain contradictions that could confuse foreign investors and make them vulnerable to arbitrary action by the state. Article 669 of the Colombian civil code stated that property "is a real right to enjoy or dispose arbitrarily of a tangible good, as long as this is not contrary to the law or an infringement of the rights of others." Article 30 stated, "private property and other rights acquired with a fair title are guaranteed by the civil law, in favor of natural or legal persons, who may not lose their rights nor be weakened in them by posterior laws." Yet, the same article states that "property is a social function which implies obligations."[60] This contradiction within the same article could be interpreted by the government for its own purposes. Folsom pointed out that the Colombian constitution did not clearly define what it meant by "social function," which he stated was one of the most problematic matters for international investors as well as for domestic ones.

Folsom also said the Colombian constitution left a great degree of freedom to the government for expropriations. Article 669 of the constitution placed the interests of the state above individual interests with regard to the application of any law: "for reasons of public utility or social interest, resulting in a conflict of the rights of individuals with the needs recognized by law, private interests must cede to public or social interests." Another section of the article stated, "for reasons of public utility or social interest as defined by the legislator, expropriation is permitted providing there is a judicial decision and prior indemnification." Folsom explained that this could generate discriminatory measures that would mitigate the legal equality of nationals and foreigners. The same paragraph did not even ensure indemnification for expropriation, when it stated, "In all matters, the legislator, for reasons of equity, may determine the cases in which indemnification will not be given, by holding a vote receiving an absolute majority of the members of both Chambers." In short, the constitution gave the Colombian government a great deal of leeway.

Folsom emphasized that not even the postrevolutionary Cuban constitution limited the payment of indemnification for expropriation. Not even Fidel Castro's government claimed that the principle of expropriation for state interests would imply a right not to give compensation. In fact, following the Cuban revolution, all nationalization of foreign property carried out by Castro respected the right to indemnification. This meant the Colombian constitution was singular in the international sphere. Folsom's statements show that Colombian constitutional principles, when compared with other nations, were seen as unfavorable by United Fruit's lawyers. This critical view of Colombia's constitution likely explains the company's aversion to direct investment in Colombia.

## The 1970s and the Colombian Government's Economic Interventionism

In the long term, United Fruit never faced a real risk of expropriation in Colombia, as feared by Folsom, but had to deal with a government that wanted to support the local banana corporations in their relationship with the foreign multinationals. In 1968, several local providers of United Fruit in Urabá decided not to renew their contracts with the company and instead created their own export company. This initiative depended on government support on several occasions. In 1970, the government intervened in favor of the Urabá banana exporters when they conflicted with United Brands over access to the canals built by the multinational in the region. The canals were conditioned by United Brands for the transportation of bananas to their ships anchored at sea. The government forced United Brands by decree to give the Colombian banana exporters access to these canals. In 1971, the government provided subsidized loans to the local exporters to build a shipyard in Urabá in order to make the local companies more competitive in the international market. In none of these occasions could United Brands do much to preclude the government action.[61]

The Colombian government also played an active role in the creation of the Unión de Países Exportadores de Banano [UPEB]. One of the main individuals behind the creation of the UPEB was the Colombian minister of agriculture, Hernán Vallejo, who became the UPEB's first president. The creation of the UPEB generated a heated conflict between United Brands and the Central American governments. The conflict did not include Colombia despite Colombia being one of the founding members of the UPEB.[62] This is partially because United Brands still owned producing assets in Central America where it was being threatened with expropriation by the local governments; in Colombia, the government had nothing to expropriate.

In the 1980s, the Colombian government had higher priorities in Urabá than the business operations of multinational enterprises. During this decade, the territory of Urabá witnessed fighting between the left-wing guerrilla groups FARC and the EPL, the right-wing militias, the drug mafia, and the national army. The violence increased in the late 1980s to unimaginable levels, each group seeking to eliminate its enemy. Complete neighborhoods were wiped out. Right-wing militias avenged the kidnapping of some farm managers by killing the activists of the Communist Unión Patriótica [UP]. Farm owners could not go back to their properties and had to manage their businesses from Medellín, giving authority to their local managers. In the 1980s, nongovernmental organizations declared Urabá the most violent place in the Western Hemisphere, while the Colombian national government declared it a war zone.[63]

Between 1982 and 1989, United Brands interrupted its operations in Colombia partly because of the political turmoil and partly because of its general international strategy. During this period, the government continued to support the national exporters through soft loans through the Export Promotion Fund (PROEXPO) and a tax credit of 10% of the export value of the bananas established in 1984.[64] In the 1990s, the government played a more active role in protecting its national production in the European market, which created new conflicts with United Brands (since renamed Chiquita).

## *The 1990s: Chiquita and the Colombian Government Conflict over the European Market*

In 1992, the members of the European Community unified their economies into a single market—the European Union. This was seen as a great business opportunity for banana growers and marketers. However, the optimism generated by this new organization in Europe rapidly waned. Several European countries advocated a banana import restriction system that favored the French and British former colonies in Africa and the Caribbean (the ACP countries), discriminating against Latin American producers and, as a consequence, against the American multinationals that marketed Latin American bananas.[65]

The tensions between the European Union and the United States around the new banana regime also created tension between the American government, Chiquita, and the Colombian government. When the Europeans announced in 1993 the establishment of a quota system that favored their former colonies, the governments of Colombia, Nicaragua, Costa Rica, and Venezuela negotiated a quota for their countries with the European Union. These negotiations led to the Framework Agreement, in which these four countries shared a quota with the former colonies of Europe. In 1994, Colombia was allocated 21% of the total EU quota with 441,000 tons of bananas, which was raised to 462,000 tons in 1995. As a way to support the national producers under this new system, in March 1995 the Colombian government increased export subsidies to the banana growers from 2.5% to 5% of the free-on-board (FOB) value.[66] The Colombian government provided the subsidies at the same time it negotiated the quota with the European Union to compensate its local growers for their loss of a portion of the European market. Not only had the national producers been severely hit by the European quota system, but the over supply created by the world producers' miscalculations on the future size of the European market also led international prices to collapse. Saving the banana sector was a particularly sensitive issue in Colombia because, by that time, the Urabá region had achieved a fragile political peace that could be shattered by an economic crisis in the zone.

The Framework Agreement counted on the strong opposition of Chiquita and the U.S. government. Even though the bananas exported to Europe under the agreement would be marketed mostly by Chiquita, the multinational believed the Colombian government initiative actually reinforced the European quota system they sought to abolish and left Chiquita with a smaller participation in the EU market.[67] By September 1994, Chiquita reacted against the Framework Agreement and filed the Section 301 petition with U.S. trade representative Mickey Kantor.

Section 301 of the 1974 Trade Act allowed American corporations to petition the U.S. government to investigate and seek redress against unfair foreign trade acts that violated U.S. rights under GATT, or discriminated and burdened or restricted American international commerce. Section 301 provided grounds for economic retaliation measures against an offending country. In October, Kantor announced the U.S. government would begin formal investigations against the EU quota system and advised the countries under the Framework Agreement not to continue with an initiative the U.S. government considered a "GATT-illegal and discriminatory policy."[68] According to the *Journal of Commerce*, in December 1994, Chiquita CEO Carl Lindner had an interview with Colombian president, Ernesto Samper, in which Lindner warned Samper (after showing Samper photographs of himself in the company of Senator Bob Dole) of the serious consequences continuing under the Framework Agreement would have for Colombia.[69]

The Colombian government protested the investigations. In February 1995, Colombian foreign trade minister, Daniel Mazuera, said the accusations were unfounded because the claim was made by Chiquita, a company that was exporting its goods to Europe. Therefore, instead of being discriminated, Chiquita had benefited from the agreement. Mazuera also warned that U.S. sanctions against Colombian banana exports would hurt the economy of a region in the midst of a civil war and threatened the stability of the whole country.[70] As a way to settle the difference with the U.S. trade representative, the Colombian government proposed an increase in the share U.S. banana producers and marketers in Colombia could ship to Europe, at the expense of local companies. Mazuera's proposal included an increase of banana shares from 6.83% to 10.9% for Chiquita and from 4.36% to 10.1% for Dole. The proposal was rejected by Kantor.[71]

In 1995, the U.S. government increased pressure on the Colombian government to change its deal with Europe. Senator Dole aggressively campaigned to impose trade sanctions on Colombia and strip the country of any trade benefit it had enjoyed until then. Colombian President Samper wrote a letter, cosigned by Costa Rican President Figueres, to President Clinton stating that trade sanctions would punish two countries already victimized by the EU quota system and insisted that the increase of the Chiquita and Dole participation was the best solution to avoid a catastrophic damage to their economies.[72] The plea did not stop Senator Dole from continuing to campaign for trade sanctions, but he did not have much support from other senators, President Clinton, or Kantor because no American jobs or American production had been hurt by the Framework Agreement.[73]

Despite Chiquita's and Senator Dole's joint campaign to impose trade sanctions on Colombia, the U.S. government backed off its threat in early 1996. The Clinton administration allowed both Colombia and Costa Rica to continue operating under the Framework Agreement in exchange for a commitment by both governments to join the U.S. effort to find a market-oriented solution to the dispute over the quotas. The U.S. government decided to focus its efforts on ending the quota system in Europe—the origin of the whole conflict. Some analysts believe Clinton's decision took into account the political stability of the two countries, both

U.S. allies in the Western Hemisphere in the war against drugs and Communism. The Colombian government received the U.S. decision with joy, but it was clearly a disappointment for Chiquita.[74]

Once the Framework Agreement dispute was settled, the Colombian government and Chiquita experienced no other serious conflict for many years. Although the Colombian government committed itself to pursuing a less restrictive system, it was concerned what effects the economic sanctions the U.S. government imposed on the European Union in 1999 would have on Colombian banana exports. During the peak of conflict between the European Union and the United States between 1998 and 2000, the Colombian government advocated for a compromise between the use of sanctions on Europe by the United States and the European Union's "first come first serve" system. This system would discriminate against non-ACP bananas, which would hurt the Colombian government, the U.S. government, and Chiquita.[75] Colombia and the rest of the banana producers did not have much influence on the settlement, which was decided between the United States and the European Union, but Colombia welcomed the final agreement with cautious optimism.[76] The agreement gave some hope of revival to the wounded banana industry as a whole and to Chiquita, which declared bankruptcy due to the huge costs and debts the company had incurred during the years of the conflict with the European Union.[77]

## Conclusion

The way United Fruit operated in Colombia during the twentieth century was heavily affected by the evolution of Colombian national politics. However, contrary to what happened in Central America, United Fruit could not do much to influence the way Colombian politics evolved. During the first half of the twentieth century, the fate of the company depended on which of the two main political parties was in power. In the latter half, it depended on the way the economic policy of import substitution industrialization and export promotion evolved.

The centralist structure of the Colombian government played an important role in the way the politics around banana exports evolved. It affected how United Fruit operated in Magdalena in two ways: first, in the competition for export taxes between the local government and Bogotá; and second, in the lack of support the Magdalena planters received from the national government when they faced their worst crisis during the 1960s. On the contrary, when United Fruit moved to Urabá, the powerful Medellín industrial lobby made the national government intervene in favor of the local growers (who, in fact, belonged to the same industrial group; see chapter 5).

During the Conservative Hegemony (1904–30) United Fruit did not face major differences with the national government. The main political conflict was the competition between the local Magdalena government and the national government for the tax revenues generated by the banana export business. United Fruit benefited from the conflict because the national government torpedoed every attempt the Magdalena assembly made to tax exports. The government of Bogotá defended the tax exemptions it granted to foreign investors as an incentive to promote the arrival of foreign capital in the country. Once the tax exemption period was over, the national government took the benefits for itself and did not permit the government of Magdalena to make use of them.

After 1930, United Fruit faced a Colombian government that was not entirely sympathetic to its interests. Both the reformist government of Alfonso López and the radical Gaitán took advantage of the tragic outcome of the 1928 strike to approach banana labor unions. The unions were some of the first that benefited from López's support. López even endorsed the banana labor unions' petitions. Gaitán supported the workers' struggle as well, which increased his popularity and political importance.

Colombia's fall after Gaitán's assassination into the tragic period of La Violencia did not affect United Fruit's businesses significantly. The company did not face problems with the local governments, the national government, or the unions. In fact, the period of the bloodiest point of La Violencia coincides with the company's managers reporting less problems with workers, the local government, and the national government. There are several probable explanations. First, the Caribbean was not as heavily affected as the rest of the country during La Violencia; it affected the most prosperous areas of the country more than the poor ones. Second, the country was ruled by arch-Conservative Laureano Gómez, who did everything possible to repress labor unionism. Third, the Gómez government remained friendly to national and foreign businesses.

As the conflict between Liberals and Conservatives diminished, the company's conflicts with local workers and the government rose. The company was helped by the economic policies of the military dictatorship of Rojas (1953–57) but faced difficulties with the protectionist governments of the Frente Nacional (1958–70).[78] These governments wanted stronger state participation in the banana export sector and higher corporate taxes. Additionally, the company began to fear that the vagueness of the Colombian constitution regarding expropriation could be used by the interventionist governments. The constitution was written in 1886, but the articles on expropriation had been added during López's administration.

Concentrating on marketing and relying on local providers did not eliminate the effects of an interventionist government for the company. When the local producers of Urabá decided to create their own company, they counted on the open support of the Colombian government. In this way, United Fruit could not impede the creation of Uniban, the local export company, in 1968.[79]

From the 1970s to the 1990s, United Fruit operated in a country in which the government provided strong support to the local banana export sector. The company did not have much power to oppose this government endorsement and continued operating in the country until 1982 when it left partly because of the violence in Urabá, but more important, because of a general strategy to concentrate the company in its Central American division. The company returned to Urabá in 1989 and had its first serious conflict with the Colombian government in the 1990s over the European market banana quota system. This conflict led the company to seek U.S. government support to pressure Colombia to drop the Framework Agreement it had signed with the European Union. The U.S. government threatened Colombia with sanctions, but Chiquita was not powerful enough (despite the resources it spent lobbying senior levels in Washington) to make the United States punish Colombia for its actions.

In summary, during the twentieth century, United Fruit had to adapt to the evolution of national politics and had little power to influence them in return. The Colombian government had been seen as weak and unable to rule the country. Nevertheless, it proved to be more effective at controlling the multinational corporation than its Central American counterparts. The Colombian government's effectiveness relies not only on the relatively smaller size of United Fruit in the Colombian economy in contrast to in Central America, but also on the institutional framework in Colombia that included a more pluralistic system and the political competition between its political parties. The evolution of Colombian politics created incentives for United Fruit to make direct investments in the first half of the century but encouraged divestiture in the second half of the century.

# 5

# The Labor Conflicts of the United Fruit Company in Magdalena in the 1920s

No issue related to the history of United Fruit in Colombia has been more studied than the labor relations with its workforce in the 1920s. Pioneering studies by Catherine LeGrand and Judith White focus on the social conflicts surrounding the 1928 strike that ended in the city of Ciénaga when the Colombian army opened fire against peaceful and unarmed demonstrators, killing several of them. The strike was made infamous by Gabriel García Márquez's novel *One Hundred Years of Solitude,* which has remained the primary point of reference for the labor history of United Fruit in Colombia. White's study is important in that it was the first serious historical account of the strike that looked at the evolution of the relationship between the planters, the workers, and the company. She shows the developments of 1928 as the inevitable outcome of the social tensions generated by the presence of the company, tensions that were a direct consequence of the dependency of the region on fruit exports. LeGrand takes a more social scientific approach to the problem using a Marxist framework and concludes that the strike was the consequence of the penetration of capitalistic social relationships in the region by United Fruit.

Most of the writings on the 1928 strike argue two points. First, that the strike was an early manifestation of the revolutionary struggle of the Colombian working class against oppressive capitalism. And, second, that the tragic outcome of the strike—the massacre of the demonstrators in Ciénaga—destroyed the region's unionism and reinforced the exploitation of the banana workers. I argue that neither of these points is accurate. I will show that the workers were not fighting against the capitalistic system created by United Fruit in Magdalena, but that they wanted to formalize their relationship with the company by being recognized as official United Fruit workers. I will also show that the military repression of 1928 did not "kill" labor unionism in the region. After 1930, Colombia went through important political and institutional changes that permitted the rise of labor unionism and the creation of a labor code similar to what the 1928 strikers wanted.

## The 1928 Strike as a Revolutionary Movement

Both the Left and the Right in Colombia portrayed the 1928 strike as "revolutionary," but they did so for different reasons. Left-wing authors have interpreted it as the first battle of the revolutionary struggle by the Colombian working class against capitalism. Historian Hugo López opens his essay on the strike with, "On December 6, 1928, Colombia witnessed its first anti-oligarchy and anti-imperialistic battle, made by the Magdalena banana zone workers. This event provides the working class with invaluable experience for the struggle currently taking place against exploitation and the bourgeois-landowning-imperialistic blackmail."[1]

In the introduction of Alberto Castrillón's book on the massacre, Rodríguez points out what he believes are the most important lessons of this event:[2] "The fundamental enemies of the Colombian working class are the Colombian bourgeoisie and American imperialism. The only way to radically eliminate the misery and exploitation of our people is by having the proletarian class taking power."[3]

Herrera and Soto's book on the history of the Magdalena banana zone, classified the region's labor movement as a "proletarian apparatus prepared as spearhead of the Revolution."[4]

While the studies written years after the massacre depict the strikers as "good" revolutionaries, contemporary documents by the Colombian government portray them as "bad" revolutionaries—a foothold of the international Communist threat in Colombia. This justified the army's attack against the demonstrators in Ciénaga. In his trial, Alberto Castrillón was accused by the government of the following charges:

> We find that responsibility rests with him (Mahecha) for the sole reason of having used the intellectual resources of easy expression and the frequent use of certain sensational tools of communist oratory, in order to induce the masses of workers with little education toward the political orientation of the accused, who considers himself its banner-holder after going to the source—Russia—to initiate himself in Soviet doctrines. We

consider those who contributed with their speeches to the organization of the strike to be its intellectual authors, because the strike would not have been sustained and nourished, and would have not eventually degenerated into acts of vandalism and the like that, in fact, transformed the strikers into a band of criminals, had it not been for the revolutionary torch sprung from Communist minds.[5]

Similarly, the Bogotá newspaper, *El Tiempo*, which represented the moderate Liberals, expressed relief after the army's intervention in Magdalena by reporting, "The Soviet spirit is as foreign to our people as the Protestant spirit, and the very painful proof has been the Magdalena strike."[6]

The above-mentioned quotations show that both the radical left-wing writers and the right-wing establishment considered the 1928 strike "revolutionary" or "Soviet-oriented." Both the Left and the Right benefit from showing the strike this way. For the left, the casualties of Ciénaga were the first martyrs of the revolution, while for the establishment, the army's action was necessary in order to defend national security. Both views might have developed for propaganda purposes because, as I will show in the following sections, both are inaccurate.

## The Magdalena Labor Relations before 1928

Prior to 1928 there was a constant struggle by the Magdalena banana workers to be recognized as formal workers of United Fruit. The company did not hire the workers directly but through subcontractors. United Fruit faced several strikes before the 1928 strike and in all of them, the workers demanded the elimination of the subcontract system and the formalization of a direct contract between them and United Fruit.

### The Contracting System in the Magdalena Banana Zone

The banana labor force of Magdalena arrived in the region from other parts of the country around the same time United Fruit began its operations in the area. The War of the Thousand Days produced an influx of immigrants into Magdalena, increasing the available labor force in the region. During the war, many liberal soldiers and their generals escaped to the Caribbean and settled there once the war was over. The newcomers eventually became an important segment of the banana industry labor force.[7] After the war, the region also absorbed people from other impoverished areas of Colombia who were looking for better prospects. The arrival of these people, many of them sympathizers of the Liberal Party, shaped the area into one with unique characteristics, different from the rest of the Colombian Caribbean.

The several thousand dock and banana plantation labor workers were not hired directly by United Fruit. The company utilized a subcontracting system, hiring a Colombian labor contractor (*ajustero*) to recruit and hire workers as needed. The *ajustero* was responsible for the worker, leaving the company free of any legal commitment to its labor force. The workers were hired for specific tasks for a specified length of time and were paid according to their production during that time. This system was an informal one with no written contract between the *ajustero* and the worker, which created uncertainty for the workers.[8] Although the workers did not oppose being paid according to their individual productivity, they disliked being hired by locals, who they accused of exploitation and abuse.[9] In some instances, the *ajustero* hired other contractors, and the latter hired the workers, making the workers' relationship with the company even more indirect.[10] Under this system, the company's payroll only showed between one hundred or two hundred workers consisting of basically the contractors and the administrative staff, despite having thousands of people working in its fields.[11] According to Pierre Gilhodes, by 1925 the company had 25,000 people working on the docks and plantations, but only 5,000, including clerical and administrative staff, were actually in the company's books.[12] This subcontracting system was the initial source of conflict between United Fruit and the banana workers.

Another source of conflict was the company's use of vouchers or tokens to pay its laborers. The vouchers were only valid at the company stores where they could be exchanged for merchandise. United Fruit was not the only employer using this system in Colombia. Before the Kemmerer mission, monetary policy had been chaotic; large parts of rural Colombia were excluded from the monetary economy. Additionally, United Fruit did not bring its boats back empty to Magdalena, the company imported merchandise and sold it below cost to workers in its stores. Some workers opposed this system because they wanted the freedom to spend their wages anywhere, and they needed to have the local shopkeepers' solidarity during the strikes.

### The Initial Labor Conflicts between United Fruit and the Labor Movement

United Fruit faced its first big strike in January 1918. The workers demanded a wage increase that matched the inflation the country was undergoing at that time, in addition to an end of the subcontracting system.[13] At the end of the strike, the workers got a 20 to 30% wage increase despite the movement's lack of organization and leadership. In 1919, the company faced another strike that led to new wage increases for the dock workers.[14] Despite these successes, the workers did not get what they considered their most important petition—the establishment of an actual contract between them and the company and the elimination of the token payment system.[15]

Although the workers lacked a formally structured labor movement, they achieved some of their demands during the 1918 and 1919 strikes. In order to improve the movement's organization, some labor leaders created *sociedades obreras* in the early 1920s. Even though some *sociedades* called themselves *sindicato* (labor union), they were basically communal organizations that gave out medicine to their members when needed or raised bail when their members were arrested. The strongest *sociedad* was the Sindicato General de Obreros de la Sociedad Unión, established in 1921.[16] The *sociedades* were the embryos of the much stronger unions of the late 1920s.

The more formal Sociedad Unión led a strike in 1924 in which they basically wanted to end the uncertainty the company's subcontracting system generated among workers—a petition similar to the demands in the 1918 and 1919 strikes. Through the Sociedad Unión workers also petitioned the national senate for legal reform that would oblige their employers to give advance notice of employee layoffs. The government, however, decided not to approve the law and declared the strike illegal.[17]

The workers' petition of nine items during the 1924 strike looked similar to those they demanded in 1928. These petitions were

1. Payment of forty pesos to the *arrumadores* (dock workers) per every thousand bananas loaded in the ships.
2. Overtime pay for the railway *braceros*.
3. A minimum *jornal* (daily wage) of two pesos in the plantations and an overtime pay of doubled wages for work on Sundays.
4. Elimination of the subcontracting system.

5. Compensation for work accidents, health insurance, and life insurance.
6. Eight-hour work days.
7. Creation of a fund to support the union.
8. Clean camps with medical service.
9. Indemnity for unemployment and lay offs.

The nine points are not much different from the kinds of labor union demands and social reforms developed countries were facing during that time. In fact, these demands were not radical by international standards. The kind of changes the workers wanted were in accord with the labor practices gradually being accepted in other parts of the world.

The failure of the 1924 strike radicalized the region's labor movement but weakened the Sociedad Unión, which, as a result, became less revolutionary and changed into a workers' organization financed by United Fruit. Its leaders signed an agreement in which they committed not to present demands to their employers. This discouraged the most radical members of the workers' organization, who decided to create separate groups, which later played an important role in the infamous 1928 strike.[18]

In the mid-1920s, the labor movement received help from Spanish and Italian immigrants who arrived in the banana zone and tried to organize the labor movement for the coming strikes. Although some studies point to the presence of the Spanish and Italian Communists as evidence of the "revolutionary" character of the 1928 labor movement,[19] the workers' main concerns did not change much from those they had in previous strikes.

In 1926, Spaniards Elías Castellanos y Abad and Mariano Lacambra and Italian Jenaro Toroni helped to create the Unión Sindical de Trabajadores del Magdalena [USTM], to fill the gap left after the failure of the Sociedad Unión in 1924. This organization faced initial problems such as internal conflicts and unclear strategies and objectives that were resolved once members of the Revolutionary Socialist Party took control. They tried to expand USTM membership to railway workers and establish an ideological goal during the railway workers' strike in February 1927.[20] The railway workers, however, refused to join the USTM and decided to renew their contract with the Sociedad Unión after the Santa Marta Railway Company, a subsidiary of United Fruit, agreed to a wage increase.[21]

The railway workers' decision was a defeat for USTM. United Fruit officials and the local government decided to recognize and support the Sociedad Unión in order to debilitate what they considered the more radical USTM. Thomas Bradshaw, then manager of the Santa Marta Railway and future manager of the United Fruit division talked of "bolshevik elements" in the USTM that made him think it was wise to give some kind of endorsement to the more moderate Sociedad Unión.[22] In fact, both the government and United Fruit had a conciliatory attitude toward the railway strikers.

USTM did not give up after its failure to include the railway workers among its members and continued its campaign to get more followers. In January 1928, USTM organized a strike for dock workers and lower-level railway employees who demanded higher wages. This time, USTM's efforts were successful. The workers joined USTM and won a pay increase.[23]

## *The Strike of 1928 and the "Masacre de las Bananeras"*

USTM's success in January 1928 encouraged them to plan a much larger strike that year. In February, the most prominent leaders of Colombian labor unionism—Ignacio Torres Giraldo, María Cano, Alberto Castrillón, and Raúl Eduardo Mahecha—toured the region to endorse USTM and instruct locals on how to organize a larger strike. These four were experienced in this issue: Ignacio Torres Giraldo was one of the most respected intellectuals of the Colombian left; María Cano led several labor unions in the Medellín textile industry and in the coffee regions; Alberto Castrillón, another influential strike organizer, was a founder of the recently formed Socialist Revolutionary Party [PSR] and took courses on unionism in the Soviet Union; and Raúl Mahecha was one of the main organizers of the 1927 strike of the Tropical Oil Company workers in the city of Barrancabermeja and was educated and trained for revolutionary action in the Soviet Union.

By mid-1928, the revolutionary character of the Magdalena labor movement was ambiguous for both the government and the union leaders. Soon after the arrival of the labor union leaders to Magdalena, the local government arrested some of the labor organizers, including Mahecha, for "subversive activities" but did not harass the labor organizations themselves. According to White, the reason the repression was not against all of those sympathizing with Mahecha and his ideas was because the members of the national congress and the Magdalena assembly could not agree on whether the Magdalena labor organizations represented a real Communist threat.[24] Shortly after his arrest, Mahecha was freed, and he returned to the banana zone to continue organizing the labor movement. However, once freed, Mahecha faced opposition by Tomás Uribe Márquez, one of the leaders of the PSR, who was highly influential in USTM. "Mahecha is confusing a strike with an insurrection," said Uribe, who did not want the workers to clash with the national government.[25]

Although a comité de huelga (strike committee) was formed, its revolutionary tactics were still unclear. Between May and October, Mahecha, Castrillón, and Russo founded the strike committee in the residence of radical leader Christian Bengal, a Dutch immigrant and then president of USTM. During these months the committee lost an opportunity to turn the movement into a revolution and unify the various labor advocates. During the 1928 strike of the Barranquilla dock workers, organized by the Confederación Obrera del Atlántico, USTM published a communiqué that said, "The USTM does not support the Atlantic Workers' Confederation, either in principle or in tactics. Therefore, it is not true that we have been in solidarity with that strike, which we in fact condemn."[26] Other communist groups in Barranquilla refused to endorse USTM's position on the strike. Meanwhile, the PSR had difficulty coordinating other labor unions across the country that were willing to go on strike simultaneously with USTM to add pressure to United Fruit and the government.[27]

The final document presented to United Fruit was approved by the USTM general assembly on October 6. Although this *pliego de peticiones* was signed by Mahecha and written by Mahecha and Castrillón, none of its demands seemed revolutionary. On the contrary, the entire document was filled with references to the current Colombian constitution and legislation. The strikers insisted that they wanted United Fruit to comply with Colombian law. The *pliego* consisted of nine points:

1. Collective insurance (which they defended by using law 37 [1921] and law 32 [1922]).
2. Indemnification for work-related accidents (according to law 57 [1915]).
3. Hygienic dwelling places and one day of rest every week (law 46 [1918], law 15 [1925], and law 76 [1926]).
4. A 50% increase for lower-paid workers.
5. Discontinuance of the company's commissaries.

6. Elimination of the use of credit slips in place of money.
7. Weekly rather than biweekly payments.
8. Replacement of subcontractors with direct contracts with the company.
9. Establishment of hospitals in sufficient number and the proper sanitation of camps.[28]

The most critical issue for USTM leadership was recognition by United Fruit. This was crucial in order to make the company obey Colombian legislation and enhance job security.

The other sensitive issue, which was harshly criticized by different politicians and journalists, was the payment of wages in tokens or credit slips. Being paid in coupons limited the workers' ability to save, invest, or simply spend the product of their work freely. It is understandable that in a monetary economy, people prefer to be paid in cash rather than in coupons. These coupons, however, could be sold, and this was a common practice. United Fruit's stores also sold goods to the banana workers at lower prices than the town's stores.[29] So if the workers got a better deal buying from the company's stores, why did they want to eliminate them?

There are different interpretations as to why the workers demanded the elimination of the voucher system. Urrutia suggests that the strikers made this request to get support from store owners.[30] Strikers needed food supplies and local stores wanted to eliminate competition from United Fruit. So local shopkeepers provided them with food in exchange for demanding the elimination of the voucher system. LeGrand highlights that local store owners turned into the strike's most enthusiastic supporters because they saw the *comisariatos* as unfair competition.[31] White quotes American consular reports in which the consul believes that discontinuing United Fruit's commissaries and eliminating credit slips were written into the *pliego* under pressure of the shopkeepers' lobby at USTM.[32] Fonnegra goes further in saying that at the beginning the workers opposed discontinuing commissaries, but after discussion they realized the need for the local shopkeepers' support.[33]

Authors from different ideological backgrounds all suggest that an elimination of the voucher system was not a good deal for the workers, despite the demand for its elimination. Fonnegra denounces United Fruit and describes the role of their stores in the local economy. Fonnegra found that the company had no other choice but to create the voucher system because after the War of the Thousand Days the nation's monetary economy fell into a crisis, forcing many small towns and haciendas to issue their own currency. The economy and individual currencies only improved after the Kemmerer mission.[34] Fonnegra writes,

> There was almost no trade in the country's interior. Both luxury goods and basic goods were imported in the Great White Fleet ships. Thus, the company stores stocked a large amount of goods allowing them to sell at a lower price. . . . From the workers' viewpoint the elimination of the company stores was prejudicial for them, because there they could get their basic goods at low prices. The union was aware of this. But it also knew that the strike could only survive with the local shopkeepers' support.[35]

In the late 1970s, *Voz Proletaria*, the official newspaper of the Colombian Communist Party, commissioned Carlos Arango to write a book to commemorate the fiftieth anniversary of the 1928 events. Arango interviewed several former workers of United Fruit who played a major role in the 1928 events. When asked about the company's stores, union leader Sixto Ospino said, "The goods sold at the comisariatos were not expensive."[36] When interviewing former workers of the banana zone, I sensed a general nostalgia for the times in which the company stores operated in the region. María Teresa Caneva, the widow of Rafael Caneva, an important Magdalena left-wing intellectual in the early twentieth century. A Socialist activist herself during the pre–World War II period, Caneva acknowledged,

> We could find everything we needed in the company's stores. From a needle to a refrigerator. . . . There they carried imported good quality furniture, food and clothes. Everything was much cheaper than in the other stores. Beforehand, the workers did not use silverware to eat and sleep on the floor. They dressed badly. . . . Thanks to the company's stores they were able to buy iron beds, silverware, and good imported clothes.[37]

Another former field worker remembered, "In those times we wore Arrow shirts to go working, while in Bogotá only the 'doctors' could afford to buy them. It was cheaper for us to drink whisky than to drink *aguardiente* [locally made liquor] in our parties."[38]

While LeGrand and Urrutia see the demand for eliminating credit slips and discontinuing commissaries as a strategic move by union leaders to widen support, Fonnegra and Arango saw a revolutionary angle behind it, saying that the workers also were heroically struggling to protect local industry against unfair competition from abroad generated by United Fruit stores.[39] Using a curious analysis, Fonnegra and Arango portray the shopkeepers as heroes of the working class because they wanted to eliminate the competition and be able to drive up their prices.

By highlighting that the company stores were cheaper than local stores I am not defending the use of the voucher system. Not being paid in cash represents an obstacle for the development of a market economy and limits workers' freedom to consume, save, or invest in the future. Even though these vouchers could be sold in the market for cash, this represented an extra operation that increased the society's general transaction costs, creating obstacles for economic growth. But that workers included the elimination of vouchers in their petitions reluctantly in order to have political support also tells us they found some advantages in the existence of these stores. It is understandable that they wanted to buy cheap goods rather than expensive goods. Additionally, it is worth mentioning that United Fruit was not the only institution paying with vouchers in the Colombian countryside in those times, and this was because of the particularities of the Colombian monetary system in those times.

By the early twentieth century, a monetary economy had not expanded throughout all of Colombia, and the countryside was still living outside of this system. There was general skepticism among the population on the value of paper currency after the disastrous monetary policy followed by the Conservative government in the late nineteenth century that ended in unprecedented inflation during the War of the Thousand Days. After the war, the Colombian government was reorganizing its financial system and was trying to expand the monetary economy around the country. So, before the 1930s, most employers in the countryside paid their workers in vouchers because there was not enough currency circulating in the economy.

United Fruit was not the only institution paying this way. It was a common practice in the Colombian countryside with large landholders ruling over inward-looking haciendas with not enough currency for their operations. According to Salomón Kalmanovitz, by 1917, there were 24 million pesos circulating in the Colombian economy, or 4.06 pesos per capita. By comparison, by the same year, the circulation in Argentina, the richest country in Latin America, was 46 pesos per capita and 16 pesos per capita in Chile.[40] Colombia's circulation increased to 7 pesos in 1922 and 19.2 pesos in 1928 after huge changes in the monetary policy and the creation of a financial sector.[41] The banana workers must have been aware of the expansion of the monetary economy and that payment in vouchers was no longer necessary, but they also wanted cheap goods. This was a moment of transition in Colombia's monetary economy, so it is understandable why, in the 1928 strike, some people defended the voucher system and some others did not.

The lack of a revolutionary tone in the workers' petitions has been discussed by the Russian Communist Arnold Lososky, who says the events in Magdalena show a lack of "revolutionary praxis," which is evident in the way USTM managed the process and in the *pliego de peticiones* itself.[42]

Even the Conservative Colombian government did not find any reason to classify the workers' petitions as subversive. United Fruit refused to talk to USTM representatives and discuss the *pliego*, so the union appealed to the national government. An envoy of the Ministry of Labor, Alberto Martínez, visited the banana zone, talked to USTM representatives and company manager Thomas Bradshaw, and requested United Fruit's management to discuss the workers' petitions on October 28. However, Bradshaw refused to talk to them.[43]

United Fruit argued that because USTM representatives were not formal workers of the company and claimed to represent people who were not formal workers of the company, there was no reason why Bradshaw should negotiate with them.[44] Given Bradshaw's response, USTM went again to Martínez and requested his intervention. Martínez informed United Fruit that the workers' petitions were legal, so Bradshaw had to listen to them. In response, USTM declared, on November 6, that if Bradshaw refused to negotiate again, they would call the workers to strike on November 10.

The partial government support by Martínez encouraged the workers to seek government endorsement of their petitions at a higher level. On November 11, Russo sent a telegram to the national congress in which he said USTM was trying to make United Fruit comply with the law "wisely written" by the national deputies.[45]

In spite of the ministry of labor's endorsement of the USTM petition, Bradshaw stubbornly refused to talk to the workers' representatives on November 10. USTM went on strike the next day.

Once the strike began, the relationship between the company and the workers worsened. The strikers organized themselves into special committees to keep the strike alive, such as food committees and watchmen committees, and they received support from local merchants. The strikers also had their own courier service (*el correo rojo*), with which they kept all workers informed of the leaders' decisions and printed newspapers and fliers. United Fruit tried to keep operations going by hiring strikebreakers. However, the strikers tried to sabotage their harvest by destroying bananas they had cut. The strikers also blocked transport in and out of the region by making women and children lie on the train tracks.[46]

The sabotage activities forced Bradshaw and the governor of Magdalena to ask the national government to intervene. Bradshaw's telegrams to President Miguel Abadía Méndez described the danger the strike could pose for Colombian national security. The governor feared that with thousands of workers on strike the region was in danger of falling into chaos.[47]

The possibility of violence led the national government to intervene. Abadía's government sent an army battalion and a negotiating commission, the latter by request of USTM. The battalion was led by General Carlos Cortés Vargas, who arrived on November 13 with troops from Antioquia. The troops were kept ignorant of the situation to avoid any sympathy with the strikers. The commission arrived on November 20 to mediate between the company and the strikers.[48]

There was no agreement among different levels of the Colombian government regarding the appropriate stance to take toward the strike. Catherine LeGrand and Judith White give excellent descriptions of the conflicts for power that rose between the local Conservative governor, the army, the local police, and the government commission.[49] For instance, Cortés arrested the inspector of the labor office for having declared the strike legal, accusing him of being a Communist. He was freed by the local courts. The minister of industries declared that the inspector's effort to let the strike take place on under the rule of law was the best way to fight against "Soviet Socialism" in Magdalena.[50] The struggle among those in charge of dealing with the conflict between United Fruit and its workers made the situation harder for both parties.

During the strike, the workers held hostage United Fruit's investments in the region to increase their bargaining power. They invaded several of United Fruit's installations to prevent the company from exporting fruit. The strikers organized themselves so effectively that the company found it impossible to export any fruit during the strike.

The first round of negotiations by the government commission resulted in some concessions by both United Fruit and the strikers and gave a glimmer of hope to both parties. United Fruit, together with some local planters, committed to housing improvement, construction of emergency hospitals, a weekly wage, and a slight wage increase. The strikers dropped their petitions for doubled wages on Sunday and the abolition of the commissaries. They also postponed their petitions for social security and indemnification for workplace accidents. The agreement, however, fell through at the last minute.[51]

The hopes of reaching an agreement faded when the strikers realized the most significant issue for them—recognition as United Fruit workers and a formalization of contracts—was not going to be addressed. The strikers wanted United Fruit to sign the agreement with them, but the company insisted on signing the labor agreement with the government commission. Signing an agreement with the workers would have meant an official recognition of the existence of a United Fruit labor force and its union; the workers wanted their negotiating organization, USTM, to be officially acknowledged by the company as their union. After United Fruit's refusal to sign the agreement with USTM, USTM delegates called for the continuation of the strike and refused to accept an agreement between the government commission and the company.[52]

The official recognition of USTM by United Fruit became the largest point of contention. The government commission began to lose patience and proposed an increase in wages in exchange for dropping the demand for USTM recognition. The workers, however, refused to renounce this crucial issue and lost the local governor's support. He approached Cortés and asked for greater vigilance over the region. The government commission, for its part, endorsed United Fruit's plan to hire strikebreakers to cut the fruit after a month of stalled operations.[53]

The breakdown of negotiations between USTM and United Fruit and the siding of the governor and the government commission with United Fruit began the countdown to the bloody outcome of December 5. The newly hired banana workers began to cut the fruit under the army's protection. The strikers did everything possible to stop the fruit from reaching the port. United Fruit manager Bradshaw talked of "gangs of Soviets scaring the peaceful workers in the plantations." On December 4, the first trainload of fruit arrived in the Santa Marta port escorted by the army. As a last resort, the strikers demanded to talk to the governor, who promised to see them in Ciénaga. The *correo rojo* spread the word and encouraged the people to gather in Ciénaga's main plaza to demonstrate and demand that United Fruit sign the final agreement with USTM. Hundreds of people gathered in the plaza waiting for the governor. Cortés dispatched his troops there. At 2:30 p.m., the demonstrators were told that the governor was on his way with Bradshaw to sign the agreement, and they began to celebrate in the plaza. Later that day, however, they were informed that neither Bradshaw nor the governor were coming. This discouraged the demonstrators, and some even attacked USTM's headquarters. In the ensuing confusion the troops surrounded the workers. General Cortés ordered the demonstrators to disperse, citing the state of siege law written by the national government for Magdalena that same afternoon, and he gave them until 11 p.m. to disperse. The workers refused and at midnight the troops opened fire on the demonstrators.[54]

## The 1928 Strike's Outcome

The army's violent response to the strike, known as *la masacre de las bananeras,* is the single event for which United Fruit is most famous among Colombians. In *One Hundred Years of Solitude,* García Márquez writes of three thousand casualties, but the range of casualties cited by other sources varies widely. In the book Cortés wrote to explain his actions, he admitted thirteen casualties.[55] Alberto Castrillón, in a document presented at the Colombian Congress, wrote of thousands of deaths.[56] Among historians, the numbers range from 60,[57] to 100,[58] 400,[59] 800,[60] 1,000,[61] 1,500,[62] and 2,000.[63] García Márquez himself has shown that he did not have any evidence of the thousands of victims he claimed, and he has admitted he inflated the number to make his novel more spectacular. He even said he was surprised to see how many people took his number seriously.

> There was talk of a massacre. An apocalyptic massacre. Nothing is sure, but there can't have been many deaths. . . . It was a problem for me . . . when I discovered it wasn't a spectacular slaughter. In a book where things are magnified, like *One Hundred Years of Solitude* . . . I needed to fill a whole railway with corpses. I couldn't stick to historical reality. I couldn't say they were three, or seven, or seventeen deaths. They wouldn't even fill a tiny wagon. So I decided on three thousand dead because that fitted the dimension of the book I was writing. The legend has now been adopted as history.[64]

Whatever the number of deaths, the army opened fire against peaceful demonstrators who could not defend themselves and were making legitimate demands that were in accordance with what the Colombian legislation stated. The debate over numbers, unfortunately, has made people forget the reason that led to the massacre in the first place—the workers' demand that they be recognized and made permanent employees of United Fruit. If this demand had been approved, the workers would have achieved a remarkable modernization of labor relations in Colombia. Even though they could have had a higher real wage when working with United Fruit, they were more concerned with having stable contracts with the company. This demand was revolutionary in itself, taking into account the prevailing labor relations and the way large corporations operated in the underdeveloped world. Had the strikers been successful, this would have forced the company to change the way it related with workers in other divisions. However, the strike did not have the revolutionary character many claim it had: workers were not trying to sow the seeds of a Communist revolution but wanted to participate in the benefits of the system created by United Fruit by being officially recognized as what they were—workers of the company.

## After the Massacre

Judith White argues that the massacre of Ciénaga "killed" labor unionism in Magdalena.[65] However, a study of the evolution of the labor movement in Magdalena in the 1930s shows a different picture. The institutional changes brought by the Liberal government that came into power in the 1930 elections allowed the Magdalena workers to get most of what they demanded in the 1928 strike. The Liberals stayed in power for over a decade, winning every elections between 1930 and 1942, which allowed the ruling party to make significant changes in Colombia's labor relations, especially during Alfonso López's administration.

### The End of USTM after the Ciénaga Massacre

The 1928 strike failed to give the United Fruit workers what they wanted most—stability and a formal contract with United Fruit. Shortly after the strike, the government destroyed USTM. Attempts to create an organization to replace it failed because the area remained under a state of martial law. Strikes were planned in July 1929 and February 1930 but were aborted because of police intervention. The Sociedad Unión was strengthened after the disappearance of USTM and remained the official representative of the workers.[66]

Despite the massacre in Ciénaga and the close links of the Liberal Party with Communist and Socialist organizations, the Magdalena workers did not see radical changes with the new Liberal government of Enrique Olaya. Although he made some labor reforms, Olaya supported United Fruit in the labor conflicts between the company and the workers during his administration.[67] Additionally, the Magdalena labor movement had been weakened after the strike and was going through a process of reorganization.

## Alfonso López Pumarejo and the Transformation of the Colombian Labor Movement

The workers' situation changed dramatically in 1934 after the triumph of Liberal Alfonso López Pumarejo. President Alfonso López crossed a threshold in Colombian history. This London-educated, upper-class, white gentleman and successful banker supported labor reforms that included the establishment of a labor code copied from the United States' New Deal, the legalization of unionism, and active government endorsement and support of the union movement. During López's administration, unions could count on government aid and police protection. López's strong support for unionism made him approachable from the radical Left and helped him receive the backing of the working class. No Colombian president besides López has invited a Communist union leader to give a speech from the presidential palace balcony nor seen Communist and Socialist parties' demonstrations with the people chanting ¡*Viva el presidente*!

The first banana strike after 1928 came in 1934, the opening year of the López administration. Even though the government sent the army to the region again, the affair did not end violently. The president personally intervened in the conflict and forced United Fruit to negotiate and sign a collective agreement with its workers—the Auli-Garcés Navas Pact.[68] By signing the pact the company agreed to recognize the people who worked for it as its own workers, accept the union as the workers' representative (a different union from Sociedad Unión), and commit itself to obey the new Liberal labor code that included paid Sundays and an eight-hour workday—in short, most of the workers' 1928 demands.

The outcome of the 1934 strike reveals several important elements that help better understand the 1928 strike. First, although López approached the Socialists and the Communists, he was not a Communist himself. But this was not an obstacle for him in getting for the workers in 1934 what they wanted in 1928. It did not generate strong opposition from the Conservative Party, the American legation, or United Fruit itself. Nobody accused López of being a Communist sympathizer for support of the banana workers. López was simply modernizing labor relations in the country, which was what the banana strikers of the 1920s also wanted.

Second, the outcome of the 1934 strike shows how the institutional environment in Colombia was changing. With the Liberals in power, United Fruit could not count on unconditional government repression of labor demands. Before López, the labor legislation was virtually ignored in the countryside, and he wanted to change this. The 1934 strike facilitated his prolabor program. Under the new legal framework created by López, the workers finally could formalize their relationship with United Fruit peacefully and become actual employees of the company.

Third, during López's administrations the workers did not request the elimination of vouchers again. Because the monetary economy dominated the entire country, vouchers were not necessary for the company to use. However, United Fruit kept the system but gave workers a choice of being paid in cash or in vouchers. Many workers accepted the vouchers and sold them to people who did not work in the banana industry. After 1928 the workers did not request the elimination of the voucher system despite the increase in their bargaining power under Liberal rule. This backs the theory that workers raised the vouchers as an issue in 1928 because they were looking for political allies among the shopkeepers. Once they no longer needed those allies, they dropped the issue because it did not directly concern them.

## Conclusion

The terrible events of December 1928 in Ciénaga have shaped the image of United Fruit and the banana workers in Colombia. On one hand, United Fruit is seen as the stubborn and exploitative agent of American imperialism in the region. On the other hand, the strikers are seen by many as representatives of the revolutionary struggle against capitalism.

Both images have been reinforced by the worldwide popularity of *One Hundred Years of Solitude*.

It is undeniable that government repression was disproportionately in favor of United Fruit so that United Fruit felt it had the power to ignore workers' demands. However, if we take into account the existence of a democratic system in Colombia in those times, we find that United Fruit paid a price for its attitude. When the Liberals came to power, especially during López's administration, it was clear the government was not un-conditionally going to protect the company's interests. The Liberals sided with the workers and endorsed their demands when the workers went on strike in 1934. United Fruit could do little to change or challenge this. The quiet and peaceful way United Fruit accepted the government deci-sion is clear evidence that the company had to adapt to the changing times.

The image of the 1928 strikers as pioneers of a Communist revolution needs to be revised. The most important issue for the workers, dating back to the early strikes of 1918 and 1924, was a lack of formal contracts with United Fruit. Thousands of people had been working for the com-pany through a system of intermediate contractors, and they wanted to become formal and full employees of United Fruit. In spite of the revolu-tionary rhetoric of some of their leaders, the workers never showed any interest in getting rid of United Fruit, destroying the banana export in-dustry, or becoming collective owners of the plantations. Had this been true, it would not have made strategic sense for them to negotiate with United Fruit. The workers wanted to join the company, so they organized themselves to negotiate with United Fruit. The company's stubbornness forced the workers to turn to the guidance of Communists and anarchists. But even with these elements present in their organization, they never dropped their most basic demand—to become full employees of United Fruit.

6

# Nobody's Triumph
## *Labor Unionism in Magdalena after World War II*

After the 1928 strike, the Magdalena banana labor unions grew stronger. Their power reached a peak after World War II when workers managed to win unprecedented benefits from United Fruit as well as win almost every conflict with the company. The labor unions became so powerful that United Fruit eventually opted to gradually divest their operations in Magdalena, transferring all the production activity—along with all the associated labor conflicts—to local producers. In this way, United Fruit freed itself from its increasingly demanding employees. When the company finally pulled out of Magdalena in the mid-1960s, workers found they could not recoup all of the benefits from local producers that United Fruit had once provided. In this chapter, I will examine the conditions that permitted the unions to become powerful and will show how they finally managed to "kill" their employer.

## *The World War II Pause: Transformation of the Colombian Labor Movement during United Fruit's Temporary Absence*

The outbreak of World War II interrupted banana exports from Magdalena and forced United Fruit to halt operations in Colombia during a critical moment for the national labor movement. The entire period of World War II witnessed a slowdown of the social and labor reforms initiated by López, a reorganization of the Conservative Party, and a growth of Conservative labor unions. When United Fruit returned to Colombia in 1946, it found a changed country with a much more powerful labor movement.

In the years preceding World War II, the Colombian left seemed unstoppable. In 1935, under the support of President López, a group of Liberals, together with a few Communists and a few anarchists, created the Confederación de Trabajadores de Colombia [CTC], a national labor federation that became one of the most important organizations in Colombian labor history. The rise of the CTC, along with López's complacency, caused a wave of strikes all over the country and growing opposition from the Conservative Party, the Catholic Church, and the moderate sector of the Liberal Party. The creation of the CTC came just one year after López openly supported banana workers in the strike against United Fruit and the arrest of United Fruit's manager. Allowing the creation of the CTC demonstrated that López not only wanted to make deep changes in the social system, but he also wanted to ensure these changes would continue after his administration.

During Colombia's presidential election in 1938, the Liberals, tired of López's leftist agenda, decided to nominate moderate Eduardo Santos as its official candidate.[1] Santos intended to cool López's social reforms and relations with the Communists. When Santos won the election, the CTC's membership was at its peak. Santos wanted to make it clear that the CTC could no longer operate under the assumption that the Liberal Party would protect and side with it during labor disputes. Although Santos did not revoke López's reforms, he did not make further transformations either. Santos did not mediate labor conflicts, a role López had developed, and Santos even declared some major strikes in 1940 illegal. This created divisions within the CTC, which always had been heavily dependent on Liberal Party support.

The Liberal Party nominated Alfonso López for a second time in the 1942 election. His nomination received enthusiastic endorsement by the Communist Party and labor unions. He won the 1942 elections easily, and as soon as López took power, a new wave of strikes swept the country. The strikers wanted the same government mediation that had existed in López's first administration. This, however, did not happen. López instead used force to repress several of the strikes but continued with his reforms on the labor code.

López faced more difficulties in his second administration than in his first. The Conservative Party organized a strong, aggressive opposition under the leadership of charismatic, ultra-right, anti-Semitic, and fanatic Catholic, Laureano Gómez. The Conservative Party had the open support of the Catholic Church, which encouraged its members to oppose López's reforms. At the same time, the Liberal Party began experiencing a rift as a growing number of Liberals felt uncomfortable with

López's close connections to labor unions and Communists. Last, López faced economic difficulties that caused discomfort for industries and landowners.

An important element of the Conservative strategy against López was to weaken the president's biggest support—the labor unions. In order to counterbalance the CTC's power, Laureano Gómez and the Church organized right-wing Catholic labor unions around the country. These unions were popular in the female-dominated industrial sector of Medellín, and the Church wanted to spread this model to the male-dominated sectors in the rest of Colombia.

The coordination and unity of the Conservative opposition contrasted with the growing internal divisions within the Liberal Party and the CTC. In 1944, López was involved in a series of scandals denounced by the Conservatives and lost his party's support, keeping only the Communists' open loyalty. Also in 1944, a sector of the military attempted to depose him with a military coup, but the group was forced to return him to power after the CTC and the Communist Party organized massive street demonstrations in major Colombian cities. Although back in power, the Liberals disliked that the president's main support came from Communists and labor unions.

After the coup attempt, López rewarded the unions' support by furthering social reforms. He established a nine-hour work day in the countryside, instituted accident indemnification, forbade payment with goods, and obliged employers to pay for overtime and work on Sundays, among other reforms. In short, López extended the achievements of the banana unions in the 1930s under his support to all agricultural workers.

López's return to power was not easy, however. Accusations of government mismanagement from the Conservatives continued until 1945, when the national congress requested that he resign. López left the presidential palace, and the Liberal Party was left with even more uncertainty. Colombia had polarized into two opposite forces that grew during López's second administration: the right-wing unions led by the Conservatives, and the Liberal movement of *caudillo* Jorge Eliecer Gaitán. Although Gaitán was popular among the working classes, his presence created more divisions during the critical moments of López's last months as president. The CTC continued to weaken due to the divisions among *Lopistas*, communists, and *Gaitanistas*. Its weakness became clear after the defeat of the Magdalena river steamship workers strike in 1945. This defeat killed the CTC.

The campaign for the 1946 presidential election divided the Liberals and the CTC even further. Gaitán decided to run as an independent Liberal, while the party nominated moderate Gabriel Turbay. With the Liberals divided, the Conservatives won the elections and Mariano Ospina became president. Once the Conservatives were in power, they took advantage of the CTC's crisis and established, in 1946, a new right-wing labor federation—the Unión de Trabajadores de Colombia [UTC]. The UTC witnessed a strong increase in membership shortly after its creation, while the CTC's membership fell. In 1946, the CTC had 66.1% of the unionized labor force, but, by 1965, the UTC had 41% and the CTC had only 34%.[2]

The evolution of the Magdalena labor movement mirrored what was happening in the rest of the country. Even though the first organizers and union leaders were committed Socialists such as Alberto Castrillón and Raúl Mahecha, the banana unions leaned more toward the Conservative UTC than to the Communist-Socialist CTC. This demonstrates the lack of a real revolutionary agenda among the banana workers. Even though the workers became much more powerful during the Liberal administrations than during the previous Conservative Hegemony, in the end, the UTC became more popular among banana workers. Moreover, the labor unions joined the Conservative federation even though the region as a whole remained Liberal.

So, by the time United Fruit returned to Magdalena in 1947, Colombia had experienced great turmoil in its labor relations. United Fruit had left Colombia under a government that strongly supported left-wing union organization and returned to find Conservatives in power and a newly created right-wing labor movement.

## Postwar Magdalena: UTC Dominance and Growing Union Power

When United Fruit returned to Magdalena in 1947, the biggest labor union operating in Magdalena was the Unión de Trabajadores del Magdalena (UTRAMAG), which was affiliated with the UTC. No union affiliated with the CTC operated in the banana zone in the postwar period. This did not mean, however, that there were no labor conflicts between the workers and the company in the postwar period.

United Fruit suffered its first postwar strike shortly after it returned to Magdalena. The strike began in April 1949 and lasted until July.[3] During the strike, the company had to reduce deliveries. In addition, the company's officials were unable to visit the facilities and provided their superiors a pessimistic outlook on the state of affairs they expected once the strike was over. The damage done by the workers was worse than company officials had imagined. Once the strike was over, the company was obliged to make large capital outlays to recover farmland, offices, and vehicles strikers had occupied and abandoned in states of disrepair. The manager reported that these problems would cause an unforeseeable increase in costs.[4]

The workers won an important benefit from the 1949 strike. In September, the company undertook large investments in equipment for hospital improvements, which provided free medical care to workers and their families.[5]

Former United Fruit workers still recall the 1950s as the "golden times" of the company's presence in the region. The company's healthcare system was considered excellent by the workers interviewed because it covered them and their families. But according to a few of those interviewed, many of workers abused the system:

[In the 1950s and 1960s] the company always gave to us whatever we asked for. Not only did we have free healthcare for our spouses and children, but also for our cousins, relatives in law, etc. In the end, people abused the system so much that they managed to get free healthcare for their lovers, and the children they had with their lovers.[6]

Additionally, John Strange, the company's manager during these years, had the reputation of being softer with employees and the union than his predecessor, Thomas Bradshaw, and others. In an interview for the journal *Economia Colombiana*, Strange proudly said, "Besides the business and in fact, as a decisive factor in the company's success, [the company] is proud to have and put into practice a socially fair and eminently humane policy." The same journal referred to him as the "affable Mr. Strange" and "the serene negotiator of disputes and differences."[7] LeGrand also writes that the company's last management was extremely lax with its workers.[8]

During the 1950s, United Fruit did not face many problems with its workers until 1958, when a new contract with the union established an increase in wages. The new labor agreement was backed by the labor policy of the military government of Gustavo Rojas Pinilla, who wanted to gain support from the working classes. Rojas wrote Decree 118 of June 21, 1957, which established salary increases.[9] The company reported this news along with a report of its first sales of land to the locals.[10]

### Increasing Labor Bargaining Power with Disappointing Results: Unionism and United Fruit's Divestiture in the 1960s

Rojas's brief dictatorship ended in 1958, beginning a new period in Colombian labor history. After a military coup against Rojas, civilians returned to power with Liberal President Carlos Lleras, the first Frente Nacional president. The CTC tried to rebuild itself but did not succeed due to the widening division between the Communists and Liberals. In 1964, after a radical wing of the CTC decided to separate and create a new labor federation, the Confederación Sindical de Trabajadores de Colombia [CSTC], the CTC and the UTC began to make amends. With the communist influences gone from the CTC and the UTC accepting the practice of strikes, Conservatives and Liberals were more alike than ever before and shared a common a fear of Communism.[11]

The changes experienced by the UTC-affiliated Magdalena banana labor unions mirrored the changes experienced by the Colombian labor movement in the rest of the country. Because strikes were not a sin for the UTC anymore, banana unions began to strike more often. Former field workers still remember that in those times, the company's unions went on strike for almost any reason and the company always ended up giving them what they asked for. One former worker said,

> People kept demanding and demanding from the company. And the company eventually gave us everything. We even managed to get milk for free. . . . The camp houses had everything: furniture, kitchenware, silverware, electric light, running water, sewage system. We had a free cleaning service. . . . We didn't have to pay any rent for living in those houses. On the contrary! They paid us to live there![12]

The union simply did not prepare for the possibility of not having the company for support in the future. One former worker said,

> In those times people never thought about whether the company would leave or not. We all wanted to get something from it. We went on strike

for everything, and everybody asked them for money for everything. It was *Mamita Yunai*! We never expected them to leave. It was like a bottomless keg![13]

However, these good times were being threatened. The sale of land proved to be an efficient way for the company to gradually rid itself of increasing obligations to the workers, who were grouped in the Sindicato de Trabajadores de la Compañía Frutera de Sevilla [STCFS].[14] When the company sold a piece of property, the people who worked on that farm changed employers. The workers could no longer belong to the STCFS and had to create their own union. Therefore, the more land the company sold, the smaller the number of STCFS members. Local farmers who bought the company's lands had to deal with a new, though smaller union.[15] Thus, even though the workers perceived an increase in their bargaining power, United Fruit had the tools to weaken the banana labor movement in the long run. The company had the flexibility, mobility, and power the labor unions did not have.

The possibility of having a weaker banana labor movement in Magdalena worried UTRAMAG, an umbrella of labor unions in Magdalena. UTRAMAG sent activists to the region to organize all the small unions of the different farms into a single banana industry union. This attempt failed, however, due to the internal divisions among the different union leaders. Additionally, according to Mario Rey, UTRAMAG president, workers affiliated with the STCFS were enjoying their good times and did not have much interest in joining forces with other unions. By this time, the United Fruit workers were privileged in their housing facilities, health insurance, and cheap goods. Rey said,

The unions were dull. They never thought what would happen in the long term. The company gave in to the workers' demands more and more [after World War II]. . . . [United Fruit] had a paternalistic attitude that spoiled the workers. The camps had everything and the workers never learned how to make a budget. They did not know how much it cost to pay for water, electricity, sewage, or cleaning. . . . The prices at the company's stores were risible. . . . When the company left, many workers ended up as owners of the camp's houses, but they didn't know how to maintain them well. They had never done that. . . . The union could have organized itself, buy the lands and exploit them as cooperatives. They could have created a housing project out of the camps' houses. But they never thought of the future. . . . Once the company left, the union was finished.[16]

The unions continued with this attitude in the early 1960s. United Fruit faced a new strike in February 1960 while it was going through the process of selling off lands.[17] The strike was resolved quickly, but the company rushed the sales and the transfer of assets tied to services and benefits for the workers. These included the hospital and the Sevilla clinic, which were transferred over to the Colombian Institute for Social Security (Instituto Colombiano de Seguro Social [ICSS]) for $58,004.[18]

The workers experienced a major loss when the company announced the elimination of the voucher payment system in 1961. The company's management had been reporting a loss in profits by subsidizing the vouchers in order for workers to obtain their basic goods at a low cost. The elimination of vouchers was part of United Fruit's plan to minimize their direct obligations to their employees. In May 1962, the company decided to completely eliminate the ration cards. This provoked a negative reaction from the union, which requested salary compensation for the loss of this subsidy.[19] The change reduced general costs but involved the company in a new conflict with the union. In June, the union requested double-time payment for Sundays and holidays, basically seeking total compensation for loss of the vouchers. The net result for the company was few immediate gains with its new policy. The benefits inevitably came from reduction of staff and sale of lands.[20] This conflict is proof of how the workers were not against the voucher system and reinforces the notion that their request for its elimination in 1928 was in order to have the shopkeepers as allies during the strike.

UTRAMAG's industry union was successful only until 1965, when United Fruit had divested itself of all its lands. The union was called the Sindicato de Trabajadores del Banano and grouped together all the small unions from different farms. Its aim was to reinforce the weakened banana labor union organizations after United Fruit's divestiture.[21] This, however, did not affect the company. By 1965, United Fruit did not have workers in Magdalena and was concentrated in Urabá, where, since the beginning, they had avoided labor problems by using only a subcontracting system.

When United Fruit ended its operations in Magdalena in 1966, the company still had to deal with its laid off and retired workers. The workers opposed a government plan to take over their pensions and unemployment benefits. The Colombian Congress considered a new law whereby companies would no longer pay unemployment benefits to their workers, but rather the government would create a special entity in charge of collecting money from the companies and distributing it to workers. According to a United Fruit report, the unions—representing the retired workers of the company—opposed the law because they did not trust the government to be efficient or timely with the payment of un-employment benefits. The workers preferred to leave this in the hands of private enterprise and trusted the company more than the government.[22] In short, even though United Fruit no longer operated in Magdalena, and even though its workers were no longer employed with United Fruit, the workers still preferred United Fruit to administer their benefits rather than the Colombian government. United Fruit, however, liked the pro-posal and wanted to transfer their obligations to the government.

## *United Fruit in Urabá: No Workers, No Strikes*

United Fruit learned its lesson from its Magdalena workers and decided to operate much differently in Urabá. There, they based their operations on a subcontracting system and acted as a service company marketing the fruit local growers produced. Not having fixed assets decreased United Fruit's risk of being a target of striking workers, and not having signifi-cant numbers of workers eliminated the hassles of dealing with labor unions.

The only employees the company had when it arrived in Urabá con-sisted of stevedores, who loaded its ships in port. The number of workers needed to load ships was far fewer than the number needed for the plan-tations. To avoid labor problems with the stevedores from the start, United Fruit organized and financed Urabá's first labor union—Sinde-bras.[23] This was a stevedores association that would provide United Fruit with laborers when they were needed. Sindebras was managed by people appointed by United Fruit[24] and had nothing to do with the plantations, limiting itself to interaction with dock workers. The collective contracts were signed by the union, which was responsible for loading the product and paying the workers. The company paid Sindebras a lump sum and the union was in charge of distribution. In this way, if there were any labor problems, the producers had to come to an agreement with the workers, not the company.[25]

The only attempt to create a labor union independent from Sindebras among United Fruit's workers in Urabá was short lived. In 1964, a group of workers, with cooperation from members of the Communist Party, created Sintrabanano. The presence of Communists in Sintrabanano caused the government to respond violently—several of its members were arrested and one was assassinated. The following year, when this small union tried to go on strike for the first time, the company fired all the workers in the union, reinforcing its role as a service company.[26]

During the failed attempt of Sintrabanano, labor unionism in Urabá was weak, in part due to the lack of support for labor unions among the workers. In the mid-1960s, the guerrillas of the EPL began to operate in the surrounding areas of the region after being pushed out from neighboring Córdoba by the army. The EPL found a new base of operation in the banana workers; they infiltrated the plantations by sending in secret agents to apply for jobs and spread word of revolution among the workers. A former member of the guerrillas who applied for a job in the plantations in the early 1960s confirmed EPL's sole goal of creating underground revolutionary groups and a strong union: "[The workers] didn't know anything about unionism. They didn't understand what we were talking about. And they weren't interested, either. They were so used to living without a salary, that anything they were paid sounded good to them. Our greatest obstacle was to change this mentality."[27]

Another former member of the infiltration group said, "In those times the workers had no idea what a union was, they did not know of labor legislation, and did not know their legal rights. . . . They had very little education. Many of them had less than three years of schooling."[28]

This viewpoint is shared by the pioneer entrepreneurs of the region: "In that period, the workers didn't consider unionism or anything like it. The guerrillas were the ones who came with those ideas. Before this, there had been good relationships and the workers really did want to work."[29]

In spite of the lack of interest in unionizing in the region, United Fruit did not change its operating system, a strategy that proved beneficial in the long run. The guerrillas' activities continued in the region through the late 1960s and 1970s with the presence of the EPL and the Colombian Revolutionary Armed Forces (FARC). The guerrillas provided armed support for the unions in their conflicts with local growers. Both the unions and the planters used violence as a mean to increase their bargaining power, which led the region to a chaotic and violent situation in the 1980s. Hundreds of workers, union members, and managers were killed in a conflict that not only included left-wing guerrillas but also right-wing paramilitary death squads.

United Fruit left Urabá in 1985 and returned to the area in 1989 when it saw a glimmer of hope for peace in Urabá in the reinsertion of the EPL guerrillas. The events that followed proved these to be false hopes. The war between the different armed groups waged for years and, by the mid-1990s, the right-wing paramilitary groups and the Colombian army had expelled the Communist guerrillas from the region. During the second half of the 1990s, the labor unions of Urabá sided with the government and local companies in their war against the Communist guerrillas, which also benefited local and foreign producers. This shift from the unions came after a systematic elimination of the labor unions' left-wing members and the defeat of the guerrillas by the Colombian army in the region.

Despite the revolutionary rhetoric of the unions and the guerrillas and the radicalism of both the Left and the Right during the conflict, United Fruit was never a target. The Left talked of local planters, the army, or the national government as the oppressors, but not the American multinational—the region's main investor. When interviewing former guerrilla members and union leaders, I found a similar attitude. They mentioned United Fruit (or its subsidiary, the Compañía Frutera de Sevilla) only when asked and did not give them much importance. Otherwise, they blamed the Urabá planters umbrella, the Asociación de Ganaderos y Cultivadores de Banano de Urabá [Augura], the drug mafia, and the government.

That the left-wing organizations of Urabá do not give much importance to United Fruit is worth noting. United Fruit traditionally has been considered the quintessential representative of American imperialism in Latin America. It financed the planters that the unions and the guerrillas fought against. It remained the main marketing company of Urabá's fruit. From Urabá's shores, the huge Chiquita ships can be seen anchored a few kilometers away. The roads of Urabá are littered with cardboard boxes with the Chiquita logo printed on them. The company's harbors have Chiquita billboards and are guarded by armed men wearing Chiquita uniforms. The local population wears Chiquita baseball caps and T-shirts. The company's presence in the region is clear to everyone. United Fruit never hid its activities in Urabá, but it did manage to keep a low political profile in the region during a heated political conflict. This demonstrates how successful United Fruit's strategy in Urabá was at keeping its distance from any kind of labor conflict by not having a significant labor force working directly for the company.

## Conclusion

Labor unionism in Magdalena after World War II was different from that in the 1920s. The influence of the left decreased significantly as the Magdalena unions affiliated themselves with the Conservative UTC. Banana unions became more powerful than ever before. During the postwar years of operation of United Fruit in Magdalena, labor unions got almost all of what they demanded from the multinational corporation. This may have benefited workers in the short run, but proved fatal in the long run. Given the impossibility of withdrawing what it had already promised its workers, the company found the best option to avoid new labor obligations was to divest from the region and decrease its direct participation in production. In this way, United Fruit gradually disconnected itself from the workers and the obligations associated with them by transferring ownership of the plantations to local growers.

The company operated solely as a marketing company when it moved to Urabá in the mid-1960s. Despite the lack of interest in unionizing in Urabá, the company kept a small number of workers, relying on local planters to provide fruit. This strategy was successful. When Urabá witnessed major labor problems in the 1960s and 1970s, United Fruit had nothing to do with them. The company managed to continue its marketing operations while local planters dealt with the conflicts.

The story of banana labor unionism in the postwar period shows that workers were always in a difficult situation to gain concessions from United Fruit. When they reached their highest level of bargaining power, the company showed it was even more powerful by transforming itself so it did not have to deal with the workers anymore. The company was more flexible and mobile than the workers. Despite their triumphs, the workers were still a weak agent in negotiating with the foreign capital.

# 7

# The United Fruit Company's Relationship with Local Planters in Colombia

United Fruit relied heavily on local planters for its banana export business even before its divestiture. However, the relationship between United Fruit and local planters in Magdalena and Urabá has not been studied by scholars, who have mainly focused on labor conflicts. Judith White interviewed some planters and described the elite's view of the 1928 strike. Catherine LeGrand went further by analyzing how the local elite benefited from the presence of United Fruit and what kind of conflicts existed between the planters and the company. Neither studied what happened to the Magdalena local planters after the 1928 strike or after United Fruit left the region. Similarly, there is no historical study of the relationship between the Urabá planters and United Fruit.

The historiography of United Fruit in Colombia has neglected or minimized the importance of the local elite. This chapter is a first attempt to create a history of the Colombian banana export's entrepreneurial class. The rise of this class was directly linked to United Fruit's investments in the region. However, long-term development and survival of the elite was not absolutely dependent on United Fruit. The Colombian exporters had agency and initiative to develop their own international business when working for United Fruit was not to their benefit. But in the long run, local businesses faced problems due to government economic policy, climatic hazards, and political turmoil. I have based my conclusions on the evolution of contractual relationship between United Fruit and local planters. In this chapter, I will study the kinds of contracts the elite had with the multinational, how these contracts affected the planters, how they evolved, and how they were enforced.[1]

## *Waking Up the Dormant Caribbean Elite: United Fruit and the Magdalena Planters, 1899–1930*

When United Fruit's founder, Minor Keith, arrived in Magdalena in the early 1890s to buy land, he found a region ruled by the impoverished aristocracy of the city of Santa Marta. The aristocracy descended from early Spanish conquerors and French colonizers who arrived in the early years of Spanish rule. This was an upper class that the traditional elite of Cartagena and the recently enriched Barranquilla merchant class disdained.[2]

When Keith merged his interests with Andrew Preston's and Lorenzo Dow Baker's to create the United Fruit Company, Keith's lands in Magdalena became part of the new vertically integrated company (see chapter 3). Besides some locally owned lands, Keith acquired 12,500 acres from the Colombian Land Company in the Riofrío area that eventually became part of United Fruit production network.[3]

By the time United Fruit began its operations in Magdalena, the region already had a railway system. The Magdalena Department gave a railway concession to two local entrepreneurs, Julian De Mier and Roberto Joy, in 1881. This concession was transferred to a British company in 1886 and was incorporated as the Santa Marta Railway Company. The concession was transferred to United Fruit in the first years of the 1900s. United Fruit expanded the railway to facilitate the transportation of its fruit from farms in the banana region, including the farms of its local providers.[4] Therefore, the lands and railways existing in the region made possible the vertically integrated operation of United Fruit in Colombia. The company eventually operated its own plantations, but it also bought a significant percentage of the fruit it shipped to the United States from local planters.[5]

### The First Unsuccessful Attempts to Develop the Banana Export Business by Locals: Why They Failed

Colombian entrepreneurs made several attempts to export bananas themselves before the arrival of United Fruit. One local entrepreneur, José Manuel González, produced the first commercial bananas in the region in 1887 and attempted the first export in 1889. This initiative failed, however, because of the lack of fast, refrigerated ships; the fruit rotted by the time it arrived in New York.[6] Other local entrepreneurs made similar attempts and met with similar results. In the early 1890s, two English immigrants, Mansel Carr (of the Santa Marta Railway Company) and Laurence Bradbury, made the first regular banana shipments in partnership with a New Orleans firm, J. Sanders.[7] Afterward, the Colombian Land Company partnered with Carr and Bradbury and became one of their suppliers. After the creation of the United Fruit Company in 1899, United Fruit acquired Keith's Colombian Land Company, continuing the deals already struck with locals.

The early efforts made by local growers to sell bananas in the international market were not successful because they lacked the capital needed to develop an international marketing system. The locals did not have a large fleet or a distribution network in the consumer markets. During the nineteenth century, local entrepreneurs never managed to create a regular and continuous banana export business because of these problems. Before 1899, 114 local banana exports had been created, but of these, only twenty-two survived, and out of twenty-two, only four were of decent size.[8] The presence of a multinational enterprise, which operated its own transportation system and marketing networks, was essential to prosper in the export business. In fact, the real beginning of banana exporting in Magdalena came after United Fruit began its operations in the area in 1899 (see figure 1.1 in the introduction).

## The Decision between Subcontracting and Producing

United Fruit did not begin as a direct producer of bananas in all of its divisions. Victor Bulmer-Thomas shows the first shipments from Central America were made under a subcontracting system the company gradually abandoned because of coordination problems with local planters and lack of incentives for locals to invest in the unhealthy lowlands.[9] The locals built their own plantations but did not have the expertise to coordinate their marketing operations as fast or with as much quality as United Fruit. In the end, United Fruit controlled most of the production it exported from Central America.

In Colombia, United Fruit combined a vertically integrated system with a subcontracting system with local growers. The high degree of local participation in the export market was particular to Colombia compared to Central American countries. Local planters in Colombia produced between 20 and 30% of the fruit exported by United Fruit in 1910, yet, by 1920, locals produced 50% and, by 1930, they produced around 80%.[10] In Central America, United Fruit controlled almost all production, keeping its own, nonlocal levels of participation as high as 90% until the 1960s.[11]

### Subcontracting in Magdalena: United Fruit's Monopsony Power in the Region

The reason United Fruit could subcontract production in Colombia successfully was because it wrote purchase contracts with local providers to assure their monopsonic advantage. The contracts left the locals little choice but to continue working with United Fruit once the contract period was over. The contracts also strongly discouraged the creation of local export companies. Under this system, local providers had to sell all their fruit to United Fruit, but United Fruit was not obliged to buy any. Additionally, the contracts protected United Fruit from any unpredicted event, leaving all risk in the hands of the locals.

From 1900 to 1942, the contracts established that the fruit belonged to United Fruit as soon as it was cut from the tree. If, however, the fruit happened to have any defect according to United Fruit's quality control officials, the property of the bananas reverted to the planter. Moreover, even if the company's officials approved the fruit and shipped it, but the bananas were later rejected by U.S. health authorities, the fruit again reverted to the Magdalena planter, who did not receive payment. The contracts also specified that the local planters could not sell any of their fruit to another company, including the fruit United Fruit rejected. If local planters sold their land, they were obliged to include a clause in the land sale contract in which the buyer was committed to continue the purchase contract with United Fruit under the seller's original conditions. In the case of the Colombian or U.S. government taxing the banana trade, locals were to bear any extra cost these taxes created for United Fruit.

Although the contracts gave detailed descriptions of the characteristics of acceptable fruit for export, the company's officials reserved the right to reject any fruit regardless of its quality. United Fruit also reserved the right to cancel any purchase contract with any local planter without indemnification in case of political conflicts or for any other reason the company considered reasonable.[12]

All contracts, especially onerous ones like these, created incentives to cheat. Thus, United Fruit created enforcement mechanisms. The main mechanisms used by the company were

1. Timing the writing of the contracts to avoid having large numbers of planters "free" at the same time. In this way the planters could not join forces to develop their own export business.
2. Enforcing the contracts through third parties. If a local tried to export fruit that (according to contract) could be sold only to United Fruit, the contract was enforced by the U.S. customs office and British courts. The fruit could be confiscated both in the United States and in Great Britain.
3. Subjecting local planters' loans to long-term contracts. United Fruit gave loans to local planters under the condition that they commit all their production to United Fruit. The company had the advantage of being the only major financial institution in the region.

Cheating, therefore, carried stiff penalties: loss of credit and financial ruin.

### Tying Planters by Timing Their Contracts

United Fruit was aware local planters would be tempted to stop working for United Fruit and create their own marketing firm. In order to tie local producers to United Fruit, the company timed the contracts with its local providers so it was impossible for them to join forces and develop their own export business.

The strategy of contract timing was carried out as follows: the company made sure the contract with every producer expired on a date when there were not many other producers with an expired contract. In this way, there was never a large number of local producers without a contract with United Fruit. Because of the nature of bananas—a perishable good—no producer could afford to wait until other planters' contracts expired. The keys to making the system work were three features of the banana business: trees keep producing regardless if the fruit can be sold, so planters could not shut down production; bananas are highly perishable and can not be stored; and the shipping and marketing of bananas have large economies of scale, so unless planters could coordinate their actions, they could not profitably end their relationship with United Fruit. Thus, every time producers' contracts were due, they had no other choice than to sign again with United Fruit.[13]

United Fruit against Independent Mavericks:
Using Foreign Courts to Enforce Contracts

Although United Fruit's contracts stipulated that all the disputes between the company and local growers should be settled in the Santa Marta courts, the company enforced its contracts using foreign courts. This happened, for instance, when local producers tried to break the company's monopsony by attempting to sell their bananas to other foreign companies.

The first such attempt came in 1920, when United Fruit tried to increase its planters' obligations and decrease the fruit price. The company's new local management introduced the clause of local responsibility for national or foreign taxes and the obligation to transfer contracts when selling property. It also sought to decrease the price paid for bananas established by the company. A group of local producers who decided not to accept the new conditions were under the leadership of Juan B. Calderón, a banana entrepreneur, president of the Ciénaga municipal council, and a fierce long-time opponent of United Fruit's power in the region. The producers made a deal with Alejandro Angel y Compañía (a local firm) and the Atlantic Fruit Company (a U.S. firm) and exported their first shipment in September 1920. The attempt to get rid of United Fruit's dominance failed. As soon as the first shipment arrived in New York, the local customs officials seized the cargo because United Fruit representatives claimed a violation of its contracts.[14]

A second attempt to create an independent exporting company came in 1930. After organizing some planters into the Cooperativa Bananera Colombiana, Calderón entered into a contract with the Robert Brinnings Company of Liverpool. Although the British firm did not pay the prices they promised, the cooperative made its first shipments to England through Robert Brinnings in June and July of 1930 using Leyland Line, a transportation company. Once the cooperative's third shipment was ready, United Fruit protested that Leyland was transporting illegal fruit to England. Leyland refused to discuss the matter with United Fruit and passed the problem to Calderón because Leyland considered any problem Calderón's fault. However, United Fruit then refused to negotiate with Calderón. Calderón proposed that United Fruit name an agent to check which fruit in the port was United Fruit's and which was not. The company refused the suggestion and proposed, instead, that future shipments be monitored by the Colombian government. United Fruit sent its proposal, including a detailed description of what the government should do to monitor the shipments, to the Colombian government, but the proposal was rejected by the government as impractical.[15]

In the end, the Colombian government forced United Fruit to settle the case in British courts. In Britain, the case was decided in favor of United Fruit, and the judge imposed embargoes on the fruit imported by Robert Brinnings Company. After the court decision, the latter decided to stop importing bananas from Colombia.[16] This ended another local effort to break the contract system with United Fruit.

United Fruit also succeeded impeding local development of business with other companies. United Fruit did so by acquiring competing companies. In 1929, the Cooperativa de Productores Colombianos de Banano, led by Calderón and Julio Charris (another local politician and entrepreneur), made business deals with United Fruit's main competitor, the Cuyamel Fruit Company.[17] Unfortunately for Charris and Calderón, Cuyamel then was going out of business. United Fruit and Cuyamel had been in price and marketing wars prior to 1928, in which United Fruit did everything possible to eliminate Cuyamel, a small but aggressive rival. In November 1929, United Fruit decided to stop the war that was damaging both sides and proposed to Cuyamel's manager, Samuel Zemurray, to sell his company to United Fruit. Zemurray sold it for 300,000 shares of United Fruit (worth $31,500,000) and was named president of United Fruit shortly after.[18] In this way, all businesses signed by Cuyamel before 1929 were transferred to United Fruit, killing the cooperative's hopes.

United Fruit also used its monopsonic power simply to persuade those who wanted to export on their own to do otherwise. Botero and Guzmán suggest that the sabotage of local entrepreneur Ricardo Echeverría, who tried to export independently from Magdalena, was orchestrated by United Fruit. In 1908, Echeverría made a deal with the J. B. Camors company in New Orleans, but he failed to ship his first load on time because he encountered a series of accidents on the train, including damaged machines, sick machinists, destroyed bridges, and other problems. By the time the load arrived in New Orleans, most of his fruit had rotted. Additionally, United Fruit offered to buy Echeverría's providers' fruit at $0.30 a bunch, when the current price in the region was $0.15 a bunch.[19]

## United Fruit as the Region's Main Banker: Loans Subject to Long-Term Purchase Contracts

One of the main problems the local entrepreneurs of Magdalena had in developing their businesses in the early twentieth century was a lack of financial institutions to finance their operations. No formal banks existed in the cities of Santa Marta or Ciénaga; the closest ones were located in Barranquilla (30 miles) or Cartagena (60 miles). The banks in these two cities, however, did not help Magdalena's entrepreneurs because the banks tended to give loans only to a close circle of the *Barranquillero* or *Cartagenero* elite.[20] Indeed, Colombia, as a whole, did not have a decent banking system in the first two decades of the twentieth century. Even when the banking system grew in the 1930s, the situation in secondary cities such as Santa Marta or Ciénaga did not change much. In fact, when the central government, following the advice of the Kemmerer mission, established rules regarding the minimum capitalization of banks in the 1930s, it left small places such as Ciénaga or Santa Marta with no possibility of creating their own banks.[21]

When United Fruit arrived in Magdalena it was the only legitimate financial institution in the region. The company gave loans to the planters who provided it with fruit. Typically, these loans were given to planters under the condition that they sold their bananas exclusively to United Fruit. For many planters, this was the only way they could get enough capital to enter banana production. Even the critical study of Kepner and Soothill admits that "the company devoted many millions of dollars at low and reasonable rates of interest to help those who otherwise would not have been able to use their lands for banana cultivation."[22]

Many of United Fruit's loans were guaranteed by the borrowers' banana growing land. The loans were known as *pactos de retroventa*. If loans were not paid after a certain amount of time, borrowers were obliged to sell their land to United Fruit at the price stated in the *pacto*. The company got a number of lands under this system.

Although the loans provided by United Fruit generated a credit system where one did not exist before, some planters did not like that United Fruit was a monopoly. In 1924, the municipal council of Ciénaga demanded that the national government establish an agricultural bank in the city to compete with United Fruit.[23] The response was delayed, and the proposal was taken seriously only after a series of natural disasters in

1927 that left dozens of farms destroyed and nearly bankrupted planters. The governor of Magdalena, Conservative Juan Cormane, allied with Ciénaga leader Juan B. Calderón, lobbied the national government to get help to create a regional bank. Calderón organized a group of planters in the Sociedad de Productores de Santa Marta y Ciénaga, which worked with Cormane to convince the government to open a branch of the Banco Agrícola Hipotecario in Magdalena. This made Cormane popular among the small producers of Ciénaga but unpopular among his fellow Conservatives, the Santa Marta elite.[24]

The long-awaited branch of the Banco Agrícola Hipotecario was a disappointment. The bank's loan requirements were even harder to fulfill than those demanded by United Fruit, and its interest rates were higher.[25] There were simply no incentives to shift to the new financial institution with United Fruit providing below market interest rates. Additionally, the contracts tied many of the planters to United Fruit anyway, and many of them were satisfied with the company's credit service. The stability of doing business with United Fruit, the convenience of having its technical assistance, and the punctuality of its payments were strong incentives for many risk-averse planters.[26] This led some of them to use the profits and loans from the company in unproductive activities including years of residence in Brussels, London, Paris, or the United States.[27]

The use of borrowed money to finance exuberant lifestyles could be seen in Magdalena from the early 1900s. As early as 1919, the company's vice-president openly criticized the profligate lifestyle of Santa Marta planters after hearing them complain about the prices the company paid. The official said United Fruit had suffered losses of $600,000 on loans to the "so-called gentlemen planters who blew the money living high in Colombia or at the Waldorf Hotel in New York."[28]

The former planters in the cities of Santa Marta and Ciénaga still long for the times of easy money when United Fruit operated in Magdalena. A former entrepreneur said,

> Getting a loan from United Fruit in those times was much easier than nowadays. A lot of people did not do anything. They did not even have to go and pick up their checks. The company sent a messenger who brought the check to your place. . . . Sometimes we got loans to go to travel in Europe for a year. . . . United Fruit gave us the tickets for free. . . . [Under those conditions] why would you invest your profits?[29]

The entrepreneur's feelings show that not all planters were as opposed to the company's credit system as Calderón. This created a self-enforcing mechanism in the contracting system. Those unwilling to develop their own business could get wealthy sticking with United Fruit. Unfortunately, available data does not permit an accurate calculation of the percentage of planters who supported Calderón and those satisfied with the system in place.

There is still evidence of the prosperous past in the banana zone. Though now damaged, facades of the 1920s and 1930s French-style mansions, since converted into liquor stores, restaurants, or even brothels can be seen in downtown Ciénaga. People still talk of the elegant parties with European musicians and unlimited amounts of champagne and whisky held at the mansions. Many did not care for the farms administered by United Fruit but rather dedicated their time to the development of arts and literature or travel abroad, while others partied in Santa Marta. Some old *Cienagueros* still proudly hang their Belgian or French fading diplomas on the walls of their living rooms in which the refined European furniture has not been refinished in decades.[30]

## The Magdalena Banana Zone in Crisis: World War II and the Withdrawal of United Fruit

In the late 1930s and early 1940s, the region of Magdalena suffered a deep crisis. An epidemic of the Sigatoka disease affected the plantations and created an emergency in which the national government intervened. In 1941, the Colombian government signed a contract with United Fruit in which the latter committed to fight Sigatoka with government support. The outbreak of World War II, however, interrupted the implementation of the contract as well as all of United Fruit's operations.[31] As a result, the region fell into crisis and both workers and planters were forced to look for other work.

Once the war ended and Caribbean trade was reestablished, locals found themselves in a new contractual relation with the company. The clause establishing that all contracts could be cancelled in the event of foreign war had been used. So for the first time during the twentieth century, a considerable number of locals were free from their contracts with United Fruit. They now could coordinate their actions and capture scale economies. They were in a position to challenge United Fruit directly.

Creative Destruction: The Emergence
of a Local Export Marketing Industry after World War II

Before World War II, not all of the planters had blown their money in
leisure pursuits. Some used their gains to get a sophisticated education in
business at American or European universities.[32] This is remarkable considering the first generation that witnessed the arrival of United Fruit had
lived in a stagnant and poor society.[33] This second generation, who got
their business educations abroad, played an important role in the 1940s
after the export crisis of World War II.

When World War II ended, the port of Santa Marta witnessed the arrival of small independent traders looking for bananas for the American
market. The traders were not connected to any of the multinational corporations and conducted their businesses in informal ways. They did not
sign contracts with local providers but simply came to the port, bought
the fruit from whomever had fruit to sell, and paid either in cash or in
goods such as whiskey, American clothes, or imported foods.[34]

The presence of small buyers and the prospects of high prices in the
United States and Europe during postwar reconstruction stimulated local
planters to grow bananas again. In the beginning, the planters that sold
their fruit were those more harshly affected by World War II. While some
planters had the capital to cultivate different crops, others were in too
precarious a situation to finance the transformation. The latter group
kept some ruined banana plantations and eventually became the first
providers of fruit in the postwar period.[35]

Independent traders had a huge impact on the region. In 1943, the region did not export a single banana; in 1944, it exported 422,561
bunches; and, in 1945, it exported 1,381,874 bunches.[36] Figure 1.2 in the
introduction to the book shows the impressive recovery of the region's
exports. The enthusiasm around the revival of banana exports led to the
creation of a multitude of small companies that worked without any mutual coordination.

The informal and chaotic situation of the early postwar years changed
when local producer Anacreonte González created an association of
Magdalena producers. His main goal was to open markets in countries
where there was no competition from United Fruit. The country Gonzalez had in mind was Sweden, so he began negotiations with import companies in that country. After signing purchase contracts with Swedish
firms, Gonzalez's conglomerate—appropriately called La Sueca ("The

Swedish")—began to export in 1946. Other producers followed suit and established other export conglomerates such as the Compañía Comercial del Magdalena, the Consorcio Bananero, the Compañía Agrícola del Magdalena, and the Compañía Bananera de Ciénaga. In 1947, the Compañía Agrícola del Magdalena made its first shipment to Miami using the West Indies Fruit Company's ships.[37]

By 1947, the Magdalena region had witnessed the emergence of what in the prewar period seemed impossible—local, independent banana export companies successfully doing businesses out of United Fruit's reach. Locals were not tied to the purchase contracts they had signed before and were associated in different conglomerates. While González's conglomerate was operating in the Swedish market, others had signed contracts in the U.S. market or were negotiating with German import firms. González's conglomerate also gave its banana growers services similar to those United Fruit had provided, such as assistance in plague control. In the first years after United Fruit's return, La Sueca used plague control methods that were even more updated than those used by United Fruit, such as spraying pesticides from helicopters—an innovation at that time.

The great potential of the postwar West German market stimulated locals to create a conglomerate that grouped together all the existing independent export companies. The conglomerate was established in 1952 as the Federación de Productores de Banano del Magdalena and fell under the leadership of the legendary José "Pepe" Vives (from Compañía Comercial del Magdalena) and Francisco Dávila (from Consorcio Bananero). The Federación was created with an initial capital of Col.$16,000 in which each shareholder had a number of shares proportional to their number of banana-producing hectares.[38] Shortly after it was created, the Federación signed a contract with the German import firms Lutten and Sons and Afrikanische and began its first exports to Germany.

The founders of the Federación did not want to deal with maverick producers that wanted to develop their own business. The way they avoided this was by organizing the Federación as a growers' cooperative. In this way, all members would want the conglomerate to grow, and it decreased the incentives to cheat.

When analyzing the profiles of the men who created the conglomerate, it is worth highlighting that they did not conform to the stereotype of the absentee enclave landowner. This is remarkable given the high levels of poverty and low industrialization of the region compared to the rest of the country. José Vives is a good example of a self-made entrepreneur in the Colombian Caribbean. Without being a member of any of the traditional, powerful families in the region and without formal education, Vives made a fortune with his own commercial, financial, and manufacturing businesses. They included agro-industrial enterprises and the Banco Bananero del Magdalena—a financial institution that financed independent exporters. Francisco Dávila, Vives's partner, gave the company a touch of sophistication. His traditional upper-class family had increased its wealth through its connections with the banana business since the arrival of United Fruit. He completed his undergraduate studies in France and earned an MBA at Stanford University and was advised by another Stanford alumnus, local politician Rafael Pérez.

The Federación began having problems after its first year, when, after a financial scandal, Dávila and the Consorcio Bananero separated from the Federación. After this event, there were two conglomerates: the Federación, which grouped together a large number of small producers (led by Vives), and the Consorcio, which grouped together a small number of big producers (led by Dávila). Both operated parallel to United Fruit.

## The Return of United Fruit: Working in a Different Scenario

When United Fruit returned after World War II, it had no choice than to adapt to a situation in which new marketing companies were operating in Magdalena. According to the former executives of the Federación and the Consorcio, United Fruit did not make a big fuss about the newcomers and simply looked for new partners in their business. Instead of trying to destroy the local export firms, it coexisted with them. As a result, by 1955, the local companies were exporting 58% of the fruit while United Fruit was exporting the other 42%.[39] This contrasts strongly with the situation in Central America during that same time, when United Fruit exported 90% of the fruit.[40]

When United Fruit restarted its operations, it gave loans to people who wanted to begin in the business and to some of its former suppliers. The loans were subject to similar conditions to those before World War II, and United Fruit also supplied technical assistance to its borrowers. Even though the contracts were similar to those of the prewar period, some local planters preferred to work for United Fruit than for the local export companies because they reasoned a big multinational with decades of experience and a solid international network was more reliable than the smaller and newer experimental Colombian firms.[41]

How could United Fruit keep writing the same kind of contracts at a time when it did not have the monopsony it once had? The local firms did not behave differently than United Fruit with regard to contracts. There are little to no differences between the kinds of contracts.[42] In fact, when asked how the local marketing corporations wrote their first purchase contracts, one of the founders said, "We just took United Fruit contracts and copied them."[43]

Previous studies show the terms of United Fruit's contracts as clear evidence of imperialistic exploitation of local resources.[44] These studies, however, do not cover the times locals were also exporters. When taking the postwar period and the national corporations into account, it is clear that local capitalists followed the same logic and behaved similarly to the multinational. It is hard to argue the problem was the presence of a multinational corporation in the region.

## United Fruit's Divestiture and the Difficulties of Getting Back Its Loans

In the 1950s, United Fruit gradually sold its assets in Magdalena and relied more and more on its local providers. The company began to divest and to increase the importance of loans to planters as a percentage of its total assets (see introduction). Also during the 1950s, United Fruit began research in the region of Urabá to study the feasibility of developing a banana export industry there (see figure 7.1).

In the early 1960s, United Fruit began its operations in Urabá and made its first exports in 1964. In 1960, the company shut down all of its production activities in Magdalena (only continuing to purchase from its associate producers) and increased its investments in Urabá. United Fruit signed a contract with José Vives, who became their representative and main provider in Magdalena. By 1964, Vives's independent producers exported 47% of the fruit in Magdalena.[45] United Fruit concentrated its efforts in Urabá where it used a subcontracting system with entrepreneurs of the city of Medellín. In 1965, when its operations in Urabá had taken off, the company decided to interrupt its operations in Magdalena without notice and gave its providers to Vives's Federación. From that moment on, all Magdalena exports were the responsibility of local planters, while exports from Urabá, operating through Colombian companies, increased dramatically in an impressively short period of time.

After the company decided to leave Magdalena, it faced the problem

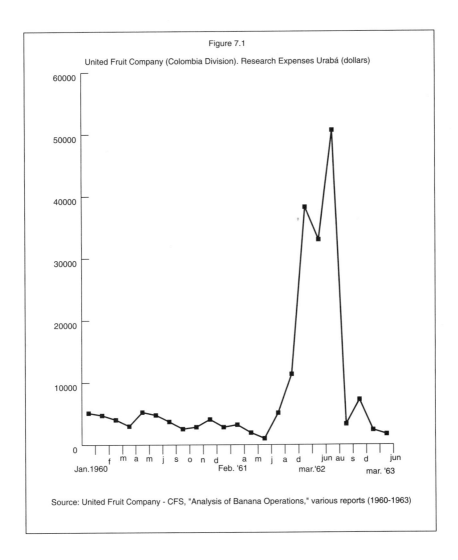

Figure 7.1

United Fruit Company (Colombia Division). Research Expenses Urabá (dollars)

Source: United Fruit Company - CFS, "Analysis of Banana Operations," various reports (1960-1963)

of getting back the money it had lent out. Some locals behaved similarly to how they did in 1943 when the company was forced to leave the region during World War II. According to Posada-Carbó, the American consul in Barranquilla reported that local planters owed two million dollars to United Fruit, which the company had little hope of recovering by the early 1940s.[46] When the company wanted to withdraw from Magdalena in the 1960s, it faced a similar problem. It transferred its purchase contracts to Vives, but he did not buy the debts. Vives must have considered them completely unrecoverable.

Not only did the company have problems getting back its loans, but also some of the buyers were not paying for assets that had already been sold. In addition, it appeared difficult to sell other assets at an acceptable price. United Fruit's manager reported to headquarters in Boston the difficulties of leaving Magdalena with a profit.[47]

Negotiations with local planters proved unsuccessful, and United Fruit looked to the Colombian government to help them withdraw from Magdalena without losing money. In the middle of 1967, the company began negotiations with the National Institute for Agrarian Reform (Instituto Colombiano para la Reforma Agraria, or Incora) in the hope that Incora would cover the debts and buy the remaining United Fruit assets.[48] The negotiations with Incora took longer than expected and continued until April 1968, when a preliminary agreement was signed. By this date, United Fruit had not been able to get rid of its last properties because a buyer who was about to take most of the properties cancelled the deal at the last minute, leaving United Fruit with one alternative—to do business with Incora.[49] Under the terms of the agreement, Incora would cover the balances of loans to planters, current accounts, and sale of the farms.[50] The manager of United Fruit reported this was a much better outcome than what he had originally hoped.[51]

Had United Fruit not been able to count on Incora's action, it would have lost the money owed by local planters. Incora took responsibility, but, according to some former planters interviewed, many of the loans were never paid to Incora. Once United Fruit had established itself in Urabá, the company created mechanisms to prevent this kind of problem in the future.

## Magdalena without United Fruit: The Local Planters in Charge of Exports

The fate of Magdalena after the withdrawal of United Fruit has been neglected by historians. Some argue that after the company left, the region fell into an economic crisis and decay from which it never recovered.[52] But in this claim, authors argue the assumptions from dependency theory regarding economic enclaves are true for the case of United Fruit in Magdalena. The dependency theory claims that an economic enclave becomes dependent on the multinational company that created it. Once the company leaves, the enclave has no means to survive on its own.[53]

I believe this is not the case for Magdalena. After World War II, locals accumulated experience and capital that permitted them to create their own export business independent of United Fruit. When United Fruit left, the local companies organized themselves to keep business alive and succeeded in their first years of operation. In the long run, however, the businesses failed and the region fell into decay. Nevertheless, the reasons for this failure are not the ones argued by *dependentistas*. Local companies could not succeed because of the way the government intervened in the banana economy and because of adverse climatic hazards that prohibited them from updating their technology and competing in international markets.

### The Shift from Gros Michel to Valery: Consequences of the Biggest Technology Change in the Banana Industry

Two important events determined the development of the banana business in Magdalena after the mid-1950s. The first was the decision by United Fruit to move to the region of Urabá while changing its operations from being both a production and marketing company to being solely a marketing company. The second was the biggest technological change in the industry since the beginning of the century. In 1956, Standard Fruit began conducting experiments to develop a new kind of banana resistant to the Panama disease that had destroyed many of its and United Fruit's plantations in Central America.[54]

Before the 1950s, all bananas traded worldwide were from the Gros Michel variety, which had a thick skin that made them easy to export in bunches, but they were not resistant to the Panama disease. The fruit developed by Standard—known as Valery—was smaller, less tasty, and had a weaker skin, but it was resistant to the Panama disease and produced more fruit per acre. Resistance to the Panama disease was enough incentive for Standard to begin a gradual change from the Gros Michel variety to Valery. Despite the advantages of changing from Gros Michel to Valery, neither United Fruit nor the independent companies in Colombia made the shift. This decision proved fatal for the independent companies.

Shifting from Gros Michel to Valery required changes. Valery's fragility made it necessary to alter the entire transportation process for the bananas from the time of harvest at the plantation to when they reach consumers. Standard Fruit developed a system of "air wires" on the plantations to avoid damaging the bunches. The air-wire system consisted of rolls of poles connected with a moving wire that travelled from the plantation to where the fruit was selected. When the workers cut a bunch off a tree, they suspended it on a hook on the moving wire, and the bananas were transported from the plantation to the packing plant. The bananas sustained minimal damage because they were not hit by anything. The stems of bananas were then cut from the bunch, and the bananas were packed in cardboard boxes.

Although the fruit was resistant to the Panama disease, it was not resistant to insect attacks. Standard solved this problem by covering the bananas with plastic bags while they were growing. These extensive new processes required changes in the plantations. Standard had to install the air-wire system, cardboard and plastic manufacturing plants, and packing plants.

In the first years Standard Fruit experimented with Valery, United Fruit did not make any changes on its plantations. United Fruit continued growing Gros Michel, even on the new lands of Urabá, while Standard Fruit decided to change all its plantations to the new variety.

By the early 1960s, Valery's advantages were unquestionable. While only 400 bulbs of Gros Michel could be planted per hectare, 1,300 bulbs of Valery could be planted in the same area, and while Gros Michel's planting-harvesting cycle was thirteen to fifteen months, Valery's was eleven to twelve months. In addition, Valery was resistant to the Panama disease.[55] Moreover, Valery's resistance to strong winds was much better than Gros Michel's. Some farms experienced total destruction due to blown down Gros Michel trees, while Valery's losses were only around 20%.[56] The change from Gros Michel to Valery brought about the biggest technological changes of the century in the banana sector. United Fruit, belatedly, began to make the shift to Valery in 1962.

While the two biggest multinationals were shifting from Gros Michel to Valery, Colombian independent exporters continued producing Gros Michel in Magdalena. In the early years, many of them were comfortable with the way the business was growing. By 1964, they provided 11% of the fruit consumed in Germany, ranking second only to United Fruit.[57] Although the American market began to demand bananas be packed in boxes (whether Gros Michel or Valery), the Magdalena exporters continued transporting them in bunches. After some visits by the Consorcio's management to the banana plantations in Ecuador, however, they proposed to their board of directors to change the way they were packing and transporting the fruit. The board did not have much time to discuss the proposal because a few days later, German firms demanded the fruit be delivered in cardboard boxes the way the multinational corporations were in Central America.[58]

### The Independents' Struggle for a Change in Banana Variety in Magdalena and the Governmental Obstacles

After the German demand, the Magdalena companies were under heavy pressure to update their processes. The Consorcio managed to transform their banana producing process after a marathon campaign that included trips to Ecuadoran and Central American plantations where they learned how to change from shipping bunches to boxes from beginning to end. In May 1965, the Consorcio made its first experimental shipment of 500 boxes. By June, they were exporting an average of one thousand boxes a week, and by January 1966, they were exporting five thousand boxes a week.[59]

The difficulty of bringing a large number of members into agreement caused the Federación to delay its transformation for some months more. The demands of its European customers, however, forced it to build a packing plant in just forty-five days.[60]

The transformation from bunches to boxes was not enough to catch up. Valery's productivity proved higher. Not only could the producers of Valery bananas plant more bulbs per hectare and lessen the time from planting to harvest, but the yield of fruit per hectare was higher. In the late 1940s and early 1950s, Colombian plantations had a higher yield per hectare than those in Central America (see table in chapter 3). However, when the multinationals made the change from Gros Michel to Valery in Central America, Colombian productivity fell far below that of Central America, reaching its lowest point in 1964. The effect on prices from the Central American and Ecuadoran competition worked against the Magdalena producers, pushing prices down from 1950 to 1976. To make things worse, in 1965 and 1966, Magdalena suffered from weather problems and a chain of diseases affecting the banana trees.

The fall in international banana price, competitors' higher productivity, and weather problems made the situation difficult for the Magdalena producers. Their only solution was to make a fast change from Gros Michel to Valery. The producers asked the central government in Bogotá for help. The 1960s were times of strong protectionism from the Frente Nacional, and the government required an import permit for almost anything introduced from abroad. Therefore, in order to change from Gros Michel to Valery, local producers needed to import the seeds and justify the importation to the central government to get an import license.

In 1966, the Magdalena growers began an aggressive lobbying effort in Bogotá to get an import license and other benefits. The exporters used Magdalena Conservative congressman and banana entrepreneur Rafael Pérez Dávila to lobby Liberal President Carlos Lleras Restrepo to get special import licenses, tax incentives, and emergency credit. The government created a commission within the Ministry of Agriculture to study the feasibility of cultivating Valery in Magdalena. The results of the commission's study would grant the government the justification to give the import license.

The commission concluded the soil and climate of Magdalena were unsuitable for the cultivation of Valery and recommended the government not grant the import license.[61] Moreover, the minister of agriculture Enrique Blair argued that if the expansion of Valery continued worldwide, the Gros Michel bananas would become a scarce good and, therefore, its price would increase.[62] Many growers in Magdalena were skeptical of Blair's optimism, and the minister's opinion was contradicted by a report published in September 1966 by a consultant hired by Incora to study the crisis of the Magdalena banana export sector. The report concluded that to "rescue" Magdalena from a deeper crisis it was imperative to replace the Gros Michel trees with Valery trees.[63] Also hindering the Magdalena growers, United Fruit officials publicly stated that it made no sense to cultivate Valery in Magalena and suggested the planters change crops.[64] This left the independent planters on their own.

### The Struggle to Keep the Magdalena Banana Export Industry Alive

The planters could afford neither to apply for the import license a second time nor to keep cultivating Gros Michel, so they decided to import Valery seeds illegally. Hundreds of thousands of seeds arrived as contraband to the port of Santa Marta and were distributed among the members of the Consorcio.[65] Unfortunately, the weather did not cooperate. In 1966, just after beginning the transformation process on some farms, a hurricane destroyed 45% of the crops.[66]

The hurricane brought major destruction to the area, and the planters took this emergency as their last opportunity to ask for government support. The Federación was so badly affected by the storm that it shut down operations completely.[67] The planters proposed a recovery plan beneficial to both parties. The plan was to reduce the banana region from 20,000 hectares down to 5,000 and to plant only the Valery variety, because according to them, 5,000 hectares of Valery had the same productivity as 15,000 hectares of Gros Michel.[68] They also asked for tax incentives for the region because of the tragedy generated by the hurricane.[69] The government, however, would not give the import license or any kind of subsidized credit to the region because of the unfeasibility of Valery in the region.[70] This led the Consorcio to decrease the purchase price it paid to its providers by 40%.[71]

The export promotion plan developed by the national government in 1967 looked like the last hope for the Magdalena exporters. President Carlos Lleras developed a policy called Plan Vallejo, which consisted of tax incentives for exports and imports. Both Magdalena and Urabá planters sought to be included in the plan, but while the government accepted Urabá planters it denied the Magdalena planters' applications. These decisions could have been made because Urabá belongs to the more wealthy and politically powerful region of Antioquia, and Magdalena does not have much presence in Colombian politics and has weaker lobbying power.[72]

The national government tried to save the Magdalena growers by creating a state-funded export company called the Cooperativa Agrícola del Magdalena. This company, however, was liquidated just months after it was created due to corruption scandals.[73] The Consorcio harshly criticized the government's initiative because it considered the solution worse than the damage they were trying to heal.[74]

Winds continued to blow against the Magdalena growers. In 1967, the region was hit by a hurricane that destroyed 4,000 hectares, reducing the banana area from 15,000 to 11,000 hectares.[75] Consorcio was the only export conglomerate left in the region after the failure of the Federación and the Cooperativa, so it decided to sign purchase contracts with the former providers of those two companies despite the fact that the international market was saturated. The survival of the region was at stake, so the planters continued with their pleas to the government requesting flexibility in its protectionist policies.

The next year, in 1968, the government finally allowed the importation of Valery seeds and gave some credit subsidies, allowing the Consorcio breathing room. With government obstacles out of the way, the Consorcio bought a new farm to develop the production of Valery as the multinationals had in Central America. The conglomerate incurred all the costs of adapting the lands of new farms, constructing roads and canals, and providing plague control with the last resources it had. However, just after the first farm was ready, all the production and infrastructure was destroyed by another hurricane.[76] The Consorcio had exhausted its finances on all these activities and plague control programs through the Ministry of Agriculture that were never carried out.[77] Calculations made by Jaime Bonet prove the precarious situation of Magdalena in the 1960s. During this decade, the exports of Urabá grew at a rate of 22% per year, while Magdalena had a growth rate of -7.4% a year.[78]

In 1970, the shareholders of the Consorcio began to lose their patience with the failures of their company and demanded its liquidation. Some even wrote letters to the government describing how the Consorcio had evaded taxes during its existence.[79] The Superintendencia de Sociedades Anónimas—the institution in charge of declaring bankruptcy for companies in Colombia—declared the Consorcio bankrupt with losses equivalent to 180% of its capital. In the court declarations the last manager of Consorcio had to give, he highlighted the patriotic role of the Magdalena entrepreneurs in providing employment and capital to an impoverished region. He pointed out what they had accomplished in spite of the many obstacles they faced. This, however, did not change the Consorcio's fate, and the last banana export company of Magdalena was liquidated.

The bankruptcy of the local conglomerates meant the decay of the region's banana exports, but it did not mean the end of them. In 1972, the Compañía Exportadora de Banano organized a new cooperative with sixty-five members. In 1973, United Brands[80] began to market the fruit of some local growers even though its main interest remained in Urabá. By this year the government had officially acknowledged the need to support and finance the conversion from Gros Michel to Valery in Magdalena and gave financial aid to the Compañía Exportadora de Banano. The Ministry of Agriculture expressed that in order for Magdalena to be successful it was imperative to have multinational corporations participating in the region.[81] In 1976, United Brands formally organized the Compañía Bananera del Magdalena to grow fruit, using the same subcontracting system it had in Urabá. The same year, the Standard Fruit Company began to produce through the Sociedad Baltime de Colombia S.A., which sold its fruit to the Compañía Exportadora de Banano.[82] In the 1980s, United Brands was again interested in Magdalena (owing to political problems in Urabá) and quietly returned to the region it had abandoned more than two decades before.

## Urabá: Doing Business with Urban Industrialists

United Fruit never had its own production farms in Urabá but used a sub-contracting system. United Fruit worked as a financial institution, technical assistant, and marketing company. The company provided loans locals needed to "adapt" the jungle of Urabá to banana production under the commitment of selling the fruit to the company when it was ready. To avoid the problem of planters defaulting on loans (as in Magdalena), United Fruit decided to use financial intermediaries. In Magdalena, the company had given loans directly to planters, but in Urabá, United Fruit used a Colombian bank that depended on capital transferred from the First National Bank of Boston. Additionally, the company arranged banana purchase contracts with its debtors to enforce the commitment.

In spite of how efficient this mechanism might sound, United Fruit could not impede its growers from becoming independent exporters. In Urabá, a conflict with the company led some of the locals to create their own export companies. This was possible in part because of the support they received from the government.

### A New Place and a New Elite: The Differences between the Local Entrepreneurs of Magdalena and Urabá

Doing business in Urabá, United Fruit had to deal with a different kind of elite than in Magdalena. Urabá was colonized late. Most of its inhabitants arrived in the 1960s, and there were no prior urban centers from earlier generations such as in Santa Marta or Ciénaga in Magdalena. Whereas the families involved in the banana business in Magdalena had been there since before the arrival of United Fruit, the Urabá entrepreneurs came from the city of Medellín and were as much outsiders as United Fruit itself. The elite of Magdalena had a tradition of working the agrarian sector, and some had built their wealth in other agricultural activities before the banana boom. In contrast, the people of Urabá had made their careers as urban professionals in the Medellín industrial sector and did not belong to landowning families.[83]

When interviewing there is a strong difference in the attitudes of the entrepreneurs of Urabá and Magdalena toward the banana business. For the people of Magdalena, the banana sector defined their society and culture. It is part of their history and tradition. On the other hand, the entrepreneurs of Urabá see it as just one more business in which they have been involved and it can change if it is not successful. In fact, all the companies working in Urabá, including United Fruit, had their central offices in Medellín, rather than in Urabá, and most of the people involved in banana exports kept working in Medellín to take care of the other businesses they had in industrial and financial sectors.[84]

There were also differences between the departments of Antioquia (where Urabá is located) and Magdalena. First, Antioquia's main economic engine has been coffee and the industrial sector and has always been considered to have the highest standard of living in the country. In fact, among Colombians, the stereotype about the people of Antioquia is that they are white pioneers and natural born entrepreneurs. Antioquia's economic power has also been reflected in its political power. Adolfo Meisel shows that during the twentieth century, Antioquia has been overrepresented in national government decisions and national resource allocation, while the Caribbean region (where Magdalena is located) has been underrepresented.[85] These differences are relevant in understanding the development of each banana export region.

In short, in Urabá, United Fruit was operating in the most prosperous and powerful Colombian region and was dealing with an entrepreneurial class who had developed sophisticated businesses themselves before going into the banana business; in Magdalena it was nearly the opposite.

### Creating the Urabá Planter Society: United Fruit's Financial Support to Its Providers

United Fruit financed its Urabá providers by using a different system than in Magdalena. The company financed its providers' first 100,000 hectares through the Corporación Financiera Colombiana de Desarrollo Industrial.[86] The financing worked in the following way: the First National Bank of Boston transferred United Fruit funds to the Corporación in Colombia, and when planters wanted credit to create a plantation, they applied for the loan from the Corporación. The Corporación loaned $693 per hectare with an interest rate of 9% to be paid in full after the first six years of operation.[87] To be eligible, the planter had to buy the land and turn it into a plantation before applying for the loan. The Corporación required United Fruit experts to evaluate the plantations for banana production feasibility along with a purchase contract between the planter and the company. The Corporación did not loan to anyone without a contract with United Fruit. The company committed itself to giving technical assistance, fertilizers, and controls against the Sigatoka disease to the planters, the cost of which was later discounted from the bananas' purchase price. Given United Fruit only purchased fruit from those evaluated by their experts and approved by the Corporación, it did not make sense for the locals to ask for the loans elsewhere because then they would not have a buyer for the fruit.[88]

In its first two years, the Corporación gave loans for the amount of $6 million, while United Fruit invested $4.5 million in the development of the first 20,000 acres used by locals. Thus, the company did not have to invest in infrastructure development, and it was up to the farmers to clear and plant their lands using the Corporación's five-year loans.[89] Hence, the company did not vertically integrate its operations, and, in terms of infrastructure, it only owned the transportation canals.

Under these dynamics, it can be seen that the Corporación played the role of an intermediary that decreased the problems United Fruit had in Magdalena. First, it saved the company the problem of giving loans to unreliable borrowers because the Corporación studied them first. Second, it minimized opportunistic attitudes from the planters by having a local agent oversee the loans in case the company left. United Fruit did not have this system in Magdalena and the locals there took advantage of it.

### The Schism of Urabá: The Locals Rebel

By the mid-1960s the local planters and United Fruit had strong ties that kept them working together. The local planters had incurred debts in order to develop their purchasing relationship with United Fruit. On the other hand, the multinational wisely had created an intermediary for the loans it had given to the locals and had many other subsidiaries in Central America that provided it with fruit for the international market. This scenario was extremely favorable for United Fruit, which wanted to get extra gains when the purchase contracts with the locals were up and they had to sign new contracts.

In 1968, changing conditions on United Fruit's Central American plantations made the company rethink its relationship with its Urabá growers. In this year, United Fruit had recovered its losses from the Panama disease in Central America. When its purchase contracts had to be renewed, in the new contracts, United Fruit offered to buy the fruit for only half the price it had previously paid.[90]

Decreasing the purchase price of bananas did not prove easy for United Fruit. Although it was the only marketing company in the area, the locals united and rejected United Fruit's proposal. The company insisted on lowering the purchase price, so, in 1968, the locals decided to continue the business themselves without United Fruit. As a result, they established their own marketing company, the Unión de Bananeros de Urabá [Uniban], as well as an association called Asociación de Ganaderos y Productores de Banano de Urabá [Augura]. While Uniban dealt with the production and export business, Augura was a lobbying organization for the banana growers' interests in the national government and at the international level. The founders of Augura and Uniban counted on open governmental support from the beginning. The Ministry of Agriculture was aware that the sector needed to update technologically and to finish the transformation from Gros Michel to Valery in order to succeed. With this goal in mind, in 1972 the Ministry of Agriculture suggested the national government provide the Urabá growers with Col.$140,000,000.[91]

After the local growers left United Fruit, United Fruit no longer provided any of the services it previously made available to the planters. The locals could not count on transportation facilities or the technical assistance they had received before. To overcome this problem, the locals contacted American fruit import firms and, in 1969, established their own marketing company in Miami, Florida, under the name of Turbana. Their efforts were so successful that by 1970, Uniban was exporting 45% of Urabá's total shipments.[92]

Once they decided to continue the business on their own, the locals faced a conflict with United Fruit on the use of the area's canals. Urabá's topography does not permit the existence of a port, so United Fruit adapted the existing rivers, turning them into canals that connected the plantations to the sea. The fruit was loaded onto boats in the canal and taken to the sea, where workers loaded the fruit onto larger ships. The company claimed ownership of the canals it had built and did not permit Uniban to use them. Augura protested to Colombian President Carlos Lleras, who personally intervened in the conflict and forced United Fruit to permit Uniban the use of the canals. The government also helped the Urabá planters by including their fruit in the export promotion project,

Plan Vallejo. Augura's lobby was much more powerful than Magdalena's (during this time, the Magdalena growers were requesting support from the government to keep the banana export sector alive and unsuccessfully applied to be included in Plan Vallejo).[93]

Government help did not stop there. In the early 1970s, the central government gave subsidized loans to Uniban so the company could continue with its vertical integration process. In 1971, the government agency Instituto de Fomento Industrial (Institute for Industrial Development [IFI]) gave Uniban a loan to build its own maritime transportation equipment, and, in 1973, the Colombian president (Conservative Misael Pastrana) inaugurated the company's shipyard.[94] In 1979, the Urabá growers also managed to get a 7% subsidy on exports from the national government.[95]

Urabá had all the infrastructure needed for the development of Valery even in the times it was exporting Gros Michel. This included the air wire, cardboard factories, packing plants, and plastic manufacturers. The factories, which were built by Colombian firms from Medellín, dramatically changed the region's landscape in a short time. A formal calculation of the linkages between the banana industry and other sectors is still necessary. However, the existence of an industrial complex of several factories— built, owned, and managed by locals—covering kilometers of territory bordering the jungle suggests that the agricultural export industry does not necessarily reinforce underdevelopment, as some studies have suggested.[96]

In the 1980s, United Brands interrupted their diversification process and concentrated its efforts on its traditional Central American operations. In 1982, it sold all of its operations to its associate producers in Urabá and signed a new contract in which the locals sold the fruit free on board [FOB] (the supplier pays the shipping and insurance costs of the fruit) and took care of all other aspects of the business. United Brands's providers decided to create their own company, called Proban, creating a situation in which there were two competing local export companies. From 1982 to 1989, the Colombian corporations controlled 100% of the banana marketing of Urabá fruit.[97]

The growth and maturation of the Colombian marketing companies paralleled the development of one of the worst political conflicts in the country (and particularly in Urabá). The conflict among the left-wing guerrillas of FARC, the EPL, the right-wing paramilitary, the drug mafia, and the government made it nearly impossible for the Medellín entrepreneurs to run their farms efficiently. Urabá fell into a spiral of violence in which farm managers were kidnapped or murdered by the guerrillas, union leaders were attacked by the paramilitary, and workers were killed by every side. The banana companies blamed the violence and the numerous strikes and destruction of the banana plantations for their poor performance in the 1980s.[98] The situation reached such a critical point, that by the mid-1980s, Uniban began buying lands in the more peaceful banana zone of Magdalena.

The war in Urabá was the main cause of the recovery of Magdalena in the 1980s and 1990s. Bonet's calculations show that from 1960 to 1969, Urabá exports grew at a rate of 22% a year, while those of Magdalena decreased 7.4% a year. In comparison, from 1980 to 1989, Urabá's exports grew at 0.1% a year, while Magdalena's grew at 7.5% a year. During the 1990s, Magdalena again grew at a faster rate than Urabá—2.3% growth versus 1.7%.[99] This was a result of higher investments of the Urabá planters in Magdalena. These planters not only invested in the more peaceful Magdalena territory but also invested in Ecuador, Honduras, and Costa Rica.

In 1989, United Brands (now Chiquita) returned to Colombia to increase banana production in anticipation of an expansion of the Eastern European market after the fall of the Soviet Union.[100] Colombian firms also increased investments to expand their production. Unfortunately, the Eastern European market did not increase as much as these companies forecasted and their initiative proved to be a disaster (see chapter 3). The huge oversupply of bananas caused prices to drop. The 1990s were a difficult decade for the locals who looked for a way to recover after the disappointment of the international market.[101]

Chiquita returned to Colombia in 1989 with different operating principles than when it left six years prior. First, the company restarted its operations by buying new land, something it had not done since it operated in Magdalena before the 1960s. Second, Chiquita related differently with the local planters. Banadex, the subsidiary Chiquita created for its operations in Colombia after 1989, was accepted as a member of Augura in 1991, and its representative had a seat on Augura's board.[102]

Chiquita's return to Colombia was aggressive. In 1989, Chiquita controlled 8.5% of the national exports, and, by 1994, it had increased its participation to 11%.[103] The purchase of land in one of the most dangerous places in the world was not consistent with the company's policies in the 1960s. However, it was consistent with the company's new management strategy and goals under Carl Lindner. Lindner anticipated a huge increase in sales to Eastern Europe in the 1990s, so potential profits were worth the risk of buying lands in Urabá. This belief was shared by the local growers, who also felt optimistic about the political future of the region after the EPL signed a peace treaty with the Colombian government in 1991, a move toward ending the fighting in the country. The banana growers had blamed the war for the decrease in production from 2,160 boxes per hectare in 1988 to 1,780 boxes per hectare in 1989.[104]

Anticipating Eastern European demand, the multinationals and locals invested heavily in increasing the acreage of land used for banana production in both Urabá and Magdalena by 20.88% between 1991 and 1993. This was a mistake for both the locals and the multinationals. The demand did not increase as expected, and they all suffered heavy losses. To make things worse, the hope created from the peace treaty between the EPL and the government did not hold, and the region remained extremely violent.

## Conclusion

There are three clearly different stages in the development of the local banana export entrepreneurs in Magdalena. The first stage is the period before World War II when United Fruit controlled the exports, leaving locals with no choice but to work for United Fruit. The second period fell between World War II and 1965, when locals managed to create their own export companies. The third stage was the period after 1965, when the local companies were in charge of all the exports after United Fruit's withdrawal.

The first period has certain characteristics that fit into the classical enclave model of a local absentee landowner elite that benefited from the rents of United Fruit and spent those gains unproductively. Some planters tried to break the company's overwhelming power but were not successful. The way the company wrote their contracts and its enforcement systems made it extremely difficult for locals to develop their own banana export business. The lack of capital in the region made it even more difficult for them to start their own business.

In the second period, characteristics of Magdalena made this region a different place from Central America. In postwar Magdalena, locals managed to break the absolute control of United Fruit in marketing and created their own export companies. This particularity of Magdalena was because locals took advantage of the break in the company's activities in the region during World War II and restarted exports independent from the multinational.

In the third period, after United Fruit departed for Urabá, locals faced incredible difficulties to keep the Magdalena banana export business alive. Weather was uncooperative, and the region suffered several damaging hurricanes. More important, the national government was not supportive. The protectionist government of the Frente Nacional did not permit the planters to import the goods they needed to survive. Additionally, Magdalena's lobbying groups proved powerless in Bogotá. Thus, the region did not benefit from the government's export promotion policies. These circumstances hindered the planters from updating their plantations and competing with the multinationals. The industry collapsed in the late 1970s.

The role of the local elite in Urabá is different from that in Magdalena. First, the company never produced the fruit directly but relied on local providers. Second, the planters that signed contracts with United Fruit came from the Medellín industrial sector and were linked to the powerful Antioqueño lobby in Bogotá. Third, Urabá was a frontier region in which all participants (multinational, local planters, and workers) were newcomers.

The history of the relationship between the Urabá planters and United Fruit can be divided in two periods. Between 1963 and 1968, United Fruit controlled all the exports and planters in Urabá. Between 1968 and the 1980s, a significant group of locals decided to abandon their contracts with United Fruit and create their own export company.

In the first period, United Fruit created a mechanism to finance its providers in such a way to avoid default. This was done by using a local financial institution as an intermediary instead of giving loans directly to the planters. The company had learned from its experience in Magdalena, where many locals never paid back their loans. In this period, business developed smoothly without relevant conflicts between the company and its providers.

The second period began when United Fruit tried to decrease its banana purchase price in 1968. Locals did not accept the new price and refused to sign the contract under the new terms. Because the company insisted on paying a lower price, the locals created their own export company, Uniban. Uniban had a moderate success in its first years of operation, but later faced problems in the international markets due to European protectionism.

The relationship between United Fruit and the local planters in Colombia shows a history of an entrepreneurial class that would not have developed a banana export business without the presence of the multinational. However, once local planters learned from the company how to do this business, they tried to create independent export companies. In the long run, however, the local planters never managed to compete at the international level, and the market remained under the control of the big American multinationals.

# 8

# Conclusion

In the early twentieth century, the United Fruit Company developed a production and distribution network of bananas from Colombia and Central America to the United States. The company vertically integrated during the first half of the century and began a divestiture process after World War II. United Fruit began its Colombian operations in the region of Magdalena in the early 1900s and exported bananas from its own plantations and local providers until World War II, which interrupted its operations. By the time United Fruit returned in 1947, Colombian-owned export companies had launched their own operations. In the early 1950s, the company went through an aggressive divestiture process leaving most of the production in hands of local planters. In the early 1960s, the company decided to move from Magdalena to Urabá. It did not produce directly in Urabá but relied on local planters. The company operated in Urabá until the early 1980s, when it withdrew temporarily and returned in 1989 to continue its operations.

This book is the first general business and political history of the United Fruit Company in Colombia.[1] The few studies that have analyzed the company's operations in Colombia have only focused on the labor conflicts with its workers in the 1920s. Because the company kept operating in Colombia for the rest of the century, it is clear we can not draw conclusions of the political economy of United Fruit's operations based solely on what happened in the 1920s. Some of the accepted views of United Fruit in Colombia have to be rethought when we study the hundred years of operations of this company in Colombia and when its strategy as a business enterprise is analyzed.

United Fruit incorporated the Colombian banana producing regions into the global economy. Thus, an analysis of the multinational's activities in Colombia or any country, must be understood in a global context.

Multinational corporations are a product of international economic integration, so its actions in a specific country can not be studied without taking into account its operations in other producing areas, its relationship with the host governments in other countries, its relationship with its home government, the development of the consumer market, the perception and the opinion of institutional investors, and the relationship between the company's owners (the stockholders) and the company's management. These factors, combined with the evolution of the Colombian political system and socioeconomic development, created a complex dynamic that directly affected the decisions of the company's managers in Colombia.

The people working on the banana plantations and the planters providing fruit for the company became part of an emerging global village by being an integral part of United Fruit's business, so the fate of these local actors can not be isolated from the national and international political and economic factors influencing United Fruit's decisions. The company affected the Colombian workers, planters, and government by making decisions based on interests of the consumer market, its home government, its shareholders, and its institutional investors. The local actors, however, did not passively accept the decisions made by the multinational. They had their own agenda and reacted to the company's decisions when these conflicted with their own interests. The banana workers wanted a higher standard of living, the planters wanted higher profits from their business, and the government wanted higher rents and political stability—goals that more often created conflicts between these groups but sometimes created alliances.

At times, the company's actions and interests concurred with some of the local groups' agenda. But when they did not, the locals reacted. They designed long-term strategies to get what they wanted. Sometimes they won, sometimes they did not, but they always had agency to reach their goals. In the one hundred years of United Fruit in Colombia, there is a long history of different forces pulling from different directions depending on how the interests of each actor (the multinational, the local government, the local entrepreneurs, and the workers) evolved. The locals had agency, and they influenced the way United Fruit made its decisions.

United Fruit had to adapt to the changing political and social conditions present in its producing divisions during the twentieth century. The main changes affecting the company were the rise of nationalist governments and stronger labor unionism. These two factors made it increasingly risky for the company to have assets in the producing countries and motivated a divestiture process. United Fruit's transformation was endorsed by its shareholders and was perceived as a positive change by institutional investors, who were aware of the lack of power the company had to change the trend the producing countries were experiencing. When analyzing the company's profitability in the long term, it tended to decrease over time and worsened after the company divested. The company's shareholders were willing to exchange profitability for security. These findings suggest that the image of United Fruit as a politically powerful institution with enormous gains from the exploitation of the "Banana Republics" has to be reconsidered.[2]

The actions of United Fruit in Colombia and other Latin American countries were motivated by one basic reason—to provide a good and secure profit rate to its investors through the sales of bananas in the United States and Europe. While the supply side of United Fruit has received attention by different historians (the production, land tenure, and labor market in the producing areas), the demand side has been neglected. In most of the studies of United Fruit in Latin America the bananas seemed to be exported into a black hole that had not yet been academically analyzed. But what happened in the consumer market was crucial. This was the company's main interest, not following a wider agenda of expanding capitalism in the Third World or exploiting labor.

Changes in the consumer market affected the relationship between United Fruit and the societies of the host countries. The consumption patterns in the United States changed throughout the twentieth century in a way that influenced United Fruit's foreign operations. Before World War II, the constantly rising demand for bananas in the United States justified and stimulated the huge investments by the company to expand its production and distribution network. However, after World War II, when Americans began to find substitutes for fresh fruit in frozen, canned, and elaborated fruit (sold in smashed, dry, or canned forms of juices), the demand for bananas plummeted, and the company decreased the relative importance of bananas in its operations to focus on elaborated fruit. This fact, together with the social and political changes in Latin America plus the legal demands made by the American government, provoked a decrease in the company's direct participation in banana production. However, by the end of the twentieth century, when fresh fruit consumption experienced a revival in the United States, the company refocused on bananas and even produced some itself, although never at its pre–World

War II levels. The market consists of supply and demand, so when studying an export economy it is imperative to take into account both sides.

United Fruit is widely perceived as a harsh exploiter in Colombia because of the events surrounding the massacre of the banana strikers in Ciénaga in 1928. Scholars have focused their attention on how the strike developed and how it demonstrated the existence of a rural proletarian class in the Colombian countryside. They suggest that the 1928 army intervention "killed" labor unionism in the region, permitting further exploitation of banana workers. My evidence shows Magdalena labor unionism did not die with the 1928 massacre. On the contrary, labor unionism grew stronger with time, especially after World War II. After 1930, Magdalena's unions had the open support of the liberal government, which permitted them to gain most of what they had demanded in the 1928 strike. In the post–World War II period, the company gave in to almost all workers' petitions to such an extreme that it made more sense for United Fruit to divest and leave production—and labor problems—in the hands of local planters.

The army's brutality against the peaceful demonstrators in Ciénaga in 1928 was a terrible event for which there is no justification. That this action was carried out by a government that claimed to be a democracy under the rule of law makes it even more immoral. The workers' demands were not different from what labor movements in the United States and Europe were demanding. They were not even different from the labor legislation some developed countries stated as minimum. Even in Colombia, the Magdalena workers' petitions eventually became law, fully endorsed and enforced by the government. After 1930, an eight-hour work day and a formal labor contract were not extreme or radical demands.

I have no evidence to contribute to the debate on the number of people killed in the massacre in Ciénaga (whether nine or two thousand). I believe, however, that debating if the action was bad because there were two thousand casualties, or not as bad because there were "only" nine casualties makes the discussion trivial. Although the number of people killed matters, that the government found it justifiable matters more. Therefore, it is necessary to study if the deaths of workers in Ciénaga because they wanted to modernize the Colombian labor legislation were in vain. I have shown they were not. Changes were made. They might not have created a perfect society, but the specific changes the 1928 strikers wanted did come true. These changes came true not only for them, but also became part of the country's institutional structure.

The role of local entrepreneurs and their relationship with United Fruit has been understudied. LeGrand and White analyzed it in the context of the relationship of the development of the 1928 strike but did not go further. Also, nothing has been written about the history of local planters when United Fruit did not operate in Magdalena (World War II and after 1965).

The way United Fruit wrote purchase contracts with locals in pre–World War II Magdalena did not leave the planters any space to develop an export business themselves. Although many planters were satisfied with United Fruit's contracts (they would not have exported anything at all otherwise), some of them tried unsuccessfully to break the company's monopsony by violating their contracts and trying to sell their fruit to other companies. United Fruit enforced the contracts by using foreign courts and impeded the locals from cheating.

The locals managed to untie themselves from United Fruit's contractual system after World War II and before United Fruit returned from its forced interruption. No longer a monopsony, the company had to work alongside other local export companies that had their own international marketing networks. Thus, the local elite did not prove to be the typical enclave parasite and landowning class but an entrepreneurial group with initiative and agency.

No historian has studied what happened to Magdalena after United Fruit left. It has been suggested that once United Fruit withdrew, the banana zone died. This is inaccurate. Once United Fruit decided to concentrate its operations in Urabá, the Magdalena local entrepreneurs kept the banana export business alive. Their effort, however, eventually failed because of devastating weather conditions and the way national protectionist economic policies were applied in that region. The weak Magdalena political lobby could not alter governmental policy toward the banana export sector, and local planters were left with no help from Bogotá. These factors created a competitive disadvantage for the Magdalena producers compared with the United Fruit-dominated Central American producers and the Ecuadoran government-supported planters, and the region fell into an economic crisis for several years. United Fruit can not only be blamed for the crisis. It was the result of a complex political economy based on a power struggle between the national government in Bogotá and the provinces as well as the Colombian government's focus on coffee promotion and industrialization in the post–World War II period.

The history of Urabá reveals what happened when the company had to deal with an urban industrial class connected to the country's most powerful political lobby. In Urabá, United Fruit tried to assure its providers' loyalty by providing loans tied to purchase contracts. As the only institution providing these loans, locals had no other option. Additionally, the company distributed loans through a local bank to avoid default on its own assets in case it had to leave the region. However, this system failed. Once the locals decided the price paid by United Fruit was not high enough, they did not renew their contracts with the company. The locals created their own export company, Uniban, and had the political endorsement of the national government. United Fruit could do little to change the situation and eventually worked together with the new local company, joining their lobbying organization.

Several studies assume United Fruit counted on a submissive government when operating in Colombia. The army's intervention in the 1928 strike backs this view. However, when analyzing the events beyond 1928, a different reality is clear. The Liberal administrations that came after 1930 (especially that of Lopez) put the company at bay by increasing its taxes, ending concessions, and supporting the unions. The following Conservative and Frente Nacional administrations, although business friendly, increased the governmental economic intervention against United Fruit's best interest. Additionally, these governments did not change the constitutional laws that permitted them to expropriate foreign assets with no compensation. The post–World War II years were times of wide nationalization and multinational-government conflicts all over the Third World. This political environment was something the company could not ignore.

In conclusion, during the years United Fruit operated in Colombia, it had to adapt to the changing social, economic, and political conditions in the country—as it also eventually did in Central America. The notions of exploited workers whose dreams died in the 1928 massacre, parasitic landowners, and a submissive government have to be reconsidered. The workers, landowners, and the government had agency, initiative, and made rational decisions. None of them were resigned to accept their fate if it meant having lower wages, lower profits, or lower rents. If they had to conflict or bargain with the multinational, they designed strategies to do so and get what they wanted. Victimizing the society in which United Fruit made its business neglects the capacity of the people to be aware of the existence of a wrong situation and organize themselves to change it. The Latin American societies are aware of their underdevelopment, and they do not want to be stagnated in it.

What are the implications of these findings? Historians studying Latin America always have been fascinated by the role played by the multinational corporations in the region. Foreign capital was seen by the ruling elite as the best means to modernize Latin American countries after they gained their independence from Spain in the nineteenth century. In order to overcome the relative backwardness of the continent with respect to Europe or the United States, the Latin American governments opened their countries to foreign investors who could create new jobs and improve the precarious local infrastructure.[3] This process, however, was not smooth but tumultuous. There were several reactions against the social, cultural, and economic changes these foreign agents created, and since the nineteenth century, many Latin American intellectuals criticized the arrival of foreign multinationals as an assault against national sovereignty and a sellout of their homeland to world powers. This has been reflected in social studies, fiction works, and political discourse in both the nineteenth and twentieth centuries.[4]

In the post–World War II period, the historical studies on Latin America were increasingly dominated by scholars of the dependency theory. Under a strong influence of Marxist thought (particularly Lenin's theory on imperialism),[5] this group of scholars attempted to understand the Latin American social and economic underdevelopment by studying the way Latin America was historically inserted in the world economy. According to these scholars, the Latin American specialization in the export of primary goods was not a result of market forces but rather an imposition from the world powers that needed a steady and cheap supply of these primary goods. *Dependentistas* concluded that this specialization did not generate economic development but rather perpetuated the problems of poverty in the continent.[6]

The *dependentistas* gave an important role to multinational corporations. The *dependentistas* saw these companies as permitting the exploitation of Latin America by world powers. The exploitation was facilitated by the local elite who repressed local workers (permitting the existence of a cheap labor force) and acted as local agents providing the companies with the goods they exported (or selling goods imported by the foreign corporations). Various sectors have received special attention by dependency theory scholars as good examples of foreign investment that did not generate local economic development, such as the case of rubber in Brazil or nitrates in Chile.[7] However, of all the foreign corporations operating in Latin America, the one that was seen as the best example of the dependency theory—the quintessential representative of American economic imperialism in the region—was the United Fruit Company. So, an understanding of how this particular corporation operated in Latin America can help us to better understand the dynamics analyzed by dependency scholars.

The dependency theory developed as a discipline parallel to, but isolated from, business history. This can be understood by taking into account the role of entrepreneurs and management among dependency scholars. Multinational corporations were part of the global expansion of capitalism, so it made more sense to analyze the political and economic relations between countries and the way foreign corporations related with local societies than to study the long-term strategy of the managers of these companies and the particular interests of their shareholders and investors.

Even though dependency scholars emphasize how these corporations represent modern capitalism in Latin America and import capitalistic relationships into local society (with which I agree), they have not studied the operations of foreign companies as capitalistic enterprises—that is, the companies have not been analyzed as business enterprises. The logic behind company operations has not been included in their analysis. A business enterprise has its own internal dynamic. Dependency scholars tend to see foreign corporations as a homogenous entity in which all its members have a well-defined agenda. No difference is made between management and ownership. As I have shown, taking this difference into account is crucial. We can not talk of American capitalism coming into Latin America as a single force in which Wall Street investors, companies' shareholders, companies' CEOs, and the Department of State share the same agenda. The complex internal dynamics of a large, publicly owned corporation have been neglected by dependency scholars and, as a result, dependency scholars have provided an incomplete picture of these companies' operations.

By taking a business–historical approach, not only can we reinterpret or have a better understanding of United Fruit's operations, but we also can take into account a social group that has not received the attention it deserves given its historical importance—local entrepreneurs. In general, in Latin American historiography, the entrepreneur is absent. This is a result of the weak development of business history in Latin America as a discipline, but it is also a result of the dominance of dependency theory. Dependency theory scholars have seen the history of Latin America as a class struggle between the oppressed lower classes and the ruling elite (backed by foreign powers and multinational corporations). With this viewpoint, analyzing local entrepreneurs was either irrelevant or a glorification of the oppressive ruling class. As a result, little has been said about the multinationals' local providers in general. By studying the banana planters in Colombia it can be seen that this group was more than a mere instrument of the foreign corporation.

The entrepreneurs managed to develop their own businesses even when United Fruit left, which goes against one of the basic assumptions of dependency theory on export enclaves. Additionally, these planters had particular contractual relationships with the multinational corporation that generated a complex dynamic of enforcement in which other agents (government and financial institutions) played an important role. Studying local entrepreneurs is not a glorification of the ruling elite but an intellectual exercise that provides a more complete picture of local society. Further studies on contractual relationships between local providers and multinational corporations in Latin America would make important contributions to understanding the region's elite.[8]

Dependency scholars have not been the only ones taking into account foreign investment when trying to understand Latin American underdevelopment. While dependency scholars believe that foreign investment perpetuates a region's poverty, neoclassical economists, on the other hand, argue that the relationships between developing and developed countries are all positive. Trade links permit underdeveloped countries to specialize according to their comparative advantage and permit them to learn and adopt superior technology, organizations, and institutions. Thus, foreign direct investment is good for them. The reason Latin America did not develop through foreign trade and foreign investments is because institutional constraints did not permit market forces to operate freely.[9]

The debate on the positive or negative role of foreign investment can be enriched and clarified by taking into account business–historical studies of multinational corporations in underdeveloped countries. Similarly, multinational corporations are nonstate actors that have generated passion among those studying politics in Latin America; the multinationals are seen by a number of scholars like states within states. Political scientists interested in international relations and the role of nonstate actors benefit from studying multinational companies' strategies dealing with the political environment in their home and host governments.[10]

The dependency theory faced a blow after the Latin American debt crisis in the 1980s and the fall of Communism in Europe in the 1990s. A theory that defended state interventionism in the economy and protectionism was considered outdated after these catastrophic failures, and both scholars studying Latin American economic development and the region's policymakers rapidly shifted to the neoclassical side. During the early 1990s, most Latin American countries elected neoliberal presidential candidates who advocated free trade, privatization, and foreign investment. The positive economic growth rates that followed convinced many that a new age of economic development had finally arrived. This period was seen as living proof that the criticisms against foreign investment made in the decades before were wrong. But this view was short lived. By the late 1990s and early years of the twenty-first century, Latin Americans elected left-wing candidates such as Hugo Chávez in Venezuela and Ignazio Lula da Silva in Brazil because they were frustrated with increasing poverty and the false promises of better times made by the neo-Liberals. The collapse of the Argentinian economy, once the most prosperous country in Latin America, increased the skepticism in neo-Liberal economics, and the region felt it had lived a second lost decade in the 1990s.[11] The 1990s crisis in Latin America did not mean a rebirth of dependency theory, but it sparked new anti-imperialistic and antiforeign investment discourse among many politicians and an increasing number of intellectuals in the region.

At the turn of the century, multinational corporations were generating debate not only in Latin America and other regions of the Third World, but also in developed countries. A French peasant like José Bové became a well-known figure (and a national hero for many of his countrymen) after destroying a McDonald's franchise in France. The huge riots at the World Trade Organization meeting in Seattle in 1999 and in Genoa in 2001 were criticisms of the operations of American and European multinationals in both the developed and underdeveloped countries. During the economic downturn of the early twenty-first century, populist politicians in Europe and the United States criticized their countries' multinational corporations for exporting jobs abroad. The debate multinational corporations generate goes beyond academic circles. They are present in people's minds and are still influencing history.

# Notes

1. See García Márquez, *One Hundred Years of Solitude*.

2. Fictional literature has also played an important role in spreading knowledge of United Fruit activities in Central America. Two other Nobel laureates, Miguel Angel Asturias and Pablo Neruda, wrote important pieces of work about United Fruit in Central America. See Asturias, *El Papa Verde, Hombres de maíz*, and *The President*; and Neruda, *Canto General*. Although less famous, the wonderful book of Alvaro Samudio, *La casa grande*, based on the 1928 strike in Magdalena, is also worth mentioning.

3. Quoted by Zamosc, *The Agrarian Question*, 1.

4. Tirado, *Introducción*.

5. Posada-Carbó, *The Colombian Caribbean*, 61.

6. Kepner and Soothill, *The Banana Empire*, 76.

7. For a detailed account of this conflict see Dosal, *Doing Business*, 75–139.

8. Ibid., 142. For a detailed description of the early twentieth-century "banana wars" in Central America, see Langley and Schoonover, *The Banana Men*.

9. The events surrounding the coup against Arbenz still generate heated debate. While some authors claim United Fruit conspired to make the U.S. government intervene in Guatemala to protect its interests (Schlesinger and Kinzer, *Bitter Fruit*), others claim the U.S. government was not going to allow a left-wing government in Central America in the height of the cold war, regardless of United Fruit's interests (see Gleijeses, *Shattered Hope*). For a study that defends the actions of United Fruit in Guatemala see, Stanley, *For the Record*.

10. Scholars studying the activities of United Fruit in other countries have made remarkable contributions using the company's records of the Costa Rica, Ecuador, and Cuba divisions. See, Bourgois, *Ethnicity at Work*, Dosal, *Doing Business*; Striffler, *In the Shadows of State and Capital*; and Zanetti and García, *United Fruit Company*. In the Colombian case, I used part of these records in Bucheli, *Empresas multinacionales*, "La crisis," and "United Fruit in Colombia."

11. Some of the results for the period prior 1970 can be found in Bucheli, "United Fruit Company in Latin America."

12. The classic early studies written during the first five decades of the century only pay attention to the vertical integration process because the divestiture came after they were written. See, Adams, *The Conquest of the Tropics*; Kepner and Soothill, *The Banana Empire*; and May and Plaza, *United States Business Performance Abroad*. Adams characterizes the process of United Fruit's expansion in Central America as the heroic and epic adventure of the company's founders—a struggle against nature in the hostile tropics, bringing civilization to the inhabitants of these regions. Kepner and Soothill make a more social scientific approach using Marxist theory on imperialism (following the lines of Lenin, "Imperialism") to show vertical integration as a process and strategy to eliminate competitors and control all phases of the production process. May and Plaza see the process of vertical integration as a means to improve efficiency, emphasizing the contributions to local societies (hospitals, roads, canals, railroads, telegraphs, and others). They address a tendency toward divestiture in United Fruit, but do not consider it a signal of major change in the long run. May and Plaza did not give an explanation for why the company vertically integrated. Among these three classic studies, the explanation that has dominated successive views is Kepner and Soothill's. Although this view makes sense to partially understand the rationale behind the company's strategy, it is not accurate when doing long-term analysis.

13. Read, "The Growth and Structure."

14. Wilkins, *The Emergence*, 157–60.

15. Barham, "Excess Capacity in International Markets."

16. There are several studies that analyze United Fruit and the politics of the countries where it operated besides Dosal's, *Doing Business*. These studies, however, do not pay much attention to how politics affected the company's strategy, although they give a good account of the history of the company in several divisions. Of these, it is worth highlighting McCameron, *Bananas Labor and Politics in Honduras*, on the 1954 banana strike in Honduras; Langley and Schoonover, *The Banana Men*, on United Fruit's involvement in several Central American military coups; Orozco, *The United Fruit Company in Central America*, on the bargaining power United Fruit had with the Central American governments; Bartres, *The Experience of the Guatemalan United Fruit Company Workers*, on the history of the Guatemalan unions during Arbenz's government; Chomsky, *West Indian Workers*, on the Costa Rican labor unions; Euraque, *Reinterpreting the Banana Republic*, on the company's political relations in Honduras; García and Zanetti, *United Fruit Company*, on the labor and political relations of the company in Cuba; and the studies on the conflict between United Fruit and the Central American governments over export taxes in 1974 by Argueta, *Bananos y política*; Urrá, *La guerra del banano*; Danilo, *La CIA*; and Ricord, *Panamá y la frutera*.

17. While White takes a more traditional historical approach, LeGrand makes an attempt to use Marxist theory to understand the class conflicts generated by the presence of the multinational corporation in the Colombian Caribbean. See LeGrand, "Campesinos y asalariados" and "El conflicto"; and White, "The United Fruit Company in the Santa Marta Banana Zone."

18. This view was developed by Rodríguez, *De cómo fue reprimida*; and Herrera and Romero, *La zona bananera*.

19. See García, *Urabá*; and Uniban, *Informe sobre Uniban*.

20. In his study on the political relationship between United Fruit and the Honduran government, Darío Euraque challenges the widely accepted view of Honduras's government as always submissive toward the multinational corporations in *Reinterpreting the Banana Republic*.

21. Colombia is politically divided into departments, which are equivalent to states in the United States.

22. Guhl, *Colombia*, 147.

23. Nichols, *Tres puertos de Colombia*, 17.

24. Jimenez and Sideri, *Historia regional de Colombia*, 134.

25. Guhl, *Colombia*, 153.

26. Krogzemis, "A Historical Geography," 34–35.

27. Parsons, *Urabá*, 13, 14.

28. Friede, "La conquista," 122–30.

29. Nichols, *Tres puertos de Colombia*, 151–58.

30. LeGrand, "El conflicto," 183–84.

31. Parsons, *Urabá*, 37–59.

32. Pardo, *Geografía económica*, 303–4.

33. Kalmanovitz, *Economía y nación*, 225.

34. Ibid., 221.

35. Parsons, *Urabá*, 59–83.

NOTES TO CHAPTER 2

1. See chapter 3.

2. Banana imports were measured only in dollars until 1904. After that year, they were also measured in stems, and since 1961, measurements were also taken in tons. Figures 2.1 and 2.2 show the trends measured in both stems and tons. A measurement of just stems would produce inaccurate results because their weight changes over time. Graph 5 shows the information in tons from 1920 according to the conversion made by ECLA. No reliable conversion was made for previous years.

3. United Fruit Company, Annual Report 1901, 6–7.

4. United Fruit Company, Annual Report 1902, 7.

5. United Fruit Company, Annual Report 1905, 5.

6. United Fruit Company, Annual Report 1906, 8.

7. Ibid., 1–16, 108–9.

8. Ibid., 107–10.

9. Ibid., 22–23.

10. Ibid., 23–24.

11. Ibid., 24.

12. Ibid., 25–27.

13. United Fruit Company, Annual Report 1919, 5.

14. Jenkins, *Bananas*, 106–7.

15. Reynolds, *The Banana*, 104–35.

16. Valles, *The World Market for Bananas*, 60–61.

17. For a more detailed description of this increase in productivity see chapter 3.

18. Putnam and Allshouse, *Food Consumption*, 33.

19. Ibid., 35

20. United Nations, FAO, Committee on Commodity Problems, *The Market for "Organic,"* 3.

21. Ibid., 2.

NOTES TO CHAPTER 3

1. In order to understand how the company adapted to a changing political and social environment, I use a set of sources and methodology that have not been utilized by other scholars. The information on the general consolidated balance of the company is taken from the United Fruit, United Brands, and Chiquita Brands Annual Reports to the Stockholders for the years 1900 to 2000. Data on dividends and stock prices come from the *Wall Street Journal*. The yields of other industries in the American economy during this period and some analyses (when quoted) of the company are taken from the *Moody's Investors Service Stock Survey* for the years 1945 to 1970. Together, these sources take us inside United Fruit itself and help us understand the motives, perceptions, and forces that were driving changes in United Fruit's corporate strategy during the post–World War II period.

2. Taylor, "Evolution of the Banana Multinationals," 2.

3. McCann, *An American Company*, 26–27.

4. Brungardt, "The United Fruit Company," 234, 244.

5. May and Plaza, *United States Business Performance Abroad*, 6–8.

6. See Read, "The Growth and Structure of Multinationals." According to Read, the international banana business followed the same pattern Alfred Chan-

dler described for American big enterprises in the second half of the nineteenth century and the early twentieth century. See Chandler, *The Visible Hand*, "The Emergence of Managerial Capitalism," "The Growth of the Transnational Industrial Firm," and *Scale and Scope*.

7. White, "United Fruit Company," 29.

8. Taylor, "Evolution of the Banana Multinationals," 72.

9. Although the company had its own production and distribution network, it also increasingly relied on local growers who provided it with part of the fruit it marketed. See Kepner and Soothill, *The Banana Empire*, 265–75. However, in spite of relying significantly on local planters, the company did not change its internal structure by the time Kepner and Soothill published their book. This means it had the structure of a production company rather than of a marketing company. The actual internal change of the company began after World War II.

10. See Adams, *The Conquest of the Tropics*.

11. See Kepner and Soothill, *The Banana Empire*.

12. Read, "The Growth and Structure of Multinationals"; Wilkins, *The Emergence*, and *The Maturing of Multinational Enterprise*.

13. See Dosal, *Doing Business*.

14. Before World War II the company did not include depreciation on fixed assets in its annual report. I took the market value of those goods for these years.

15. Equity and assets are different measures of the company's capital. Total assets is the value of all assets held, regardless of how they were financed. For instance, the company could have bought its assets using debt. Equity is the capital provided by shareholders plus the profits reinvested. So, assets financed through debt are not included in the equity measure. Return on equity treats interest and debt payment as a cost. Return on assets does not.

16. This trend holds true despite the fact that the company tried to diversify its holdings during this period. Bananas remained the main source of income and profit for United Fruit prior to 1970.

17. For the years before 1962 and after 1968, the company did not record this information and only published an aggregate of sales of products and services.

18. During the diversification phase from 1959 to 1961, the company's management made it clear that its earnings would still depend on bananas. In his letters to the shareholders during these years, president Thomas Sunderland emphasized that bananas continued to be the most important good in the company's business: "Of course, bananas will be our principal source of income for some time in the future" (United Fruit Company, Annual Report 1959, 2); "The mainstay of our business is and will continue to be bananas" (Annual Report 1960, 2); "Bananas are and will continue to be the principal source of our income" (Annual Report 1961, 2).

In the years to follow, the studies of analyst firms also showed the company as highly dependent on bananas despite its diversification efforts. In 1963, a

Standard and Poor's report on the company's diversification program stated, "Bananas represent around 70% of the company's business" (Standard Corporation Description 1962, 7311). The Standard and Poor's reports continued giving the same percentage for the next three years. In its 1967 report, Standard and Poor's data showed the success of the diversification: "In 1967 bananas represented 63.8% of sales, sugar 11.9%, fruits and vegetables 3.5% fast food operations 3.5%, communications 1%. In 1966 it had been 65.2%, 13.2%, 8.2%, 6.1%, 3.6%, 1.6%, 1%, and 1.1% respectively" (Standard Corporation Description 1968, 9123). What the information of the company's annual reports and the analyses of Standard & Poor's suggest is that the company's business was heavily influenced by its banana operations. Therefore, it makes sense to analyze the trends on profitability as largely the result of the banana business behavior.

19. Moody's Investors Service, Moody's Stock Survey (April 1949), 528.

20. United Fruit Company, Annual Report 1949, 7.

21. Moody's Investors Service, Moody's Stock Survey (March 20, 1950), 561.

22. Moody's Investors Service, Moody's Stock Survey (November 26, 1951), 133.

23. Moody's Investors Service, Moody's Stock Survey (November 17, 1952).

24. United Fruit Company, Annual Report 1951, 9–10.

25. For a good analysis of the Arbenz affair, see Coatsworth, *Central America and the United States*; Gliejeses, *Shattered Hope*; and Schlesinger and Kinzer, *Bitter Fruit*. Thomas McCann's insider view is worth reading in *An American Company*.

26. United Fruit Company, Annual Report 1954, 4.

27. Moody's Investors Service, Moody's Stock Survey (March 30, 1953), 561.

28. The story of Guevara and Castro is in Castro's memoirs. See Castro, *Che*.

29. United Fruit Company, Annual Report 1954, 3.

30. Moody's Investors Service, Moody's Stock Survey (March 14, 1955), 589.

31. Moody's Investors Service, Moody's Stock Survey (December 24, 1956).

32. In 1959's annual report, the company's president wrote, "The estimated present value of these [expropriated] properties is two and one-half million dollars. Occupation of these lands has not been carried out in conformance with the terms of the law. The company is taking every legal recourse open to it under the laws of Cuba against these illegal occupations, but thus far without results" (8).

33. United Fruit Company, Annual Report 1959, 6.

34. Moody's Investors Service, Moody's Stock Survey (August 17, 1959).

35. Larrea, *El banano en el Ecuador*, 46.

36. See United Fruit Company, Annual Report 1960.

37. Thomas Sunderland, quoted by Arthur, Houck, and Beckford, *Tropical Agribusiness*, 147.

38. May and Plaza, *United States Business Performance Abroad*, 170.

39. Organization of American States, *Sectoral Study*, 20; Larrea, "Los cambios recientes," 165.

40. In his analysis on United Fruit in Ecuador, Steve Striffler shows how peasant activism in this country also encouraged the company to follow a process of divestiture. See Striffler, *In the Shadows of State and Capital*. Also, see Glover and Larrea, "Changing Comparative Advantage," 95.

41. Ellis, *Las transnacionales del banano*, 174.

42. Taylor, "Evolution of the Banana Multinationals," 78, 81.

43. Arthur, Houck, and Beckford, *Tropical Agribusiness*, 148.

44. United Fruit Company, Annual Report 1960, 2.

45. United Fruit Company, Annual Report 1961, 1.

46. Arthur, Houck, and Beckford, *Tropical Agribusiness*, 148.

47. Moody's Investors Service, Moody's Stock Survey (March 26, 1962).

48. Moody's Investors Service, Moody's Stock Survey (January 14, 1963), 772.

49. Moody's told investors that "United Fruit's antitrust difficulties were aggravated last month when it was indicted on a charge of trying to monopolize the banana market in seven western states. This could dampen the investment appeal of the stock, particularly in view of recent weak earnings. . . . Despite the company's capabilities for eventually solving its current problems, the new antitrust suit adds to the intermediate uncertainties. Hence we should feel holdings of this stock should be disposed of" (Moody's Investors Service, Moody's Stock Survey [August 12, 1963]), 455.

50. United Fruit Company, Annual Report 1965.

51. Glover and Larrea, "Changing Comparative Advantage," 95.

52. United Fruit Company, Annual Report 1968.

53. United Brands Company, Annual Report 1970.

54. For an explanation of how I calculated this yield, see appendix to chapter 3.

55. United Fruit Company, Annual Report 1960 and 1961.

56. The opinion about the company did not only change among investors or within the company itself. A recent study shows that the American media, represented in the *New York Times*, also changed its perception of United Fruit through the twentieth century. While before the 1940s the company was perceived as "civilizer" of the Caribbean and as an important ally in World War II, after the war, the media became more concerned on the way the company managed its labor conflicts. See Read, "Reinterpreting the United Fruit Company."

57. For a detailed explanation of how I calculated United Fruit's yield on common stock, see appendix.

58. The comparison between United Fruit's and the top 200 companies' yields is also shown in graph 8.

59. United Brands Company, Annual Report 1972, 5.

60. Ibid., 38.

61. Ibid., 38–39.

62. "La UPEB, el problema bananero, inversión extranjera y empresas multi-nacionales," *Augura*, vol. 2, no. 5; United Nations, FAO, *La economía mundial del banano*, 79–80; Vallejo, *Productos básicos*, 83–88.

63. López, *La Economía del banano*, 33–34.

64. United Nations, FAO, *La economia mundial del banano*, 79–80.

65. Vallejo, *Productos básicos*, 284; Presa Fernández, *Aportes*, 11, 54, 55; Clairmonte, "El imperio de la banana," 21, 22.

66. Vallejo, *Productos básicos*, 285.

67. Ibid., 286–87.

68. United Brands Company, Annual Report 1975, 1, 2, 4, 10.

69. Ibid., 3.

70. According to the FAO, Comunbana failed because it never managed to create a marketing infrastructure and organization similar to that of the multinational corporations. Additionally, this company could never reduce production costs enough to become competitive at the international level (United Nations, FAO, *La economía mundial del banano*, 80). Roche, *The International Banana Trade*, 50. The companies' individual shares in the market increased from 28% to 30% for United Brands between 1973 and 1981, 22% to 25% for Standard Fruit, and 8% to 15% for Del Monte. United Brands increased its participation even in Panama where the most heated debate took place. In 1973, the company controlled 100% of exports, by 1975 it had decreased to 97%, and to 90% in 1977. However, by 1983, it had recovered to 97%. In fact, the market participation of the independent producers never reached levels above 12% (López, *La economía del banano*, 94–98).

71. López, *La economía del banano*, 122, 123. López also shows that Standard Fruit and Del Monte chose a different strategy. These two companies decreased the participation of their associate producers and decided to refocus on producing the fruit themselves in a smaller number of plantations of higher productivity.

72. Ibid., 124, 125.

73. "Honduran Bribery," *Time Magazine* (April 21, 1975): 46. McCann, *An American Company*, 232–34.

74. United Brands Company, Annual Report 1974.

75. Taylor, "Evolution of the Banana Multinationals," 80.

76. United Brands Company, Annual Report 1979, 1.

77. Taylor, "Evolution of the Banana Multinationals," 80; Stein, "Yes, We Have No Profits," 190.

78. Chiquita Brands International, Annual Report 1991, 1.

79. In his letter to the stockholders of 1990, Lindner showed great optimism

on the possibilities of the new European market. That year, the company forecasted a potential increase of European customers from 180 million to 675 million (Chiquita Brands International, Annual Report 1990, 3, 10).

80. Chiquita Brands International, Annual Report 1991, 4.

81. Stein, "Yes, We Have No Profits," 192; Chiquita Brands International, Annual Report 1990, 9.

82. United Nations, FAO, *Intergovernmental Group on Bananas*, 2–10.

83. In his 1992 letter to shareholders, Lindner expressed his concern on this unexpected change in policy by the European Union and gave it partial blame for the company's poor performance in that year (Chiquita Brands International, Annual Report 1992, 2).

84. Tangermann, "European Interests," 21–24.

85. The bananas imported into Germany could not be re-exported to the other EU members that had established restrictive quotas. Although one of the main goals of the European Union is to eliminate tariffs between countries, this restriction was legally acceptable under EU legislation. For a detailed explanation, see ibid., 28–31.

86. By 1997, a kilo of bananas cost the Russians 40.7% of the price of a kilo of beef, and, by 1998, bananas were 25% more expensive than apples (ibid., 27–28).

87. The Lomé Convention guaranteed a market for bananas in favorable conditions to some former European colonies over the Latin American producers.

88. Tangermann, "European Interests," 33–36.

89. Taylor, "Evolution of the Banana Multinationals," 85.

90. Ibid., 86.

91. Chiquita Brands International, Annual Report 2000, and Form 10-K 2000, 0.

92. Senator Bob Dole has no relation with Dole Corporation, Chiquita's main rival.

93. Stein, "Yes, We Have No Profits," 194.

94. Stovall and Hathaway, "U.S. Interests," 154.

95. Harding, "U.S. Banana Exporters File 301 Petition," 36; "Banana Republican," 48.

96. "Senator Dole: Frequent Flier in Battle for Chiquita Bananas," *Associated Press*; Collymore, "Trade-Bananas"; Sanger, "Dole at the Forefront of the Trade Battle to Aid Donor's Banana Empire."

97. In 1998, Chiquita also made headlines for a different reason. The *Cincinnati Enquirer* published an eighteen-page article that accused Chiquita of hidden political, environmental, and human rights abuses in Central America. The article claimed the company had several dummy companies in the region and manipulated local politicians using bribery and threats. Reporter Mike Gallagher got this information by hacking the company's voicemails from general head-

quarters in Cincinnati. Chiquita sued the newspaper for $14 million for having hacked its voicemails illegally. The newspaper was forced to publish an apology to Chiquita and fired Gallagher. However, the actual charges made in Gallagher's articles were never dismissed. If ever proved true, they will make it imperative to do new studies of the company's operations in the 1980s and 1990s. Gallagher, "Chiquita Secrets Revealed," *Cincinnati Enquirer*, May 3, 1998.

98. Stovall and Hathaway, "U.S. Interests," 161.

99. Ibid., 164.

100. Stein, "Yes," 194.

101. Ibid., 192.

102. Van de Kasteele, "The Banana Chain," Appendix A, 2.

NOTES TO CHAPTER 4

1. See, Argueta, *Bananos y política*; Danilo, *La CIA*; Dosal, *Doing Business*; Langley and Schoonover, *Banana Men*; McCameron, *Bananas*; Orozco, *The United Fruit Company*; Ricord, *Panamá*; Urrá, *La guerra del banano*; and Zanetti and García, *United Fruit Company*.

2. Some historians believe the cause of the War of the Thousand Days was the differences between Conservatives and Liberals on what to do with the coffee export gains. While the Liberals, led by Uribe Uribe, promoted the idea of using the export boom to decrease taxes and to open Colombia to free markets, the Conservatives, led by Miguel Antonio Caro, wanted to increase taxation on exports during the boom to finance local industry and social investments. Uribe's strong opposition led to the war, which makes his appointment by Reyes even more remarkable. See Bergquist, *Coffee and Conflict*.

3. Pardo, *Geografía económica*, 303–4.

4. Jimenez and Sideri, *Historia regional*, 137.

5. Posada-Carbó, *The Colombian Caribbean*, 51.

6. Although Reyes was a strong promoter of Magdalena's export he was not a pioneer in this. In the last two decades of the nineteenth century, Conservative President Rafael Núñez and Conservative Governor Ramón Goenaga created incentives for the private sector such as grants on baldíos and the concession of the Santa Marta Railway (see Corso, "El gravámen bananero", 41). Reyes's contribution, therefore, was more by way of tax exemptions than in the form of land grants.

7. Corso, "El gravámen bananero," 43.

8. White, "The United Fruit Company in the Santa Marta Banana Zone," 28.

9. United Nations, FAO, *The World Banana Economy*, 3.

10. Kalmanovitz, *Economía y nación*, 225.

11. See Corso, "El gravámen bananero."

12. Ibid., 106–7.

13. Ibid., 58; White, "The United Fruit Company in the Santa Marta Banana Zone," 41. Both Calderón and Charris were also banana growers who tried, in several occasions, to break United Fruit's monopsony in the region. All their attempts failed (see chapter 5).

14. Corso, "El gravámen bananero," 63. This clearly indicates that the loans given by United Fruit were actually quite favorable, despite the company having a monopoly before the opening of the Banco Agricola Hipotecario branch.

15. White, "The United Fruit Company in the Santa Marta Banana Zone," 46.

16. Corso, "El gravámen bananero," 125.

17. LeGrand, "El conflicto."

18. Calculations made with information taken from Posada-Carbó, *The Colombian Caribbean*, 239.

19. Author's calculations made from data taken from Bushnell, *The Making of Modern Colombia*, 291.

20. Ibid., 180.

21. Author's calculations made from data taken from Posada-Carbó, *The Colombian Caribbean*, 239.

22. White, *La United Fruit*, 112–13.

23. Corso, "El gravámen bananero."

24. The Kemmerer mission was a group of economic experts, led by economist Edwin Kemmerer, that traveled through Latin America advising local governments in the restructuring process of their financial systems. For a more detailed study on the effects of the Kemmerer missions, see Drake, *The Money Doctor*.

25. Corso, "El gravámen bananero," 123–25.

26. Ibid., 128–49.

27. See chapter 5.

28. Corso, "El gravámen bananero," 126–27.

29. Bushnell, *The Making of Modern Colombia*, 185.

30. Ibid., 188–89.

31. Backus and Phanor, *A Guide*, 100.

32. Bushnell, *The Making of Modern Colombia*, 189.

33. Ibid., 189.

34. Cepeda and Pardo, "La política exterior," 23.

35. Author's calculations with data taken from Bushnell, *The Making of Modern Colombia*, 291; and Posada-Carbó, *The Colombian Caribbean*, 239.

36. Author's calculations made with data taken from Bushnell, *The Making of Modern Colombia*, 291.

37. United Fruit Company—CFS, Monthly Report, Monthly Letter, Honiball to Sisto, March 1948.

38. Ibid., May 1949.

39. Ibid., July 1948.

40. Ibid., February, April, and May 1949; Hall to Sisto, October and December 1949; August and September 1950.

41. Bushnell, *The Making of Modern Colombia*, 208.

42. "El dólar libre."

43. United Fruit Company—CFS, Monthly Report, Monthly Letter, Hall to Sisto, December 1956.

44. I examine this issue in more detail in chapter 5.

45. United Fruit Company—CFS, Monthly Report, Monthly Letter, MacMillan to Walwood, February 1961.

46. United Fruit Company—CFS, Monthly Report, Monthly Letter, various years.

47. Colombia, Ministerio de Hacienda, "Intervención del Sr. Ministro."

48. During this time, Minister Sanz was not the only one proposing a tax increase to national and foreign corporations. The International Bank for Reconstruction and Development was also strongly encouraging the Colombian government to reform the taxation and agrarian systems. See "Carta remisoria del Informe de la Misión del Banco Internacional de Reconstrucción y Fomento dirigida al Sr. Presidente Dr. Alberto Lleras, por el Presidente de dicha Institución," and "Política Fiscal 1958–1961," in Colombia, Ministerio de Hacienda, *Memoria de Hacienda* (1962).

49. United Fruit Company—CFS, Monthly Report, Monthly Letter, MacMillan to Walwood, August 1963.

50. Ibid., February 1963.

51. Ibid., Bosy to Chagnot, August 1966. In his comparative study of both regions, Kamalprija points out the high difference in quality among the fruit produced in Magdalena and Urabá in *Descriptive Survey*, 37–48.

52. The main purpose of this decree was to restructure the Colombian economy toward export promotion of industrial goods. Its protectionist frame made the neoliberal government of César Gaviria finish it in 1991.

53. Colombia, Ministerio de Hacienda, *Memoria de Hacienda* (1970), 78.

54. United Fruit Company—CFS, Monthly Report, Monthly Letter, Bosy to Mason, May 1967; Bosy to Chagnot, June 1967.

55. Ibid., Bosy to Ronan, July and October 1967; Management Comments, December 1967.

56. Ibid., Management Comments, December 1967.

57. By this date, United Fruit had not been able to get rid of the last properties because the buyer of most of them canceled the deal at the last minute, which left the company with one alternative—to do business with Incora (United Fruit Company—CFS, Monthly Report, Monthly Letter, Bosy to Ronan, February 1968).

58. Ibid., Lascano to Mullin, December 1969.

59. Folsom, "The Taking by a State."

60. Colombia, *Constitución Política*.

61. For a more detailed history of the creation of the local banana export companies and their relationship with the government, see chapter 7.

62. See chapter 3 for a history of the creation of UPEB and the political conflicts it generated.

63. Comision Andina de Juristas, *Informes regionales*, 149. Also see García, *Urabá*; and Ramírez, *Urabá*.

64. See chapter 3.

65. For a more detailed description of this process see chapter 3.

66. Roche, *The International Banana Trade*, 163.

67. Chiquita Brands International, Annual Report 1994, 2.

68. Chiquita Brands International, "Chiquita Applauds U.S. Intervention in Banana Dispute," Public Relations Newswire (October 17, 1994); Harding, "U.S. Banana Exporters," 36; and Brewer, "Kantor Probes," 10.

69. Maggs, "Dole," 1A.

70. "Colombian Government Rejects U.S. Investigations of Banana Exports," *Interpress*; "Colombia Warns against Banana Sanctions," *United Press*.

71. Lane, "Kantor Rejects Colombian Offer to Raise Banana Quota to EU," 5A.

72. Lever, "Three-Way Banana Dispute."

73. Sanger, "Dole at the Forefront," A1.

74. Collymore, "Trade-Bananas;" Crutsinger, "Costa Rica and Colombia Avoid Trade Sanctions;" "U.S. to Withhold Sanctions in Tri-Continental Banana Rift," D4.

75. "Colombia—Estados Unidos—UE: Preocupación por efecto de roce comercial por banano a la UE."

76. "Latin American Nations Mostly Praise New E.U.-U.S. Banana Deal."

77. For an explanation on the final agreement see chapter 3.

78. In chapter 7, I show how these protectionist policies also had a negative effect on the Magdalena independent banana export companies.

79. See chapter 5.

NOTES TO CHAPTER 5

1. Rodríguez, *De cómo*, 1.

2. Alberto Castrillón was one of the leaders of the 1928 strike.

3. Castrillón, *Ciento veinte días*, 8.

4. Herrera and Romero, *La zona bananera*, 26.

5. Castrillón, *Ciento veinte días*, 10–11.

6. White, *La United Fruit*, 104.

7. LeGrand, "El conflicto," 186.

8. Herrera and Romero, *La zona bananera*, 24.

9. LeGrand, "El conflicto," 187–88.

10. Arango, *Sobrevivientes*, 39.

11. Fonnegra, *Bananeras*, 55.

12. Gilhodes, "La Colombie," quoted by White in "The United Fruit Company in the Santa Marta Banana Zone," 82.

13. White, "The United Fruit Company in the Santa Marta Banana Zone," 74.

14. Ibid., 76.

15. Urrutia, *Historia del sindicalismo*, 89.

16. LeGrand, "El conflicto," 200.

17. White, "The United Fruit Company in the Santa Marta Banana Zone," 78–79.

18. Ibid., 79; LeGrand, "El conflicto," 200.

19. Herrera and Romero say, "In the workers' movement, there was a coterie of Spanish and Italian anarchist-unionist advisors, as well as a clearly communist group led by the Colombian José Garibaldi Russo" (*La zona bananera*, 25).

20. LeGrand, "El conflicto," 200; Urrutia, *Historia del sindicalismo*, 129; White, "The United Fruit Company in the Santa Marta Banana Zone," 78–81.

21. White, "The United Fruit Company in the Santa Marta Banana Zone," 81.

22. Ibid., 79.

23. Ibid., 82.

24. Ibid., 83–84.

25. Ibid., 85.

26. Ibid., 87.

27. Ibid., 86–87.

28. Kepner and Soothill, *The Banana Empire*, 327; LeGrand, "El conflicto," 202.

29. White, *La United Fruit*, 43.

30. Urrutia, *Historia del sindicalismo*, 130.

31. LeGrand, "Campesinos."

32. White, *La United Fruit*, 88.

33. Fonnegra, *Bananeras*, 193.

34. Ibid., 51.

35. Ibid., 193.

36. Arango, *Sobrevivientes*, 46.

37. Interview with María Teresa Caneva. Ciénaga, Magdalena, July 1999.

38. Interview with a former field worker of the banana zone. He requested to remain anonymous.

39. Arango, *Sobrevivientes*, 53–54; Fonnegra, *Bananeras*, 53, 193; LeGrand, "El conflicto," 204; Urrutia, *Historia del sindicalismo*, 130.

40. Kalmanovitz, *Economía*, 259.

41. Ibid., 274.

42. Lososky is quoted by Herrera and Romero in *La zona bananera*, 30–35.

43. White, *La United Fruit*, 88–89.

44. Herrera and Romero, *La zona bananera*, 31.

45. Similar to what happened with the *pliego de peticiones*, Russo's telegram was far from being "revolutionary." He said, "Our demands do not respond to politics, but to justice and respect for the current legislation. We are prepared to declare a strike supported by the Colombian proletariat if the laws wisely written [by the Senate] are not enforced." Quoted by White in *La United Fruit*, 89.

46. LeGrand, "El conflicto," 204.

47. White, *La United Fruit*, 91.

48. White, "The United Fruit Company in the Santa Marta Banana Zone," 94; Herrera and Romero, *La zona bananera*, 38–39.

49. LeGrand, "El conflicto," 208–9; White, "The United Fruit Company in the Santa Marta Banana Zone," 93–96.

50. LeGrand, "El conflicto," 209.

51. Ibid., 208–9.

52. Ibid., 209–10, White, "The United Fruit Company in the Santa Marta Banana Zone," 96–98.

53. LeGrand, "El conflicto," 210–11, White, "The United Fruit Company in the Santa Marta Banana Zone," 99–100.

54. Herrera and Romero, *La zona bananera*, 25–32, 38–70; LeGrand, "El conflicto," 211–15; Urrutia, *Historia del sindicalismo*, 130–31; White, "The United Fruit Company in the Santa Marta Banana Zone," 100–106.

55. Cortés, *Los sucesos*.

56. Castrillón, *Ciento veinte días*.

57. Brungardt, "Jorge Eliécer Gaitán," 53–54.

58. Urrutia, *Historia del sindicalismo*, 130.

59. LeGrand, "El conflicto," 215.

60. Kalmanovitz, *Economía y Nación*, 252.

61. Fajardo, *Haciendas*, 33–34.

62. Rodríguez, *De cómo*, 1.

63. White, "The United Fruit Company in the Santa Marta Banana Zone," 106.

64. Quoted in Posada, *The Colombian Caribbean*, 61.

65. White, *La United Fruit*, 102.

66. White, "The United Fruit Company in the Santa Marta Banana Zone," 123.

67. Cepeda and Pardo, "La política," 17.

68. LeGrand, "El conflicto," 217.

NOTES TO CHAPTER 6

1. The Colombian constitution did not permit the re-election of a sitting president, so López could not run again anyway, even with the party's support.

2. Londoño, "Crisis."

3. United Fruit Company—CFS, Monthly Report, Monthly Letter, Honiball to Sisto, April 1949 to May 1949; Hall to Sisto, June 1949 to September 1949.

4. Ibid., Hall to Sisto, September 1949.

5. Ibid., September 1949, April 1950.

6. Interview with a former United Fruit employee. Aracataca, Magdalena, June 1999. The employee requested that his name not be disclosed. This opinion was shared by other workers interviewed in Aracataca and Ciénaga.

7. Interview of John Strange with *Economia Colombiana*, 35.

8. Letter from LeGrand to Bucheli, 1991.

9. Interview of Francisco Dávila with *Economia Colombiana*, 35.

10. United Fruit Company—CFS, Monthly Report, Monthly Letter, Hall to Sisto, January, March, and November 1950.

11. For the development of the labor union movement after Gaitán's assassination, see Londoño, "Crisis."

12. Interview with a former worker of United Fruit. Aracataca, Magdalena, July 1999.

13. Interview with a former worker of United Fruit Company. Ciénaga, Magdalena, July 1999.

14. After returning to Magdalena after World War II, United Fruit's subsidiary took the name of Compañía Frutera de Sevilla (CFS).

15. Interview with Mario Rey, former president of the Unión de Trabajadores del Magdalena. Santa Marta, Magdalena, May 1999.

16. Ibid., July 1999.

17. United Fruit Company—CFS, Monthly Report, Monthly Letter, Hall to Carpenter, February 1960.

18. Ibid., MacMillan to Walwood, August 1961.

19. Ibid., May 1962.

20. Ibid., June 1962.

21. Interview with Mario Rey, July 1999.

22. United Fruit Company—CFS, Monthly Report, Monthly Letter, Bosy to Ronan, October 1967.

23. Marín, "Configuración del Municipio," 37.

24. Interviews with Guillermo Rivera, union leader and former member of the guerrillas of Apartadó (Urabá), August 1997.

25. Kamalprija, *Descriptive Survey* (1986), 12.

26. Garcia, *Urabá: Región, actores y conflicto*, 118–19, 206–9.

27. Interview with Osvaldo Cuadrado, Urabá union leader and former member of the EPL. Apartadó (Urabá), August 1997. This summarizes the perspective shared by other union leaders and ex-guerrilla members interviewed in the field research of 1997 and 1998. For a detailed study of the general characteristics of the labor force in the Urabá banana industry, see Botero and Sierra, *El mercado*.

28. Interview with Mario Agudelo, former member of the Communist Marxist-Leninist party and former guerrilla member of the EPL. Medellín, September 1997.

29. Interview with Eliseo Restrepo, a former pioneer entrepreneur in the region of Urabá from Medellín. His viewpoint is similar to other entrepreneurs. The entrepreneurs were interviewed in the cities of Medellín and Bogota in 1997 and 1998.

NOTES TO CHAPTER 7

1. It is possible to approach the contractual relationship between United Fruit and the Magdalena and Urabá planters using the theoretical framework developed by the New Institutional Economics theory of contracts, similar to what Alan Dye did for the Cuban sugar industry (see Dye, *Cuban Sugar*). A good explanation of this theoretical approach can be found in Furubotn, *Institutions*. However, we only have information on the dynamics between the company and the planters and do not possess the quantitative information the contractual model requires for its analysis. James Robinson made a remarkable contribution to building a mathematical model of the contractual relations of United Fruit in Magdalena and Urabá that influenced my analysis. See, Robinson, "Hold Up in the Tropics."

2. A complete history of the ports of Santa Marta, Cartagena, and Barranquilla can be found in Nichols, *Tres puertos*.

3. White, "The United Fruit Company in the Magdalena Banana Zone," 12. The Riofrio area constitutes part of the main core of what is known as the Magdalena banana zone.

4. White, *La United Fruit*, 20.

5. According to calculations made by Eduardo Posada-Carbó in "Imperialism" before World War II, United Fruit purchased between 50 and 80% of the fruit it exported from local growers (7).

6. Herrera and Romero, *La zona bananera*, 6.

7. Ibid., 6; White, "The United Fruit Company in the Magdalena Banana Zone," 13–14.

8. Posada, "Imperialism," 12.

9. Bulmer-Thomas, *The Political Economy*, 15–16, 35–37.

10. Posada-Carbó, *The Colombian Caribbean*, 53–54.

11. Ellis, *Las transnacionales*, 116, 129, 133, 138, 143, 145.

12. This description is a summary of the information I gathered from dozens of contracts between United Fruit and different local growers from the 1900s until the early 1940s. The contracts I consulted belong to the notary records of Notaría Primera de Santa Marta, Santa Marta, Magdalena.

13. Information from interviews with former planters and dates of contracts from the notary records.

14. White, "The United Fruit Company in the Magdalena Banana Zone," 54; Kepner and Soothill, *The Banana Empire*, 288.

15. Kepner and Soothill, *The Banana Empire*, 288–89.

16. Ibid., 289–90; Herrera and Romero, *La zona bananera*, 10–11.

17. LeGrand, "El conflicto," 198.

18. May and Plaza, *United States Business*, 17.

19. Botero and Guzman, "El enclave," 356–57.

20. Meisel and Posada-Carbó, "Bancos y banqueros."

21. See Mora, "Transformación."

22. Kepner and Soothill, *The Banana Empire*, 290. The amount of United Fruit loans was incredibly high by local standards. By 1921, the company had lent one million dollars to locals (see White, "The United Fruit Company," 19). The amount continued to increase as some studies suggest. According to Posada-Carbó, in 1931, the company was struggling to get loans for three million dollars repaid, and, by 1943, some growers still owed two million dollars. See Posada-Carbó, *The Colombian Caribbean*, 56.

23. White, "The United Fruit Company," 55.

24. Ibid., 56–59.

25. Corso, "El gravámen bananero," 63.

26. Posada-Carbó, "Imperialism," 16.

27. Information taken from interviews with former banana planters in Santa Marta and Ciénaga, July 1999.

28. Quoted by Posada-Carbó in *The Colombian Caribbean*, 56.

29. Interview with José Rafael Dávila, a former entrepreneur member of the landowning families in the banana zone. Santa Marta, June 1999. This view was shared by other landowning families interviewed in the region.

30. I had these impressions while doing my field research in Magdalena. A good study of the cultural life of the Ciénaga elite during the times of the banana boom before World War II can be found in LeGrand, "Living in Macondo."

31. Cepeda and Pardo, "La política exterior," 23.

32. Posada-Carbó has shown that during the 1920s there was a group of planters that also decided to invest their profits in other businesses. These included beer, cattle, and trade. *The Colombian Caribbean*, 204.

33. For a good study of the development of the city of Santa Marta before the banana boom, see Nichols, *Tres puertos*, 151–66.

34. Interviews with Luis Riascos, Eduardo Solano, and José Manuel Dávila. They were all members of families involved in the banana export business, and Riascos and Solano were exporters themselves. Santa Marta, July 1999.

35. Ibid.

36. Arthur, Houck, and Beckford, *Tropical Agribusiness*, 182. Although these authors only studied the imports of fruit to the United States, this data can be considered accurate because by that year, 100% of Colombian bananas were exported to the United States. See Valles, *The World Market*, 208.

37. Herrera and Romero, *La zona bananera*, 12.

38. Camara de Comercio de Santa Marta, Articles of Incorporation of the Federación de Productores de Banano de Magdalena, Santa Marta, 1952.

39. May and Plaza, *United States Business*, 76.

40. Ibid., 76.

41. Interview with Ismael Correa Diaz-Granados, former provider of United Fruit after World War II. Ciénaga, Magdalena, July 1999. He also wrote his memoirs, which include a description of everyday life in Ciénaga during the United Fruit era. See Correa Díaz-Granados, *Anotaciones*.

42. I got this impression by reading the contracts between the local planters and United Fruit, Federacion, and Consorcio Bananero held at the Notaría Primera de Santa Marta.

43. Interview with Rafael Pérez Dávila. Santa Marta, Magdalena, July 1999.

44. See White, "The United Fruit Company"; Botero and Guzmán, "El enclave agrícola"; and LeGrand, "El conflicto."

45. Calculation made using data taken from Arthur, Houck, and Beckford, *Tropical Agribusiness*, 55.

46. Posada-Carbó, *The Colombian Caribbean*, 56.

47. United Fruit Company—CFS, Monthly Report, Monthly Letter, Bosy to Mason, May 1967; Bosy to Chagnot, June 1967.

48. Ibid., Bosy to Ronan, July and October 1967.

49. Ibid., February 1968.

50. Ibid.

51. Ibid., Lascano to Mullin, December 1969.

52. White, *La United Fruit*, 120–21.

53. Castells, "Urbanización," 84–85.

54. Ellis, *Las transnacionales*, 174.

55. Valles, *The World Market*, 111–15.

56. Arthur, Houck, and Beckford, *Tropical Agribusiness*, 151.

57. Consorcio Bananero S.A., Informe de la Junta Directiva y del Gerente del Consorcio Bananero S.A. a la Asamblea General Extraordinaria de Accionistas, March 7, 1965.

58. Interview with Eduardo Solano, last manager of Consorcio Bananero. Santa Marta, Magdalena, July 1999.

59. Kamalprija, *Descriptive Survey*, 28; Consorcio Bananero S.A., Informe de la Junta Directiva, August 27, 1965.

60. Interview with Eduardo Solano, Consorcio's last manager, and Luis Riascos. Santa Marta, Magdalena, July 1999.

61. Consorcio Bananero, Memorando de la Comision de Bananeros para Enrique Blair, Ministro de Agricultura, Bogotá, August 3, 1967.

62. Herrera and Romero, *La zona bananera*, 13.

63. Incora and Ilaco, *Estado actual*, 2–5.

64. Interview with Eduardo Solano and Luis Riascos.

65. Ibid.

66. Consorcio Bananero, Asamblea de Accionistas, Acta 4, Santa Marta, September 10, 1966.

67. Consorcio Bananero, Asamblea de Accionistas, Acta 6, Santa Marta, March 30, 1967, 5.

68. Interview with former Magdalena congressman, Rafael Perez Dávila, Santa Marta, Magdalena, March 1999.

69. Consorcio Bananero, Asamblea de Accionistas, Acta 4, Santa Marta, September 10, 1966, 6–7.

70. Consorcio Bananero, Informe de la Junta Directiva y del Gerente de Consorcio Bananero S. A. a la Asamblea General de Accionistas para el Primer Semestre de 1967, 7.

71. Colombia—Superintendencia de Sociedades Anónimas. Expediente 267. Consorcio Bananero. Letter from Francisco Dávila, president of the board of directors of Consorcio Bananero to the president of Colombia, Carlos Lleras Restrepo, Santa Marta, August 10, 1968, 3.

72. Although a deeper study on the regional lobbying power is needed, the analysis of Adolfo Meisel on the presence of the Caribbean representatives in Colombian politics sheds light on how weak this lobbying could have been. See Meisel, "¿Por qué perdió?" 97–101.

73. *El Estado de Santa Marta*, various issues, 1967.

74. Consorcio Bananero. Informe de la Junta Directiva, October 28, 1967, 2.

75. Ibid.

76. Interviews with several former banana entrepreneurs. Santa Marta, Magdalena, July 1999.

77. Colombia. Superintendencia de Sociedades Anónimas. Expediente 267. Consorcio Bananero. Letter from Edgar Villafañe, chair of Operating Division, Ministerio de Agricultura, to Luis Carlos Diaz-Granados, chair of the Zona Agropecuaria de Santa Marta. Bogotá, August 14, 1968; Memorandum of Consorcio Bananero to the Junta de Rehabilitación y Desarrollo de la Zona Bananera de Santa Marta, February 2, 1970.

78. Bonet, *Las exportaciones*, 11.

79. Colombia. Superintendencia de Sociedades Anónimas. Expediente 267.

Consorcio Bananero, Letter from Nicolás Hernández to the director of the Superintendencia de Sociedades, Ciénaga, December 23, 1969; letter from Nicolás Hernández to the director of the Superintendencia de Sociedades, Ciénaga, December 21, 1970.

80. United Fruit changed its name to United Brands in 1970.

81. Colombia, *Evaluación 1973*, 191–98. Aware of the potential economic, social, and political problems a total economic collapse of the Magdalena region could create, the Colombian government created an agency in charge of the recovery of the banana zone called the Junta de Rehabilitación y Desarrollo de la Zona Bananera del Magdalena (Banadelma). See Colombia, "Programas Agrícolas para 1972," 143.

82. Herrera and Romero, *La zona bananera*, 14.

83. I found this difference when asking the entrepreneurs I interviewed for their backgrounds and the backgrounds of the other people involved in the business. The studies of LeGrand, "El conflicto"; Botero and Guzmán, "El enclave"; and White, "The United Fruit Company" describe the origins of the Magdalena elite. García, *Urabá*, shows the origins of the Urabá planters.

84. This contrast was evident when interviewing the people involved in the banana business in both Magdalena and Urabá during my field research trips to these regions.

85. Meisel, "¿Por qué perdió?" 97–101.

86. Garcia, *Urabá*, 38.

87. Kamalprija, *A Descriptive Survey*, 90–91.

88. For detailed information on how these loans were provided, see Kamalprija, *A Descriptive Survey*, 91; Garcia, *Urabá*, 38; and Goedicke, *The Colombian Banana*, 51–52. I also based this description on interviews with Aurelio Correa, former president of the Corporación Financiera de Desarrollo Industrial, Bogotá, June 1998; Andrés Restrepo, pioneer entrepreneur of Urabá, Bogotá, July 1999; Eliseo Restrepo, pioneer entrepreneur in Urabá, June 1998; and Irving Bernal, pioneer entrepreneur in Urabá, July 1999.

89. Arthur, Houck, and Beckford, *Tropical Agribusiness*, 65.

90. For a chronology of the events of this period, see Turbana, *A History*; and Uniban, *Informe*. I also used the interviews quoted in note 67.

91. Colombia, "Programas Agrícolas," 146. The report of the Ministry of Agriculture also proposed a loan of Col.$9,000.000 for the Magdalena growers through Banadelma.

92. United Nations—FAO, *The World Banana* (1971), 19. Uniban continued increasing its participation. In 1971, it exported 56% of the fruit, and, by 1973, it exported 58%. See, United Nations—FAO, *The World Banana* (1986), 15.

93. The United Nations report highlighted how favorable the conditions of Uniban were for using the depots and water transportation facilities of United Fruit. See ibid., 19.

94. Uniban, *Informe*, 12.

95. Uniban, *Informes y Balance 1979*, 5.

96. In 1998, I visited the industrial complex of Urabá and interviewed dozens of managers, technicians, and employees of all levels and in every stage of the production process. For the classic studies that suggest this kind of cause-consequence dynamic, see Furtado, *Development*; and Frank, *Capitalism*.

97. Sierra, *El cultivo*, 19.

98. Ibid.

99. Bonet, *Las exportaciones*, 12.

100. For a detailed account of this process see chapter 3.

101. For an analysis of this period based on a comparative study between the flower export sector and the banana export industry in Colombia, see Bucheli, Eslava, and Hofstetter, "Empresas multinacionales."

102. Sierra, *El cultivo*, 24.

103. Author's calculation made with information from Montoya, *Anuario*, 31.

104. Sierra, *El cultivo*, 22.

NOTES TO CHAPTER 8

1. Some other important factors still need to be studied for this period regarding the operations of United Fruit in Colombia, such as the cultural and social impact of the presence of the company in this country.

2. Steve Striffler also shows how the locals' agency in Ecuador strongly affected the way United Fruit operated in that country. See, Striffler, *In the Shadows*. The adaptation of foreign multinational corporations to the local social, cultural, and political conditions has been studied for other sectors in other areas of the world. Scholars studying the manufacturing sector for the case of Singer, General Motors, IBM, and Ford have found how the companies' headquarters gave great freedom to their subsidiaries so they could adapt their companies' operations and corporate culture to the realities of their host country. See Dassbach, *Global Enterprises*; and Carstensen, *American Enterprise*.

3. Several nineteenth-century Latin American leaders praised the benefits of modernization through foreign capital, ideas, and culture to overcome what they perceived as the "barbarism" that dominated those societies. The best example can be found in the writings of Argentinian leader, Domingo Sarmiento in *Life in the Argentine*.

4. The number of works criticizing foreign influence in Latin America written in the nineteenth and twentieth centuries is vast, and any attempt to reduce them to a short list would do injustice the immense number of important and influential works on this topic. However, the early essays of José Martí, Francisco Bil-

bao, José Rodó, José Carlos Mariátegui, and José Vasconcellos can be considered a starting point. A good collection of these authors' writings can be found in Burns, *Latin America*.

5. See Lenin, "Imperialism."

6. Some of the classic works on this subject are Cardoso and Faletto, *Dependency*; Frank, *Capitalism*; Bendaña, *British Capital*; Dos Santos, *Imperialismo y dependencia* and *Imperialismo y empresas*; Evans, *Dependent Development*.

7. See Weinstein, *The Amazon*; O'Brien, *The Nitrate Industry*; Monteón, *Chile*.

8. The works of Dye and Ayala significantly contributed to this area by studying the sugar multinational corporations' local providers as profit-seeking entrepreneurs that made rational decisions when signing contracts with foreign companies in Cuba and Puerto Rico. See Dye, *Cuban Sugar*; and Ayala, *American Sugar*.

9. For this line of analysis, see Haber, *How Latin America Fell Behind*; and Coatsworth and Taylor, *Latin America*. Other works that challenge the traditional *dependentista* view on foreign investment and international economic relations of Latin America are Salvucci, *Latin America*; Bushnell and Macaulay, *The Emergence*; Davis and Cull, *International Capital*; Blakemore, *British Nitrates*; Mayo, *British Merchants*; Miller, *Britain*; and the works of Platt, *Business Imperialism*, *Trade*, and *Latin America*.

10. For a discussion on how the business-historical studies on multinational corporations can contribute to wider political and economic studies, see Hertner and Jones, "Multinationals."

11. The 1980s are known as the "lost decade" in Latin America because of the region's poor economic performance.

# Bibliography

PUBLISHED BOOKS AND ARTICLES

Abel, Christopher. and Colin Lewis, ed. *Latin America, Economic Imperialism, and the State: The Political Economy of the External Connection from Independence to the Present.* London: Dover, 1985.

Acevedo, Albeiro. "La producción bananera en Urabá: una economía de enclave?" *Revista Antioqueña de Economía,* January–March 1984.

Adams, Frederick U. *The Conquest of the Tropics.* New York: Page, 1914.

Arango, Carlos. *Sobrevivientes de las Bananeras.* Bogotá: Colombia Nueva, 1981.

Argueta, Mario. *Bananos y política: Samuel Zemurray y la Cuyamel Fruit Company en Honduras.* Tegucigalpa: Editorial Universitaria/Universidad Autónoma de Honduras, 1987.

Arthur, Henry B., James P. Houck, and George L. Beckford. *Tropical Agribusiness Structures and Adjustments: Bananas.* Boston: Harvard Business School, 1968.

Asturias, Miguel Angel. *El Papa Verde.* Barcelona: Salvat, 1971.

———. *Hombres de maíz.* Buenos Aires: Losada, 1966.

———. *The President.* London: Harmondsworth-Penguin, 1963.

Ayala, César. *American Sugar Kingdom: The Plantation Economy of the Spanish Caribbean, 1898–1934.* Chapel Hill: University of North Carolina Press, 1999.

Backus, Richard, and Eder Phanor. *A Guide to the Law and Legal Literature of Colombia.* Washington, D.C.: Library of Congress, 1948.

"Banana Republican," *Economist,* November 18, 1995.

Barbero, María Inés. "Business History in Latin America: Issues and Debates," in Jones, Geoffrey and Franco Amatori, ed. *Business History around the World.* Cambridge: Cambridge University Press, 2003.

Bartres, Alejandra. *The Experience of the Guatemalan United Fruit Company Workers, 1944–54: Why Did They Fail?* Austin: University of Texas Press, 1995.

Bejarano, Ana María. "Violencia regional y sus protagonistas: el caso de Urabá." *Análisis Político* 4, 1994.

Bendaña, Alejandro. *British Capital and Argentine Dependence, 1816–1914.* New York: Garland, 1988.

Bergquist, Charles. *Coffee and Conflict in Colombia, 1886–1910.* Durham: Duke University Press, 1978.

Blakemore, Harold. *British Nitrates and Chilean Politics, 1886–1896.* London: Institute of Latin American Studies, 1974.

Bonet, Jaime. *Las exportaciones colombianas de banano, 1950–1998.* Cartagena: Banco de la República, 2000.

Bonilla, Heraclio. *Guano y burguesía en el Perú: el contraste de la experiencia peruana con las economías de exportación del Ecuador y de Bolivia.* Quito: FLACSO, 1994.

Botero, Fernando, and Alvaro Guzmán. "En enclave agrícola en la Zona Bananera de Santa Marta," *Cuadernos Colombianos* 8, 1977.

Botero, Fernando, and Diego Sierra. *El mercado de la fuerza de trabajo en la zona bananera de Urabá.* Medellín: Universidad de Antioquia, 1981.

Bourgois, Philipe. *Ethnicity at Work: Divided Labor on a Central American Banana Plantation.* Baltimore: Johns Hopkins University Press, 1989.

Brewer, James. "Kantor Probes EU Banana Import System," *Lloyd's List*, October 9, 1994.

Brungardt, Maurice. "Jorge Eliécer Gaitán: La masacre de las bananeras," *Revista de Estudios Colombianos* 6, 1990.

———. "The United Fruit Company in Colombia," in Dethloff, Henry, and Joseph Pusateri, *American Business History: Case Studies.* Arlington Heights: Harlan Davidson, 1987.

Bucheli, Marcelo. *Empresas multinacionales y enclaves agrícolas: el caso de United Fruit en Magdalena y Urabá, Colombia, 1948–1968.* Bogotá: Universidad de los Andes-Facultad de Administración, 1994.

———. "La crisis del enclave bananero de Magdalena durante los sesenta," *Revista Historia Crítica* 5, 1992.

———. "United Fruit Company in Colombia: Impact of Labor Relations and Governmental Regulations on its Operations, 1948–1968," *Essays in Business and Economic History* 15, 1997.

———. "United Fruit in Latin America," in Steve Striffler and Mark Moberg, *Banana Wars: Power Production and History in the Americas.* Durham: Duke University Press, 2003.

Bulmer-Thomas, Victor. *The Economic History of Latin America Since Independence.* Cambridge: Cambridge University Press, 1994.

———. *The Political Economy of Central America Since 1920.* Cambridge: Cambridge University Press, 1987.

Burns, Bradford. *Latin America: Conflict and Creation: A Historical Reader.* Englewood Cliffs: Prentice Hall, 1993.

Bushnell, David. *The Making of Modern Colombia: A Nation in Spite of Itself.* Berkeley: University of California Press, 1993.

Bushnell, David, and Neill Macaulay. *The Emergence of Latin America in the Nineteenth Century.* Oxford: Oxford University Press, 1994.

Cardoso, Fernando H., and Enzo Faletto. *Dependency and Development in Latin America.* Berkeley: University of California Press, 1979.

Carstensen, Fred. *American Enterprise in Foreign Markets: Studies of Singer and International Harvester in Imperial Russia.* Chapel Hill: University of North Carolina Press, 1984.

Castells, Manuel. "Urbanización Dependiente en América Latina," in Martha Schteingart, ed. *Urbanización y Dependencia.* Buenos Aires: Ediciones Nueva Visión, 1973.

Castrillón, Alberto. *Ciento veinte días bajo el terror militar.* Bogotá: Editorial Tupac Amaru, 1974.

Castro, Fidel. *Ché: A Memoir by Fidel Castro.* Melbourne: Ocean Press, 1991.

Cepeda, Fernando, and Rodrigo Pardo. "La política exterior colombiana (1930–1946)," in Alvaro Tirado, ed. *Nueva Historia de Colombia,* vol. 3. Bogotá: Planeta, 1989.

Cepeda Samudio, Alvaro. *La casa grande.* Buenos Aires: J. Alvarez, 1967.

Chandler, Alfred D. "The Emergence of Managerial Capitalism," *Business History Review* 58, 1980.

———. "The Growth of the Transnational Industrial Firm in the United States and the United Kingdom: A Comparative Analysis," *Economic History Review* 58, 1984.

———. *Scale and Scope.* Cambridge: Harvard University Press, 1990.

———. *The Visible Hand.* Cambridge: Harvard University Press, 1977.

Chomsky, Aviva. *West Indian Workers and the United Fruit Company in Costa Rica, 1870–1940.* Baton Rouge: Louisiana State University, 1996.

Clairmonte, Frederick F. "El imperio de la banana," *Augura* 3.

Coatsworth, John. *Central America and the United States: The Clients and the Colossus.* New York: Twayne, 1994.

Coatsworth, John, and Alan M. Taylor, ed. *Latin America and the World Economy since 1800.* Cambridge: Harvard University Press, 1999.

Collymore, Yvette. "Trade-Bananas: U.S. Backs Off Dispute with Colombia and Costa Rica." *Inter Press Service,* January 10, 1996.

"Colombia Warns against Banana Sanctions," *United Press International,* January 20, 1995.

"Colombian Government Rejects US Investigations of Banana Exports," *Inter Press Service,*

"Colombia—Estados Unidos—UE: Preocupación por efecto de roce comercial por banano a la UE," *EFE,* December 22, 1998.

Comisión Andina de Juristas, Seccional Colombiana. *Informes regionales de derechos humanos: Urabá*. Bogotá: Comisión Andina de Juristas, 1994.

Correa Díaz-Granados, Ismael. *Anotaciones para una historia de Ciénaga (Magdalena)*. Medellín: Editorial Lealon, 1996.

Cortés Vargas, Carlos. *Los sucesos de las bananeras*. Bogotá: Editorial Desarrollo, 1979.

Crutsinger, Martin. "Costa Rica and Colombia Avoid Trade Sanctions for Now in Banana Dispute," *Associated Press*, January 10, 1996.

Dassbach, Carl. *Global Enterprises and the World Economy: Ford, General Motors, and IBM, the Emergence of the Transnational Enterprise*. New York: Garland, 1989.

Danilo, Héctor. *La CIA, Washington, y las transnacionales*. Havana: Editorial de Ciencias Sociales, 1977.

Davies, Peter N. *Fyffes and the Banana: Musa Sapientum, A Centenary History, 1888–1998*. London: Athlone Press, 1990.

Dávila, Carlos, and Rory Miller, ed. *Business History in Latin America: The Experience of Seven Countries*. Liverpool: University of Liverpool, 1999.

Davis, Lance, and Robert Cull. *International Capital Markets and American Economic Growth, 1820–1914*. Cambridge: Cambridge University Press, 1996.

"El dólar libre salva a la industria," *Economía Colombiana* 35, vol. 11, March 1957.

Dosal, Paul. *Doing Business with the Dictators: A Political History of United Fruit in Guatemala, 1899–1944*. Wilmington: Scholarly Resources, 1993.

Dos Santos, Theotonio. *Imperialismo y dependencia*. Mexico: Ediciones Era, 1978.

———. *Imperialismo y empresas multinacionales*. Buenos Aires: Galerna, 1973.

Drake, Paul W. *The Money Doctor in the Andes: The Kemmerer Missions, 1923–1933*. Durham: Duke University Press, 1989.

Dye, Alan. *Cuban Sugar in the Age of Mass Production: Technology and the Economics of the Sugar Central, 1899–1929*. Stanford: Stanford University Press, 1998.

Ellis, Frank. *Las transnacionales del banano en Centroamérica*. San José: Editorial Universitaria Centroamericana, 1983.

Euraque, Darío A. *Reinterpreting the Banana Republic: Region and State in Honduras, 1870–1972*. Chapel Hill: University of North Carolina Press, 1996.

Evans, Peter. *Dependent Development: The Alliance of Multinational, State, and Local Capital in Brazil*. Princeton: Princeton University Press, 1979.

Fajardo, Darío. *Haciendas, campesinos, y políticas agrarias en Colombia, 1920–1980*. Bogotá: Oveja Negra, 1986.

Folsom, Victor. "The Taking by a State of the Property, Acquired Right, or Other Interest of a Foreign National When No Contract Is Involved," in *Rights and Duties of Private Investors Abroad*. Dallas: The South-Western Legal Foundation, 1965.

Fonnegra, Gabriel. *Bananeras: Un testimonio vivo*. Bogotá: Círculo de Lectores, 1986.

Frank, Andre Gunder. *Capitalism and Underdevelopment in Latin America: Historical Studies on Chile and Brazil*. New York: Monthly Review Press, 1967.

Friede, Juan. "La conquista del territorio y el poblamiento," in *Manual de Historia de Colombia*, vol. 1. Bogotá: Instituto Colombiano de Cultura, 1982.

Furtado, Celso. *Development and Underdevelopment*. Berkeley: University of California Press, 1964.

Furubotn, Eirik G., and Rudolf Richter. *Institutions and Economic Theory: The Contributions of the New Institutional Economics*. Ann Arbor: University of Michigan Press, 1997.

García, Clara Inés. *Urabá: Región, actores y conflicto, 1960–1990*. Medellín: Universidad de Antioquia—Instituto de Estudios Regionales, 1996.

García Márquez, Gabriel. *Cien Años de Soledad*. Bogotá: Editorial Norma, 1997 [1967].

———. *La Hojarasca*. Bogotá: Editorial Zipa, 1955.

Gilhodes, Pierre. "La Colombie et l'United Fruit Company," *Revue Francaise de Science Politique*, 1967: 307–17.

Gliejeses, Piero. *Shattered Hope: The Guatemalan Revolution and the United States, 1944–1954*. Princeton: Princeton University Press, 1991.

Glover, David, and Carlos Larrea. "Changing Comparative Advantage, Short-Term Instability and Long-Term Change in the Latin American Banana Industry," *Canadian Journal of Latin American and Caribbean Studies*, vol. 16, no. 32, 1991.

Goedicke, Peter T. *The Colombian Banana Export Industry: Production and Market Patterns*. Bogotá: Instituto Latinoamericano de Mercadeo Agrícola (ILMA), 1966.

Guhl, Ernesto. *Colombia: Bosquejo de su geografía tropical*. Rio de Janeiro: Instituto Panamericano de Geografia e Historia, 1967.

Haber, Stephen, ed. *How Latin America Fell Behind: Essays on the Economic Histories of Brazil and Mexico, 1800–1914*. Stanford: Stanford University Press, 1997.

Hamilton, Shane. "The Economies and Conveniences of Modern-Day Living: Frozen Foods and Mass Marketing, 1945–1965," *Business History Review* 77, 2003: 33–60.

Harding, James. "U.S. Banana Exporters File 301 Petition." *Financial Times* (London), September 8, 1984.

Herrera Soto, Roberto, and Rafael Romero Castañeda. *La Zona Bananera del Magdalena: Historia y Léxico.* Bogotá: Instituto Caro y Cuervo, 1979.

Hertner, Peter, and Geoffrey Jones. "Multinationals: Theory and History," in Peter Hertner and Geoffrey Jones. *Multinationals: Theory and History.* London: Gower, 1986.

Instituto Colombiano para la Reforma Agraria (Incora) and International Land Development Consultants (Ilaco), *Estado actual y perspectivas agroeconómicas de la Zona Bananera de Santa Marta y el area de influencia en el Departamento del Magdalena (Proyecto Magdalena 4).* Bogotá: Incora, 1967.

Jenkins, Virginia S. *Bananas: An American History.* Washington, D.C.: Smithsonian Institute, 2000.

Jimenez, Margarita, and Sandro Sideri. *Historia regional de Colombia.* Bogotá: Universidad de los Andes/CIDER, 1985.

Josling, Timothy. *Banana Wars: Anatomy of a Trade Dispute.* Cambridge: CABI, 2003.

Kalmanovitz, Salomón. *Economía y nación: una breve historia de Colombia.* Bogotá: Siglo XXI/Universidad Nacional/CINEP, 1988.

Kamalprija, Val. *Descriptive Survey of the Colombian Banana Market Structure for Export.* Bogotá: Instituto Latinoamericano de Mercadeo Agrícola, 1966.

Karnes, Thomas L. *Tropical Enterprise: The Standard Fruit and Steamship Company in Latin America.* Baton Rouge: Louisiana State University Press, 1978.

Kepner, Charles D., and Jay Soothill. *The Banana Empire: A Case Study of Economic Imperialism.* New York: Vanguard Press, 1935.

Kujawa, Duane. *The Labour Relations of U.S. Multinationals Abroad: Comparative and Prospective Views.* New York: United Nations, World Trade Organization, 1980.

LaBarge, Richard. *Impact of the United Fruit Company on the Economic Development of Guatemala, 1946–1954.* New Orleans: Tulane University, 1968.

Lamoreaux, Naomi. *The Great Merger Movement in American Business, 1895–1904.* Cambridge: Cambridge University Press, 1985.

Lane, Patti. "Kantor Rejects Colombian Offer to Raise Banana Quota to EU," *Journal of Commerce,* May 12, 1995.

Langley, Lester D., and Thomas Schoonover. *The Banana Men: American Mercenaries and Entrepreneurs in Central America, 1880–1930.* Lexington: University of Kentucky Press, 1995.

Larrea, Carlos. *El banano en el Ecuador: transnacionales, modernización y subdesarrollo.* Quito: FLACSO, 1987.

———. "Los cambios recientes en el subsistema bananero ecuatoriano y sus consecuencias sobre los trabajadores: 1977–1984," in FLACSO, *Cambio y continuidad en la economía bananera.* San Jose: FLACSO, 1988.

"Latin American Nations Mostly Praise New EU–U.S. Banana Deal," *Agence France Presse.* April 12, 2001.

LeGrand, Catherine. "Campesinos y asalariados en la zona bananera de Santa Marta (1900–1935)." *Anuario Colombiano de Historia Social y de la Cultura* 11, 1983: 235–50.

———. "El conflicto de las bananeras," in Alvaro Tirado, ed. *Nueva Historia de Colombia*, vol. 3. Bogotá: Planeta, 1989.

———. "Living in Macondo," in Joseph M. Gilbert, Catherine LeGrand, and Ricardo Salvatore. *Close Encounters of the Empire Kind: Writing the Cultural History of U.S.–Latin American Relations*. Durham: Duke University Press, 1998.

Lenin, Vladimir. "Imperialism: The Latest Stage of Capitalism," in *Essential Works of Lenin*. New York: Bantam Books, 1966 [1916].

Levenstein, Harvey. *Paradox of Plenty: A Social History of Eating in Modern America*. Oxford: Oxford University Press, 1993.

Lever, Rob. "Three-Way Banana Dispute Heats Up with EU, U.S., and Latin America," *Agence France Presse*, February 15, 1995.

Londoño, Rocío. "Crisis y recomposición del sindicalismo colombiano (1946–1980)," in Alvaro Tirado, ed. *Nueva Historia de Colombia*, vol. 3. Bogotá: Planeta, 1989.

López, José Roberto. *La economía del banano en Centroamérica*. San José: Editorial DEI, 1986.

Maggs, John. "Dole May Use Budget Bill to Strip Colombia of Trade Benefits," *Journal of Commerce*, October 5, 1995.

Marx, Karl. *Capital*. Provo: Regal Publications, 1993.

May, Stacy, and Galo Plaza. *United States Business Performance Abroad: The Case Study of the United Fruit Company in Latin America*. Washington, D.C.: National Planning Association, 1958.

Mayo, John. *British Merchants and Chilean Development*. Barbados: Westview Press, 1987.

McCameron, Robert. *Bananas, Labor, and Politics in Honduras: 1954–1963*. Syracuse: Syracuse University Press, 1983.

McCann, Thomas. *An American Company: The Tragedy of United Fruit*. New York: Crown, 1976.

McIntosh, Elaine N. *American Food Habits in Historical Perspective*. London: Praeger, 1995.

Meisel, Adolfo. "¿Por qué perdió la Costa Caribe el Siglo XX?" in Haroldo Calvo and Adolfo Meisel, ed. *El Rezago de la Costa Caribe Colombiana*. Bogotá: Banco de la Republica, 1999.

Meisel, Adolfo, and Eduardo Posada-Carbó. "Bancos y banqueros de Barranquilla," *Boletín Cultural y Bibliográfico de la Biblioteca Luis Angel Arango*, vol. 25, no. 17, 1988.

Miller, Rory. *Britain in Latin America in the Nineteenth and Twentieth Centuries*. London: Longman, 1993.

Monteón, Michael. *Chile in the Nitrate Era*. Madison: University of Wisconsin Press, 1982.

Montoya, Fernando A., comp. *Anuario Estadístico Bananero, 1985–1994*. Medellín: Augura, 1995.

Mora, Mauricio. "Transformación del sistema bancario colombiano, 1924–1931," *Desarrollo y Sociedad* 30, 1992.

Neruda, Pablo. *Canto General*. Berkeley: University of California Press, 1991.

Nichols, Theodore E. *Tres puertos de Colombia: Estudio sobre el desarrollo de Cartagena, Santa Marta y Barranquilla*. Bogotá: Biblioteca Banco Popular, 1973.

O'Brien, Thomas. *The Nitrate Industry and Chile's Crucial Transition, 1870–1891*. New York: NYU Press, 1982.

Orozco, Constance. *The United Fruit Company in Central America: A Bargaining Power Analysis*. Austin: Institute of Latin American Studies, University of Texas, 1991.

Pardo, Alberto. *Geografía económica y humana de Colombia*. Bogotá: Tercer Mundo, 1972.

Parsons, James. *Urabá: Salida de Antioquia al mar*. Bogotá: Banco de la República, 1979.

Platt, Desmond C. M. *Business Imperialism, 1840–1930: An Inquiry Based on British Experience in Latin America*. Oxford: Clarendon, 1977.

———. *Latin America and the British Trade, 1806–1914*. London: A and C, 1972.

———. *Trade and Politics in British Foreign Policy, 1815–1914*. Oxford: Clarendon, 1968.

Posada-Carbó, Eduardo. *The Colombian Caribbean: A Regional History, 1870–1950*. Oxford: Oxford University Press, 1996.

Presa Fernández, Julián. *Aportes para la historia de la UPEB*. Panama: UPEB, n.d.

"Prettying Up Chiquita," *Time International*, September 3, 1973, 40.

Ramírez, William. *Urabá: Los inciertos confines de una crisis*. Bogotá: Planeta, 1997.

Read, Robert. "The Growth and Structure of Multinationals in the Banana Export Trade," in Mark Casson, ed. *The Growth of International Business*. London: Allen and Unwin, 1983.

Reynolds, Philip K. *The Banana: Its History, Cultivation, and Place among Staple Foods*. Boston: Houghton Mifflin, 1927.

Ricord, Humberto. *Panamá y la frutera: una batalla contra el colonialismo*. Panama City: Editorial Universitaria de Panamá, 1974.

Roche, Julian. *The International Banana Trade*. Cambridge: Woodhead, 1998.

Rodríguez, Hugo. *De como fue reprimida violentamente la primera gran lucha de los obreros colombianos: la masacre de las bananeras contra el imperialismo norteamericano, 1928.* Bogotá: Ediciones siete de enero, 1974.

Rodríguez-Clare, Andrés. "Multinationals, Linkages, and Economic Development," *American Economic Review*, vol. 86, no. 4, 1996.

Salvucci, Richard. *Latin America and the World Economy: Dependency and Beyond.* Lexington: D. C. Heath, 1996

Samudio, Alvaro. *La casa grande.* Buenos Aires: J. Alvarez, 1967.

Sanger, David. "Dole at the Forefront of Trade Battle to Aid Donor's Banana Empire," *New York Times*, December 5, 1995.

Sarmiento, Domingo F. *Life in the Argentine Republic in the Days of the Tyrants: Or, Civilization and Barbarism.* New York: Hafner, n.d.

Schlesinger, Stephen, and Stephen Kinzer. *Bitter Fruit: The Untold Story of the American Coup in Guatemala.* New York: Anchor, 1990.

"Senator Dole: Frequent Flier in Battle for Chiquita Bananas," *Associated Press.* December 5, 1995.

Sierra, Luis Eduardo. *El cultivo del banano: producción y comercio.* Medellín: Gráfica Olímpica, 1993.

Stanley, Diane K. *For the Record: The United Fruit Company's Sixty-Six Years in Guatemala.* Guatemala: Centro Impresor Piedra Santa, 1994.

Stein, Nicholas. "Yes, We Have No Profits: The Rise and Fall of Chiquita Banana: How a Great American Brand Lost Its Way," *Fortune*, vol. 144, no. 11, November 26, 2001.

Stovall, John G., and Dale E. Hathaway. "U.S. Interests in the Banana Trade Controversy," in Timothy E. Josling and Timothy G. Taylor, *Banana Wars: The Anatomy of a Trade Dispute.* Cambridge: CABI, 2003.

Striffler, Steve. *In the Shadows of State and Capital: The United Fruit Company, Popular Struggle, and Agrarian Restructuring in Ecuador, 1900–1995.* Durham: Duke University Press, 2002.

Tangermann, Stefan. "European Interests in the Banana Market," in Timothy E. Josling and Timothy G. Taylor. *Banana Wars: The Anatomy of a Trade Dispute.* Cambridge: CABI, 2003.

Taylor, Timothy. "Evolution of the Banana Multinationals," in Timothy E. Josling and Timothy G. Taylor. *Banana Wars: The Anatomy of a Trade Dispute.* Cambridge: CABI, 2003.

Tirado, Alvaro. *Introducción a la historia económica de Colombia.* Bogotá: Universidad Nacional, 1971.

———, ed. *Nueva Historia de Colombia.* Bogotá: Planeta, 1989.

Turbana. *A History of Turbana and Uniban and Banana Growing in Colombia.* Medellín: Elena Mogollón, n.d.

"La UPEB, inversión extranjera y empresas multinacionales," *Augura*, vol. 2, no. 5.

Uribe, María Teresa. *Urabá: región o territorio.* Medellín: Universidad de Antioquia, 1992.

Urrá, Pedro. *La guerra del banano: de la Mamita Yunai a la UPEB*. Buenos Aires: Colección Tierra Nueva, 1975.

Urrutia, Miguel. *Historia del sindicalismo en Colombia*. Bogotá: Universidad de los Andes, 1969.

"U.S. to Withhold Sanctions in Tri-Continental Banana Rift," *New York Times*, January 11, 1996.

Vallejo Mejía, Hernán. *Productos básicos, dependencia y subdesarrollo: el problema bananero*. Bogotá: Tercer Mundo, 1982.

Valles, Jean-Paul. *The World Market for Bananas, 1964–72*. New York: Praeger, 1968.

Weinstein, Barbara. *The Amazon Rubber Boom, 1850–1920*. Stanford: Stanford University Press, 1983.

Weisskoff, Richard, and Edward Wolff. "Linkages and Leakages: Industrial Tracking in an Enclave Economy," *Economic Development and Cultural Change*, vol. 4, no. 25, July 1977.

White, Judith. *La United Fruit en Colombia: historia de una ignominia*. Bogotá: Editorial Presencia, 1978.

Wilkins, Mira. *The Emergence of Multinational Enterprise: American Business Abroad from the Colonial Era to 1914*. Cambridge: Harvard University Press, 1970.

———. *The Maturing of Multinational Enterprise: American Business Abroad from 1914 to 1970*. Cambridge: Harvard University Press, 1974.

Zamosc, León. *The Agrarian Question and the Peasant Movement in Colombia: Struggles of the National Peasant Association, 1967–1981*. Cambridge: Cambridge University Press, 1986.

Zanetti, Oscar, and Alejandro García, ed. *United Fruit Company: un caso de dominio imperialista en Cuba*. Havana: Editorial de Ciencias Sociales, 1976.

## UNPUBLISHED RESEARCH DOCUMENTS

Barham, Bradford. "Excess Capacity in International Markets: An Application to the Banana Industry in Latin America." Diss., Stanford, 1988.

Benavides, Eduardo. "Urabá: Gobierno, guerrilla y multinacionales en el proceso socio-economico de produccion bananera." MS, Universidad de San Buenaventura, Medellín, 1996.

Bucheli, Marcelo. "La teoría de la acumulación originaria del capital y su aplicación al caso de United Fruit Company en Magdalena, Colombia." MS, Universidad de los Andes, 1991.

Bucheli, Marcelo, Marcela Eslava, and Marc Hofstetter. "Empresas multinacionales y comercializadoras locales: un estudio comparativo entre los sectores floricultor y bananero en Colombia." MS, Universidad de los Andes, 1998.

Colombia. Ministerio de Agricultura, "Programas Agrícolas para 1972." MS, Oficina de Planeamiento del Sector Agropecuario (OPSA), Bogotá, 1972.

Corso, Adriana. "El gravámen bananero: un caso de historia política en el Magdalena, 1925–1930." MS, Universidad del Norte, Barranquilla, Colombia, 1996.

Krogzemis, James. "A Historical Geography of the Santa Marta Area, Colombia." Diss., University of California, Berkeley, 1967.

Marín, Freddy. "Configuración del Municipio de Chigorodó como objetivo de planificación." MS, Universidad Nacional de Colombia, Medellín, 1991.

Martin, Gerard. "Desarrollo económico, sindicalismo y proceso de paz en Urabá." MS, Universidad de los Andes, School of Business, 1986.

Posada-Carbó, Eduardo. "Imperialism, Local Elites, and Regional Development: The United Fruit Company in Colombia Reconsidered, 1900–1945." MS, University of London, n.d.

Read, Ian. "Reinterpreting the United Fruit Company: The Role of the U.S. Government and American Popular Perception." MS, Stanford University, 2000.

Robinson, James. "Hold-Up in the Tropics: United Fruit Company in Magdalena and Urabá, Colombia." MS, University of California, Berkeley, 2001.

Van de Kasteele, Adelien. "The Banana Chain: The Macroeconomics of the Banana Trade." MS, Amsterdam, 1998.

White, Judith. "The United Fruit Company in the Santa Marta Banana Zone, Colombia: Conflicts of the '20s." MS, Oxford University, 1971.

PRIMARY SOURCES

Statistical

Colombia. Contraloría General de la República. *Anuario General de Estadística.* Bogotá, various issues, 1928–49.

Colombia. Departamento Administrativo Nacional de Estadística. *Anuario de Comercio Exterior.* Bogotá, various issues, 1950–70.

Comisión Económica para America Latina (CEPAL), *Boletín Estadístico de América Latina.* Santiago: CEPAL, 1960.

International Monetary Fund, *International Financial Statistics.* Washington, D.C., various issues, 1965–70.

Moody's Investor Service, *Moody's Stock Survey.* New York, various issues, 1936–70.

Organization of American States. *Sectoral Study of Transnational Enterprises in Latin America: The Banana Industry*. Washington, D.C., 1975.

Putnam, Judith J., and Jane E. Allshouse. *Food Consumption, Prices, and Expenditures, 1970–1997*. Washington, D.C.: USDA, 1999.

Standard and Poor's, *Standard Corporation Description*. New York, 1962 and 1968.

United Nations, Economic Commission for Latin America. "Evolución y Perspectivas del Mercado Internacional del Banano," *Revista Económica de la CEPAL*, vol. 3, no. 2, October 1958.

———. Food and Agriculture Organization [FAO]. *La economía mundial del banano 1970–1984: estructura, desempeño y perspectivas*. Rome, 1986.

———. Committee on Commodity Problems, *The Market for "Organic" and "Fair-Trade" Bananas*. Rome, 2001.

———. *Intergovernmental group on bananas and on tropical fruits, Russian Banana Market in 1994–1998*. Rome, 1999.

———. Food and Agriculture Organization [FAO]. *The World Banana Economy*. Rome: United Nations, FAO, 1971.

———. *The World Banana Economy, 1970–1984*. Rome, 1986.

U.S. Department of Agriculture, Bureau of Statistics, Bulletin 74, *Imports of Farm Products into the United States, 1851–1908*. Washington: U.S. Department of Agriculture, 1909.

———. *U.S. Food Consumption: Sources of Data and Trends, 1909–63*. Washington, D.C., 1965.

———. Economic Research Service, *U.S. Food Consumption*, Statistical Bulletin 364. Washington, D.C., 1965.

*Wall Street Journal*. "Stock Exchange Quotes." Various issues, 1936–70.


Corporate Documents

*Consorcio Bananero (Colombia)*

Colombia. Superintendencia de Sociedades Anónimas. File 267: Consorcio Bananero S.A., Informe de la Junta Directiva y del Gerente del Consorcio Bananero S.A. a la Asamble General Extraordinaria de Accionistas reunida el 7 de marzo de 1965, el 27 de agosto de 1965, el primer semestre de 1967.

———. Memorando de la Comisión de Bananeros para Enrique Blair, Ministro de Agricultura, Bogotá, Agosto 3, 1967.

———. Asamblea de Accionistas, Acta 4, Santa Marta, Septiembre 10, 1966.

———. Asamblea de Accionistas, Acta 6, Santa Marta, Marzo 30, 1967.

———. Letter from Francisco Dávila, president of the board of directors to the president of Colombia, Carlos Lleras Restrepo, Santa Marta, August 10, 1968.

————. Letter from Edgar Villafañe, chair of Operating Division, Ministerio de Agricultura, to Luis Carlos Díaz-Granados, chair of the Zona Agropecuaria de Santa Marta. Bogotá, August 14, 1968.

————. Memorandum of Consorcio Bananero to the Junta de Rehabilitación y Desarrollo de la Zona Bananera de Santa Marta, February 2, 1970.

————. Letter from Nicolás Hernández to the director of the Superintendencia de Sociedades, Ciénaga, December 23, 1969, December 21, 1970.

*United Fruit Company*

Annual Report *to the Stockholders*, various issues, 1900–1970.

CFS. "Detail Contribution and Welfare Expenses Requested by Mr. J. R. Herbig's Radiogram of January 17, 1964."

CFS. "Land Investigation of Urabá Lands at Turbo." Various Reports, 1960–1962.

CFS. *Management Comments*. December 1967.

CFS (Colombia Division). Monthly Report, Monthly Letters:

Honiball to Sisto, April 1948–May 1949

Hall to Sisto, June 1949–December 1957

Hall to Carpenter, December 1958–September 1960

MacMillan to Carpenter, October 1960–December 1960

MacMillan to Walwood, January 1961–April 1965

Bosy to Walwood, May 1965

MacMillan to Walwood, June 1965–August 1965

Bosy to Walwood, September 1965–December 1965

Bosy to Chagnot, March 1966–December 1966

Bosy to Mason, April 1967–May 1967

Bosy to Chagnot, June 1967

Bosy to Ronan, July 1967–May 1968.

Lascano to Mullin, October 1967–December 1969

CFS. "Monthly Report, Analysis of Banana Operations, Profit and Loss," Colombia Division (Santa Marta-Turbo), various reports, 1948–1968.

*Unión de Bananeros de Urabá*

Uniban. Informe Anual a los Accionistas. Medellín, various issues, 1968–78.

Uniban. Informe sobre Uniban. Medellín. No date.

Uniban. Informe sobre Uniban. Medellín: Uniban, 1980.

## Government and Notary Records

Colombia. *Constitución Nacional de la República de Colombia.* Bogotá: Imprenta Nacional, 1986.

Colombia. Ministerio de Agricultura. *Evaluación 1973, Programación 1974, Proyecciones 1975.* Bogotá: Oficina de Planeamiento del Sector Agropecuario, OPSA, 1973.

Colombia. Ministerio de Hacienda. *Memoria de Hacienda.* Bogotá: Imprenta Nacional, 1962, 1970.

Colombia. Ministerio de Hacienda. "Intervención del Sr. Ministro de Hacienda Dr. Carlos Sanz de Santamaría, correspondiente a la sesión vespertina de la Cámara de Representantes del 25 de julio de 1963." In *Memoria de Hacienda.* Bogotá: Imprenta Nacional, 1964.

Colombia, Ministerio de Hacienda, "Dirección General de Aduanas. Contabilidad de Bienes Fiscales." In *Memoria de Hacienda.* Bogotá: Imprenta Nacional, 1964.

Notaría Primera de Santa Marta (Magdalena, Colombia), Purchase contracts of United Fruit and the local planters, 1900 to 1955.

Notaría Primera de Aracataca (Magdalena, Colombia), Purchase contracts of United Fruit and the local planters, 1900 to 1955.

## Interviews

Ciénaga, Magdalena, Colombia.

María Teresa de Caneva. Widow of former Socialist intellectual and activist Rafael Caneva. July 1999.

Rafael Correa Díaz-Granados. Former banana planter and United Fruit provider in the 1960s. July 1999.

Several former workers in Cienaga and Aracataca requested me not to disclose their names.

Santa Marta, Magdalena, Colombia

Mario Rey. Former president of the Unión de Trabajadores del Magdalena, July 1999.

Luis Riascos. Entrepreneur in the banana export sector of Magdalena who was close to the businesses developed by United Fruit, Consorcio Bananero, and the Federación de Bananeros de Magdalena. July 1999.

Eduardo Solano. Last manager of Consorcio Bananero. July 1999.

José Manuel Dávila. Member of a banana planter family of Santa Marta who lived during the 1940s crisis and the postwar recovery. July 1998, 1999.

Rafael Pérez Dávila. Banana exporter of Magdalena; as a former congressman for Magdalena he negotiated with President Carlos Lleras Restrepo for emergency aid for the region's banana sector in the 1970s. March 1999.

Francisco Dávila Riascos. First president of Consorcio Bananero. July 1999.

Camilo Larrazábal. Former member of the labor unions in Magdalena. July 1999.

Other former entrepreneurs and field workers requested me not to disclose their names.

Apartadó, Urabá, Colombia

Guillermo Rivera. Former guerrilla member of the People's Liberation Army (EPL) and current union leader of the banana workers in Urabá. August 1997.

Oswaldo Cuadrado. Former guerrilla member of the People's Liberation Army (EPL) and current member and organizer of the banana labor unions of Urabá. August 1997.

Medellín, Colombia

Mario Agudelo. Former member of the Colombian Marxist-Leninist Communist party and former guerrilla member of the People's Liberation Army (EPL). Current assemblyman at the Antioquia Departmental Assembly. September 1997.

Juan Felipe Gaviria. Former president of Uniban. August 1998.

Gabriel Harry. Pioneer banana entrepreneur in the Urabá banana zone, August 1997.

Eduardo Benavides. Former manager of a banana farm in Urabá in the early 1960s. August 1997.

Oscar Ochoa. Pioneer banana entrepreneur in Urabá. August 1998.

Several former entrepreneurs and union members of Urabá requested their names not to be disclosed.

Bogotá, Colombia

Irving Bernal. Pioneer entrepreneur in the Urabá banana zone and current exporter in the same region. June 1998.

Andrés Restrepo. Pioneer entrepreneur in the Urabá banana zone, June 1998.

Eliseo Restrepo. Pioneer entrepreneur in the Urabá banana zone, June 1998.

Aurelio Correa. Former president of the Corporación Financiera de Desarrollo Industrial, June 1998.

New Orleans

Marc Johnson. Former Standard Fruit official in charge of quality control in Central America in the 1960s. May 2001 (Phone interview).

Interviews via letters and emails

Thomas McCann. Former public relations director of the United Fruit Company in the 1950s, 1960s, and early 1970s.

William Mason. Former director of United Fruit International Operations in the 1960s. He was in office when United Fruit decided to move from Magdalena to Urabá.

Lloyd Poland. Former plantation manager in Honduras in the 1940s and 1950s.

# Index

# About the Author

Born in Venezuela, Marcelo Bucheli grew up in Chile and Colombia. He received his Ph.D. in history from Stanford University and is Newcomen Fellow in business history at Harvard Business School and Professor of Economic History at Universidad de los Andes, Bogotá, Colombia.